MAGAZINE EDITING—
ITS ART AND PRACTICE

Magazine Editing—
Its Art and Practice

by Jim Mann

THE MAGAZINE FOR MAGAZINE MANAGEMENT

CONTENTS

INTRODUCTION

by Norman Cousins

Editing a magazine is as much a matter of individual style and purpose as writing a book. Some magazines are the product of systematic market surveys generally directed at these questions: 1. Is there an unmet need for a certain kind of magazine? 2. What is the nature of the audience for this magazine? 3. What kind of magazine is this audience prepared to support? 4. What editorial content would be most appealing to this audience? 5. What advertisers would be interested in reaching this audience?

Such systematic and scientific approaches are no guarantee of success, of course; indeed, the roster of early deaths among magazines employing such techniques raises questions about the efficacy of market surveys (even though it hasn't discouraged their sponsors).

Counterposed against the market survey is the gizzard system, than which nothing could be more unscientific. The gizzard system, simply put, is an editor putting his or her hunches to work. This system subscribes to the theory that you don't look to the audience but to a strong editor to define your project. You can't expect an audience to create or run an editorial product any more than a brain surgeon should feel justified in asking a patient how to operate.

My personal theology favors the latter course, but I readily acknowledge that this approach has also produced an impressive group of failures. What, then, *is* the formula for magazine success? The answer is that no one knows in advance, any more than anyone can come up with a sure-fire prediction for a best-seller or a small Broadway success.

This book doesn't presume to provide instructions in the theory and practice of editing a successful magazine. What it does do, however, is to identify the wide range of techniques, problems, and challenges that belong to editing—whether the editing of specialized or general magazines. It is concerned not just with the processing of words but with the management of people who are engaged in the highly pluralistic enterprise of magazine publishing. It's main value is represented by the authority it brings to bear on this particular form of communication.

In this sense, I believe this volume is unique. I know of no single book which has assembled so much editorial experience to be shared with all those who are interested in the inner workings of magazines, whether from the standpoint of readers or perspective editorial workers.

Indeed, there are very few editors who have achieved prominence during the past quarter-century who are not represented in this volume. One of the values of this book is the extended biographical material about the contributors. In toto, their introductions serve as something of a listing of contemporary magazine publishing. Their observations and counsel have been superbly orchestrated in a book which, if it had been available when I was starting out as an editor, would have made my life not just simpler, but much more focused and productive. Mr. Mann does me profound honor in inviting me to roll out the carpet for such distinguished company.

PREFACE

WHY

This book was prepared on the assumption that the better an editor understands what he or she is doing, the higher the odds are that he or she will do it right. It is an unproved assumption. I consider magazine editing an art. And many will argue that in art, instinct is a more reliable guide than intellect—that many great artists did not understand, in the philosophical sense, what they were doing or why they did it.

That does not mean that thought, understanding—even philosophy has to be a barrier to great art. It certainly was not for Leonardo da Vinci or Jean Paul Sartre.

I feel strongly that understanding helps, and I am convinced that great artists do understand. If few have explained what they understood, it is because most artists are too much in love with the concrete expression that is art to waste time on the abstract expression that is philosophy.

All editors are not geniuses. Some will develop into great editors, others never will. But it is possible to be very good at our craft even when greatness eludes us. And if understanding cannot of itself make us great, it can at least help to make us good, for it is a marvelous auxiliary to instinct.

To express it in another way, as artist and craftsman, the editor must depend on his or her instincts. But instincts can be sharpened, and there are two honing tools for sharpening them: experience and understanding.

There are no short cuts to editorial experience. There are short cuts to editorial understanding. I hope this book will be one of them.

HOW

Had I wanted to be pretentious, I would have called the five parts of this book the Etiology, Ontology, Technology, Psychology and Pathology of magazine editing. But I would rather be helpful, so I will describe the order of this book as follows:

Part One: "Understanding the Magazine Medium" analyzes some basic concepts on the nature of magazines and how they work. It is this area that makes magazine editing different from other forms of editing.

Part Two: "The Theory of Successful Editing" examines the magazine editor's job in its essentials. We want to understand precisely what the editor brings to the magazine to make it successful.

Part Three: "The Practice of Successful Editing" goes beyond the basics into specific techniques that editors use to make their magazines work.

Part Four: "The Basics of Editorial Management" studies the function of the editor as an executive, as the boss of organization, the leader of a creative staff.

Part Five: "Change: Editorial Threat or Challenge" considers the toughest problem a magazine editor confronts: how to manage change, whether internal or external.

WHO

It is evident from the very format of this book that the author owes a lot to other people. There are 22 interviews, each with a different expert. I am proud to say that each of these contributors is a friend, and that their contribution to this book, in information and inspiration, goes far beyond the interviews themselves. I want to thank each one of them, and use this occasion to point out that the titles and companies on these pages are the titles they had, and the companies for which they worked, at the time of the interview. Several have moved on to bigger and better positions, as was to be expected.

I would also like to thank two people whose names do not appear on the following pages: my good friend and adviser, Wallace Wegge, on whose suggestions and criticisms I have relied for years, and who provided both for each chapter as it was written; and my wife, Mary, who has been, in addition to so many other things, my reliable and patient proofreader.

PART ONE

Understanding the Magazine Medium

Magazines are periodicals. They are published to be read periodically. Hence, when you market a magazine, you are marketing a service rather than a product. There are exceptions, but most readers are buying your magazine's promise whether they sign up for a subscription or purchase a copy from a newsstand. They are paying to have an editor serve them with a selection of appropriate reading fare at regular intervals.

To put it another way, editors are restaurateurs, not grocers.

This is why the manner in which the editorial package is prepared and presented is as important as its content. This is also why it is so important for editors to know and understand their customers.

Our first questions: Who are those customers, what is a magazine market, and how is it formed? Chapter 1 attempts to answer these questions with the help of George Hirsch.

Once you know who the people in your market are, how do you define their special need—the one your magazine is supposed to fill? Should your "restaurant for the mind" cater to all the needs of a special group of people, or attract a special group by serving a special kind of fare? Chapter 2, with Don Wall, discusses the importance of that distinction.

Whatever the nature of your specialization, is your restaurant's ambiance more important to your customers than the food, or the food more important than the ambiance? That is the basic question we analyze with Jim Horton in Chapter 3.

Or look at it in another way—through the principal classification in the magazine world. What is the difference between consumer and business publishing? How distinct are the editorial objectives and techniques? That is the subject we explore with Joel Harnett in Chapter 4.

Finally, lest we overlook the element that pays the bills for most magazines, what has all this editorial effort to do with advertising? Do editors work for advertisers? Can they serve two masters, readers and advertisers? See Chapter 5 and the results of the interview with Gil Chapman.

CHAPTER ONE

Which Comes First:
Market or Magazine?

Featuring an Interview with
George A. Hirsch
Founding Publisher of The Runner

No endeavor fits the chicken-vs.-egg riddle more precisely than editing a magazine. Does the audience define what the magazine should be, or does the editorial product define the audience? How extensively should editors study their readers before they begin to edit? Can editors rely on their gut instincts and expect an audience to form around the editorial bait their instincts create? Is it enough to give readers what they want, or is it the editor's function to give them what they need, even when they do not know they want it?

When a magazine serves two markets, advertisers as well as readers, the problem is even more complex. Advertisers tend to define a market before they decide to use a magazine. Does this change the editorial approach? In business publications, especially, should editorial content be indirectly dictated by advertisers' needs?

Before we discuss any of the particulars of magazine editing, we must examine the magazine-audience relationship and how it is established.

To break ground for this investigation we interviewed George Hirsch, publisher of *The Runner*. We intentionally chose a publisher rather than an editor. We wanted someone who had worked with more than one editor, someone whose objectivity would not be influenced by editing habits or preferences. Over a period of 11 years, George was involved in starting three magazines, each with a different editor. And each of the magazines was very different: in frequency, in editorial focus, and in the way each had to find its audience.

In 1967, George Hirsch and Clay Felker launched *New York* magazine. George was publisher and president; Clay, editor. Due to disagreements between the two, George left at the end of 1971 to start another magazine, *New Times*. He chose John Larsen as editor, and the two worked together from the first issue in 1973 until the magazine folded in 1979. In 1978, George launched *The Runner*. John Larsen edited *The Runner* for a while, but Marc Bloom, who was with the magazine from its first issue, soon became editor. Although George sold *The Runner* to Ziff-Davis Publications in 1981, George remains publisher and Bloom editor.

One of Hirsch's proudest boasts is that his 1979 Boston Marathon time was 2:38:54. Running in the fast lane has been a habit since he graduated from Princeton (magna cum laude) in 1956. Before he started founding magazines, he spent three years in Italy as a Navy LST gunnery officer, two years at the Harvard Business School, and five years at Time Inc. as assistant publisher of *Life International* and *Life en Espanol*.

INTERVIEW

Q: Was there a big difference in initial reader-market analysis for New Times *vs.* New York *and* The Runner?

A: There was. For *New Times*, we knew there was a special interest in current events. Vietnam and Watergate had moved magazines off newsstands and indicated a thirst for investigative reporting. There were extraordinary changes in society: concern for black rights, the sexual revolution, feminism, new life styles. Our target market was the segment of the population at the cutting edge of these changes. Almost every metropolitan center had an underground publication reacting to these changes. We felt a need for a national, truly professional publication directed at this market. The market existed, but is wasn't as large as we expected.

Q: With New York *and* The Runner?

A: *New York* was the right magazine at the right time—and it took off almost immediately. There was a need for a magazine helping people cope with New

York City living. With *The Runner*, it was even easier to determine the size and interest of the audience. We knew there were 30 million people running and that many of them were very serious about it.

Finding prospects

Q: How did you select the direct-mail lists to launch each of these magazines?
A: It was toughest for *New Times*. There were no specific lists for that audience. We had a similar problem with *New York*, but there, at least, we could select the New York area names from lists of other magazines. We did a particularly successful campaign for *New York* with a sweepstakes mailing which offered prizes such as dinner with Mayor John Lindsay, bar hopping with Jimmy Breslin, and movie screenings with Judith Crist. The lists that worked best were readers of other magazines. We tested $5 and $6 a year. The sweepstake, at $5 returned approximately 4%. But the $6, without the sweepstakes, did very poorly. New Yorkers weren't waiting for this kind of magazine. The terrific editorial product made the difference. With *New Times*, we looked for lists that might indicate an ideological stance. We got lists of political groups, environmental groups. But none of these lists worked, and we had to depend on lists from other magazines. A haunting fact in our business is that people who buy magazines by mail are the best prospects for other magazines ordered by mail.

Q: What lists did you use for The Runner?
A: We tested a lot of magazine lists. But we did far better with lists of runners: 25,000 people who enrolled for a marathon, for instance. Runners lists worked like gangbusters, while non-runner lists were mediocre. So we put together our own list-gathering operation, which got us involved in organized racing. There are tens of thousands of participants in such races.

Q: With New Times, *people active in fields the magazine discussed responded poorly, while with* The Runner, *active participants responded wonderfully. Why the difference?*
A: With *New Times* there were a lot of other publications that touched on our subject matter. With *The Runner* the subject matter is more clearly defined. You are either a runner's magazine or you aren't.

Q: In the second case you identified the magazine with a specific interest, while in the first, it wasn't identified with a specific cause. Activists don't identify with all causes, only with their cause or causes.

A: Well said. *New Times* had to force its way into the market. And, although we did not ultimately succeed, we lasted five years, won lots of prizes, and had real impact. Circulation reached 350,000, but got very expensive to maintain. The market wasn't looking for us. With *The Runner* it's different. The readers know who they are. If you're a runner, you put on running shoes and go out and run. There's no half way, no relying on temporary inpulse. The magazine doesn't depend on being picked up by people passing through an airport.

Q: Did any of the three magazines take off on the newsstands faster than the others?
A: *The Runner*. It has the largest single-copy sales and is on the largest number of stands. It gets asked for.

Q: Do you sell it in specialty stores?
A: We have a special department for placing it in stores that sell running shoes and apparel.

Gauging the size of the audience

Q: The Runner *is a special-interest magazine. What did you consider* New Times?
A: It was aimed at a special audience, but the interests were more general: social issues, investigative reporting and politics.

Q: It's my theory that when a magazine tackles such general subjects, it cannot succeed without a very strong editor—one who can gather a following by the sheer force of personality and ideas. If you edit such a magazine by committee, with editors who are capable but do not have the genius of leadership, nothing happens.
A: I totally agree. *New Times* had a very strong editor, John Larsen, and it won a very loyal following, but the following wasn't large enough.

Q: Many new magazines die because they're overextended. New Times *might have been a successful smaller property.*
A: I disagree. A loyal following doesn't work unless it can raise enough revenue to meet certain fixed costs. Magazines are expensive to produce and distribute.

Q: Only if you bring to the enterprise a preconception of the medium, a basic concept of what a magazine has to be. The modern way to market is to study the market and gear the product to fit it, not to start out with a product and look for a market that fits.
A: True, you may publish a newsletter or a book. But if you want a magazine

for butterfly collectors, you must first measure the universe, its interest and what butterfly collectors will pay for a magazine. You have to judge the potential for advertising. Are there advertisers aiming directly at this audience? If not, what qualities does this audience have to interest other advertisers? There may be 15,000 butterfly collectors who would appreciate a high-quality magazine on butterfly collecting, but those numbers won't justify that kind of magazine. Here the answer may well be a book.

Renewability and price sensitivity

Q: Was there much difference in the conversion rate of the three magazines?
A: First year conversions were very good for all three. With *The Runner*, they continued to be good. With *New Times*, as we built higher numbers, conversions began to slide.

Q: There are three possible causes of such a phenomenon. First, the magazine's editorial quality disintegrates. I presume that was not the case with New Times. *Second, the audience changes and loses interest. The third, and most common, is that promotion starts to attract too many secondary readers.*
A: With *New Times*, it was the second reason as well as the third. Many readers were very interested for a time, but lost interest as times changed.

Q: Analogous to, but not the same as, the bridal books.
A: But with the bridal books the readers are constantly replaced. Marriage doesn't go out of style.

Q: Did the nature of the magazines have any bearing on the way subscriptions were priced?
A: *The Runner* was the only one of the three that relied solely on full-price offers: $12 a year.

Q: What was the reason for this—the audience's readiness to pay, or your need to make money from circulation, since the potential for advertising is not that great?
A: In each case we tested prices. You have to do that. But there's no question that the audience for a special-interest publication is far less price-sensitive.

Advertiser acceptance

Q: What differences were there in introducing the three magazines to advertisers?
A: *The Runner* had a base of primary advertisers: running shoes, running apparel, digital watches—things that runners use. Once we had our basic audience, such advertisers had to advertise in *The Runner*.

Q: Was it easy to estimate how much you could expect to bring in from primary advertisers?
A: Very easy. There are only so many shoe companies, so many companies making running apparel. A lot of the companies are small and can't advertise every issue. It isn't hard to estimate what they will spend. With *New Times* there was no such base. Absolutely no advertiser had to be in *New Times*.

Q: Were there categories that could be considered primary for New York?
A: Not primary, but *New York* had major advantages over many national magazines. The New York market is such an exciting market, with so many companies to go after. The number and diversity of local advertisers are unusual, as are the upper demographics that make it a natural for certain kinds of national advertising.

Q: When you sell advertising to agencies, you almost always have to fit into a media category. Was it easier for some of these magazines to find a category?
A: *The Runner* and *New York* had distinct categories. *The Runner*'s category was special-interest sports magazines. *New York* was a city magazine. It was really a forerunner of that category. There were city magazines prior to *New York*—such as *Philadelphia* and *San Diego*. But *New York* had more to do with developing the genre.

Q: New Times *was fitted into the category of egghead magazines, but that's not a rich advertising category.*
A: We did better in advertising than a number of them, and weren't quite categorized with any of them. We were biweekly, but weren't identified with the newsweeklies. Sometimes we were associated with *Rolling Stone* or *Esquire*, but we never had a precise position.

Frequency

Q: What effect did the difference in frequency have? All three had different frequencies.
A: Frequency tends to be ignorned in publishing analysis. The decision is made early, and after that, you don't think of it again. *New York* is the only city or regional magazine in the United States that's a weekly. The others are monthlies. But New York is the only metropolitan area big enough to support a weekly. In New York City there's a velocity of events and ideas that requires a weekly.

Q: Is it the city's velocity, or its numbers?
A: In other cities there's not that much going on: there aren't that many movie theaters, that many dance companies, that many legitimate theaters—an off-Broadway and an off-off-Broadway. No city in the world is like it.

Q: Did you ever regret making New Times *a biweekly?*
A: There's a certain value in that frequency for publications commenting on news. *Forbes* is biweekly. *Fortune* has changed from monthly to biweekly. The frequency was right for *New Times*.

Q: Have you any basic advice for launching a magazine?
A: Starting a magazine is one of the most difficult jobs a person can undertake. It requires a sort of romance with an idea. In that stage, it's not easy to do negative thinking. You don't want your optimism dimmed. But you have to face reality. The crucial thing is that you find a real market. Don't mislead yourself. Don't imagine that you can create your own market.

ANALYSIS

The Recognition Factor in Magazine Marketing

New Times and *The Runner* seem to exemplify two fundamental approaches to publishing: 1) select an audience and build a magazine to serve it, or 2) build a magazine and find readers who like it—what business schools call the marketing-oriented vs. the production-oriented business. The first selects a target market and develops a product for it. The second makes a product and looks for customers who can use it.

But magazine publishing is communications, and communications require listening as well as talking. Both the editor who has an audience and looks for something to say, and the editor who has something to say and looks for an audience, must tailor what they say and how they say it to the audience. *New Times* and *The Runner* were both marketing-oriented. Both were developed for what George Hirsch saw as specific target markets.

What, then, was the difference?

It lay in the extent of the audience's recognition of the magazine's ability to fill its needs. Most magazines serve two markets: readers and advertisers. And the recognition factor applies to both. Thus *The Runner* was in the advantageous position of targeting readers fully conscious of their interest in running and advertisers fully conscious of their need to be in a runners' magazine. In contrast, *New Times* had to target potential readers and advertisers, neither of whom were convinced they needed the magazine.

As a city magazine, *New York* had an easily-defined audience, yet its situation was closer to that of *New Times* than to that of *The Runner*. New Yorkers were not convinced a magazine could fill their need—not until they had sampled the magazine and learned how it worked.

Needs vs. wants

To need something is not, necessarily, to want it. There are two fundamental acts of acceptance that precede any sale. First, prospects must recognize that they have a need. Then, prospects must recognize that a particular product or service can fill or satisfy that need. We do not know whether Walter Annenberg was right in seeing a widespread need for a magazine like *Panorama*. What we do know is that he was wrong in thinking that enough people wanted it.

We can distinguish between three kinds of markets according to how prospects recognize their need:

1) Primary, where the majority knows its need and considers it important.

2) Secondary, where the majority knows its need but does not consider it important.

3) Potential, where the majority of prospects does not yet recognize the need.

We can also distinguish between three kinds of markets by the ease with which the prospects recognize that they want the product, i.e., that it fills their need:

1) Spontaneous, where the majority automatically accepts the product or service as filling its need.

2) Inducible through persuasion, where the majority needs convincing that the product or service fills the need, but is open to persuasion.

3) Inducible only through trial, where only experience with the product or service can convince the majority.

Evaluating target markets

The prudent publisher evaluates his or her target market first according to need, then according to want. Need determines the feasibility of the project; want, the cost of launching it.

A magazine's economic foundation can be built on a primary market with regard to need, whether it is a reader market, an advertiser market, or both. To depend on a secondary market is foolhardy. It is difficult enough for a publication to persuade prospects that they want it without taking on the burden of convincing them that they have a need for such a product and that the need is important. (See *Solving Publishing's Toughest Problems* by Jim Mann, FOLIO, 1982, Chapter 18, ''The Art of Launching a New Publication.'')

The reason for this seems to be that people expect to be educated in how you can fill their needs, but resent attempts to convince them that needs they consider non-existent or unimportant are really important. In the first case you are answering questions they are asking. In the second, you are challenging their judgment.

After a magazine is established on a firm foundation of acceptance by primary readers and/or advertisers, it can profitably exploit secondary markets. Changing secondary prospects to primary requires peer pressure and happens slowly. Hence, the need to be established and the high cost of promoting secondary prospects.

Pursuing a potential magazine market is almost always too costly to be practical. U.S. economic history may be full of examples of how advertising and marketing converted latent needs into important real needs, but, even with mouthwash, personal deodorants and cosmetics, no product has ever gotten off the ground without the help of an economically feasible base of prospects.

In like manner, magazines like *Reader's Digest, TV Guide* and *National Geographic* have converted millions of latent prospects to real prospects, but only after success had triggered enough herd instinct to work in their favor.

Once it is clear that an adequate primary market exists with regard to need, the publisher must judge how much it will cost in effort, money and time to get those prospects to want the magazine. Will they recognize it spontaneously as joggers recognized *The Runner* the instant it was described to them? Will it require considerable education, as *New York* magazine discovered? Or will a long, slow trial period be necessary while the audience discovers the magazine for itself, as was the case with publications as diverse as *Sports Illustrated* and *Prevention*?

Business papers (particularly when they depend on controlled circulation) are seldom successful unless the market is primary according to need and spontaneous according to want. Hence the importance of a title that clearly designates the publication's coverage. Thus, Cahners' *Institutions* changed its name to *Restaurants & Institutions*.

Establishing recognition of want

One of the most common mistakes in magazine promotion is the use of identical introductory techniques regardless of whether want is spontaneous, inducible through persuasion, or inducible only through trial.

The success of Bernard Goldhirsh in launching *Inc.*, *Sail*, *Motorboat*, *Marine Business* and *High Technology* is due, at least in part, to the fact that his launching techniques and timetables have been more or less different for each publication.

Some examples of how initial planning for new publications has to differ according to the recognition factor as it affects want:

1. When the reader market is spontaneous:
   * Direct mail is the best means of promotion, provided mailing lists accurately target the market.
   * Promotion approach should be straightforward, describing the magazine and its editorial plans.
   * Single-copy sales will work if logo and cover are unambiguous as to the magazine's purpose, and copies are displayed in locations where traffic includes a high percentage of prospects, e.g., *People, Woman's Day, Colonial Homes*.
   * Subscription and cover prices may be relatively high. Cut rates are usually a waste of money. Short-term offers (but at a premium per-issue price) are smart.
   * Breakeven should take place early, usually by the end of the first year when renewals begin to come in.

2. When the reader market is inducible by persuasion:
   * Direct mail is best means of promotion, but returns will be smaller and various packages should be tested.

- Promotion should describe the magazine's usefulness for the reader.
- Single-copy sales are useful only as a trial device, and then require heavy promotion. It is a mistake to depend on newsstand sales as the prinicpal source of circulation, as *Inside Sports* discovered.
- Bargain prices and short-term rates are needed to persuade the dubious to try the publication.
- Breakeven may not take place until the third or even the fourth year.

3. When a reader market is inducible only through trial:
   - Sampling is the only effective promotion, whether by a barrage of soft offers, or the usually more efficient free-sampling period directed to a carefully selected list. Also practical, when possible: purchase a discontinued magazine's list.
   - Best promotion approach: sweepstakes and premiums (enabling the magazine to piggyback on a spontaneous want).
   - Best technique for single-copy sampling: persuade another magazine to carry a prototype issue, as *Ms.* did with *New York*.
   - Bargain and short-term rates encourage sampling, but cut rates should not be needed when converting from free to paid (with the exception of a courtesy discount to ease transition).
   - Breakeven depends on size of audience need. Magazines requiring inducement by trial do best if they are geared to break even at very low numbers, allowing gradual growth over a number of years.

4. When the advertiser market is spontaneous:
   - Since these are always primary advertisers, selling methods require only that appropriate data be presented to the right people.
   - Advertising rates should be competitive, but no trial incentives are needed.
   - Advertising objectives should be attained by the first issue if the number and quality of readers is right and sales communications are adequate.

5. When the advertiser market is inducible through persuasion:
   - Initial buys will be experimental. Hence sales will have to be made to principals, not agents.
   - Advertising rates should be as low as possible to encourage experimentation.
   - Advertising objectives will not be reached until the magazine is successful in other ways, e.g., with primary advertisers or with readers.

6. When the advertiser market is inducible only through trial:
   - These advertisers need tangible proof. Per-response deals and coupon offers should be encouraged.
   - Advertising rates should be geared to results rather than cost per thousand. If possible, free effectiveness research should be offered to advertisers.
   - Advertising objectives should be structured for slow buildup. Look for suc-

cess first in direct-response advertising, then in couponing, and—only after long efforts—in areas like image advertising.

Creator's myopia

Some magazines—like *New Times,* the original *Media People* and *Geo* — fail because there is insufficient need for them. Others, and they are more numerous, die because their creators are so blinded by the need for the publication that they cannot see the lack of want. *Panorama* and *Viva* were examples. But most magazines that die do so because their creators (and/or financial backers) expect the want market to be spontaneous when it is really inducible by persuasion (the mistake Newsweek Inc. made with *Inside Sports*), or because they presume it is inducible by persuasion when it is inducible only through trial (probably the reason why Rodale Press had to fold *Spring*).

As George Hirsch points out, it is difficult to dim the magazine's entrepreneur's optimism with negative thinking. Yet it is crucial to face reality. Nothing collapses more quickly than a publishing venture built on false hopes.

MANAGEMENT REVIEW

Check List for the Recognition Factor's Bearing on Marketing a Publication

I. Does the publication depend on revenue from:
_____readers only?
_____advertisers only?
_____both readers and advertisers?

II. With regard to recognition of need:
A. Are the targeted readers
_____a primary market?
_____a secondary market?
_____a potential market?
B. Are the target advertisers
_____a primary market?
_____a secondary market?
_____a potential market?

C. If the publication's revenue base depends on a targeted market which is not primary, the publication is in serious trouble.

    1. If the publication is still on the drawing board, abandon present plan and start fresh.

    2. If the publication is established, consider repositioning to target a primary market.

III. With regard to recognition of want:

A. Are the targeted readers

    _____a spontaneous market?

    _____a market inducible through persuasion?

    _____a market inducible only through trial?

B. Are the targeted advertisers

    _____a spontaneous market?

    _____a market inducible through persuasion?

    _____a market inducible only through trial?

C. If the publication's revenue base depends on a targeted market that is spontaneous:

    1. Initial investment required is relatively small.

    2. A straightforward, expository approach is the best sales technique.

    3. It can fail with no cause other than a lack of professional implementation.

D. If the publication's revenue base depends on a targeted market that is inducible through persuasion:

    1. Initial investment required is relatively large.

    2. Sales technique should have high persuasive content and use promotional aids that will stir interest.

    3. A common cause of failure is insufficient or ineffective promotion.

E. If the publication's revenue base depends on a targeted market that is inducible only through trial:

    1. Initial investment must be large enough to subsidize the publication for a long time before breakeven.

    2. Sales technique should provide as many sampling devices as possible.

    3. A common cause of failure is inadequate provision for sampling or lack of patience on part of investors.

F. If the publication's revenue base depends on both reader and advertiser markets, and recognition of want differs in each case:

    1. Initial investment required for each market should be calculated separately according to III C, D or E above.

    2. Sales techniques should similarly be different for each market, as above.

3. A common cause of failure is the apportioning of attention and investment according to amount of revenue expected from each source instead of by extent of recognition of want in each.

CHAPTER TWO

Editing for a Special Audience vs. Editing for a Special Interest

Featuring an Interview with Donald R. Wall

President, Magazine Division of Whitney Communications Corp.

The future—some would say the present—belongs to specialized publications. Hence magazine editing is almost always specialized editing. But just what does this mean?

Every well-edited publication has a special focus, but is it focused on a special audience? Is *Esquire* specialized in the same way as *The Runner*, or *Good Housekeeping* as focused as *Modern Bride?*

If there is a difference, what is it? And how much difference does it make in editing the magazine, in attracting and holding readers?

To get some initial answers we interviewed Donald Wall, the president of Whitney Communication's magazine division. We chose Don because he has a reputation for skill in positioning publications in special markets and, more precisely, because he had been largely responsible for transforming the special-interest magazine, *Retirement Living*, into the special-audience magazine, *50 Plus*.

In 1949, after three years at Boston University's School of Business Administration, Don began his business career as assistant advertising manager at Bostitch, Inc., the stapling equipment manufacturer. Four years later, after moving into market planning and public relations, Don left to join Atlas Plywood Corp. as director of advertising and public relations.

In January 1957, Don switched from the client to the agency side and became an account executive at Bresnick Co., a Boston advertising agency. In December of the same year, McGraw-Hill asked him to become New England district manager for its Sweet's Construction Division.

At Sweet's he worked his way up to advertising and promotion manager (1960), director of staff activities (1963), and general manager (1964). Then, in 1969, he was promoted to group vice president for the McGraw-Hill Information Systems Company with total responsibility for Sweet's and four other publishing properties serving the construction industry.

In 1970 Cahners Publishing lured him away to solve some pressing problems in that company's construction-publication unit.

Ten months later Walter Thayer offered Don the presidency of the magazine division at Whitney Communications Corp. There he reorganized Whitney's three unrelated publishing properties (*Interior Design*, *Harvest Years* and *Art in America*) into one integrated company, and then acquired *The Hockey News*, *Boating Industry* and *Oil Daily*. When Don became president, Whitney's magazine division was grossing $2.5 million. At the time of this interview, annual volume was $16 million.

Don has since left Whitney, and is now a magazine consultant working out of Boston.

INTERVIEW

Q: Why was Retirement Living *changed to* 50 Plus?
A: To broaden its base. *Retirement Living* was devoted purely to the challenges of growing older, particularly to those of retirement. *50 Plus* keeps a lot of that, but broadens the editorial to appeal to people as young as 50. We couldn't expect anyone much under 60 to read *Retirement Living*, so we've added a whole ten years.

Q: What made you choose 50?
A: A lot of demographics cut at 50. Fifty is old enough to be concerned about retirement, young enough to be active and at the peak of the average person's income cycle.

Q: How did the editorial content change?
A: We still have a very strong service orientation: recreation, housing, money

management, food, health. We have changed more in style than in substance. Articles are shorter, more punchy. The material, always sugar-coated to some degree, is much more sugar-coated. We are more oriented to news and people in the news.

Repositioning and the reader

Q: Has the change affected your reader market much?
A: It's too early to tell. We do have a barometer most publications don't have. About 70,000 of our 170,000 circulation is subscriptions paid by companies who include the magazine as part of their programs for pre-retirement counseling. So we can phone 40 or 50 people in benefits departments at large corporations and get an instant readout. We've done that, and there wasn't one complaint—unlike seven years ago, when we changed from *Harvest Years* to *Retirement Living. Harvest Years* catered to the really old, 75 and over. It was kind of cuddly. We lost at least 100 such people in protest against our becoming too "young."

Q: Are renewal rates changing?
A: We used a bit of Publishers Clearing House offers in our testing, and that is bound to bring renewal rates down. Otherwise, they should remain high. Our direct-payment renewal rate is now over 70%. In corporate-benefit subscriptions, of course, the renewal rate drops much more. Many companies pay part or all of the subscription a year or so after retirement. Then the retiree gets a "you-have-to-pay" notice from us or the company. Naturally, there's a lot of attrition.

Repositioning and the advertiser

Q: How did the repositioning affect advertising sales?
A: Advertising growth is very modest. There's a lot of questioning as to whether this market has really arrived, although our repositioning intrigues a lot of advertising people. Our agency presentations get larger audiences than ever before. There's a lot of interest in this market, because of its affluence. But growth will not be sudden or sensational. Advertising never starts that way. The big agencies are conservative. But they are studying this market, and we are getting ads featuring older people, from coffee, analgesic, energy and other advertisers.

Q: Despite high disposable income, I doubt if consumers in this market will ever be as attractive to many big advertisers as the young marrieds. Advertisers are not interested in where money is, but in where it turns over fastest. You can't get over-50 consumers to eat as much, do as much laundry, buy as many cosmetics.
A: Your point is well taken. By the time people are 50, not only are the children gone, but they have done most of their home furnishing.

Special-audience vs. special-interest

Q: We can distinguish between a special-audience magazine and a special-interest magazine. The former defines a special demographic class, and is a publication about interests common to that class. The latter defines a certain subject, and is a publication about the subject. Does this distinction make sense to you?
A: Yes. Our *Hockey News* is a special-interest publication. *50 Plus* is a special-audience magazine. *Boating Industry* is special-interest. But with *Oil Daily* it is hard to be sure.

Q: In the trade field, vertical books are usually special-audience; horizontal books, special-interest. A publication that covers all the interests of a particular industry is really directing its editorial at a class of people, a special audience.
A: True. Yet in some books the distinction is hard to make. *Art in America* covers all the interests common to people in the art world, so it is special-audience. Yet a large segment of its circulation, readers who are interested in art but not part of the art world, look at it as special-interest.

Q: I'd call it special-interest. That's why it appeals to people in and out of the art world, and that is why it can't afford to give too much space to subjects of interest to the art world but not directly concerned with art.
A: You're probably right.

Q: Do you think special-audience books are as easy to market to advertisers as special-interest books?
A: No. Special-interest publications, like *Hockey News* or *Interior Design*, are well-defined as to what they do. Special-audience magazines tend to be broader. And the broader you get, the more you run into agency computers and comparisons with mass-circulation media.

Q: Don't advertisers usually prefer special-interest media for their products, if they can find them?

A: Sure. They're easier to understand. Their audience and appeal are much easier to define. Although we know certain demographics about the *50 Plus* special audience, its appeal to advertisers is very broad, whereas readers who are interested in retirement are of very specific interest to certain advertisers, to marketers of annuities, for instance.

Q: But does a strong special-interest always mean a strong advertising market? People who are interested in hockey do not necessarily buy hockey sticks.
A: That's right. *Hockey News*'s audience is half watchers, half players, and the watchers don't need hockey sticks. A special-interest need not be a buying interest. We have had some bloody experiences with this phenomenon. In football, there is a lot of equipment, but most of it, with the possible exception of shoes, and depending on the age of the player, is purchased by an institution. In basketball, there is relatively little equipment, basically sneakers. But hockey demands $200 to $300 on your back before you get out on the ice, and frequently, especially at lower levels, it has to be purchased by the player. That's why a good part of *Hockey News*'s success is due to equipment advertising.

Q: What about marketing to readers?
A: Special-audience is more expensive. Special-interest magazines are easier to find lists for, and they tend to be much more self-contained.

Q: And special-interest magazines can be sold in single-copy outlets closed to special-audience magazines. You can put a plumbing magazine in a hardware store.
A: We sell *Hockey News* at ice rinks, where they sell no other publications. We sell *Art in America* in art museums and highly-specialized art bookstores.

Moving from one category to another

Q: Consider editing. Can a special-interest book like Boating *run articles on automobiles because boating enthusiasts usually own cars?*
A: I think it would be reaching, and I think it's very hard to sell advertising through that kind of editorial. If you are selling car wax in the boating field, it has got to be related to the waxing of the boat, not the car.

Q: Judging purely by the names Harvest Years, Retirement Living, 50 Plus, *it looks as if you changed from special-audience (65 and over) to special-interest (retirement) back to a larger special-audience (50 and over).*
A: We never conceived it in those terms. In both cases, we tried to broaden

the base of the magazine to attract a larger audience with more attractive demographics.

Q: Many special-interest books have successfully broadened their base by becoming special-audience publications. Saturday Review *was a book-review magazine at one time.* Rolling Stone *was strictly a music publication.* Women's Wear Daily, *once 100% a trade paper, has taken on many elements of a consumer newspaper. Others have tried and failed.* American Girl *closed down, and* Crawdaddy *did not make it as* Feature. *As to going the other way—from special-audience to special-interest—the farm publications are a successful example.*
A: Many trade papers made the switch, either by splitting one special-audience magazine into two special-interest publications, or through repositioning. They have been forced to do this as the interests of their readers grew more and more specialized. The electronics field, where there once were only two or three big magazines, is now served by about 20 or so very specialized publications.

Q: According to your description in SRDS, Interior Design *is edited for professional designers of commercial and residential interiors. Doesn't that sound as if it were a special-audience publication?*
A: But its editorial and its reason for being, as an ad medium, really make it special-interest; it is about the design and decoration of interior space.

Q: Doesn't Interior Design *run articles telling interior designers how to run their businesses?*
A: It is only recently that we have started to run articles on subjects like how to run your business, how to do your own public relations, etc. So we are moving in the direction of special-audience. Approximately 85% of the editorial is special-interest, but 15% (and it is growing larger) is special-audience.

Potential and flexibility

Q: Would you agree that a special-interest publication is easier to keep current and ahead of its audience?
A: Yes. Special-audience publications tend to follow trends rather than generate them, while the sources from which a special-interest magazine gets its information are apt to be much more controllable. It goes back to what we were saying earlier: It's easier to manage a special-interest publication because it has narrower parameters.

Q: Yet magazine publishers are constantly tempted to move from special-interest to special-audience. Most successful publications sooner or later get to a point where they have saturated their advertising market and begin to reach a plateau in advertising sales. Their first thought, then, always seems to be to broaden the editorial base to attract more advertising. It doesn't always work.

A: I think it will work with *50 Plus*, but it is going to take a lot of effort and perseverance.

Q: Falling back on an earlier example, if you bring enough readers into your audience who are not thinking about retirement, don't they become waste circulation for marketers of annuities? By going after the more general advertisers, you could lose the more specific advertiser. There is a delicate balance to be maintained there.

A: We watch that very closely.

ANALYSIS

Audience vs. Interest: A Matter of Method

Years ago there were general-interest magazines that catered to everyone's interests. No subject was beyond the scope of the old *Saturday Evening Post*—and no reader. There were editorial features for mom, for dad, even for the kids. General-interest/general-audience magazines like that are no longer viable.*

Today there are still big-circulation magazines and limited-circulation publications, and either type can have either a special-audience or special-interest focus, e.g.:

•Big-circulation special-audience: *Cosmopolitan, Family Circle, Ladies' Home Journal, Playboy, Seventeen, Ebony.*

•Big-circulation special-interest: *Field & Stream, National Geographic, Sports Illustrated, TV Guide.*

---

*Is *Reader's Digest* a general-interest magazine? You can call it the exception to the rule, or you can call it a big-circulation magazine dedicated to the special interest of self-improvement.

•Limited-circulation special-audience: *Coal Age, Diversion, New Yorker, Rolling Stone, Saturday Review.*

•Limited-circulation special-interest: *AOPA Pilot, Cycle, Machine Design, Medical Economics, Popular Photography.*

Although the basic difference between big and limited circulation is in numbers, the important distinction is not in the number of actual readers, but in the number of potential readers. Thus a "big-circulation" magazine that has not reached its potential audience should not be considered a limited-circulation publication.

This chapter, however, is concerned less with the difference between big and limited circulation than the distinction between special-audience and special-interest publications, a difference much more significant for publication management.

Special-audience magazines tend to define their readership first, then choose the subject matter to interest those readers. Special-interest publications define their subject matter first, then look for readers interested in the subject. The key is in the editorial approach or method of editing. This holds true even for special-audience magazines like *The New Yorker* or *The National Review*, where the editor defines the audience as "people like myself," i.e., with similar interests and tastes.

Bob Guccione's *Omni* is a good example of a special-audience magazine. There are a lot of people intrigued by science and its implications for the present and future. If *Omni* continues its success, it will be because Guccione knows how to satisfy that special audience's need for knowledge, entertainment, fantasy, opinion, even news. Contrast *Omni*'s editorial approach with those of special-interest publications such as *Scientific American, Science,* and *Popular Science.*

If you find it difficult to decide whether a particular magazine is special-audience or special-interest, examine how its customers, i.e., those who provide most of its revenue, look at the publication.

A limited-circulation book supported by advertising is usually special-interest if the majority of the ads sell products or services directly related to its editorial subject matter. If the core advertisers fall into a variety of advertising categories, it is probably special-audience.

A limited-circulation book sustained by circulation is usually special-interest if its core readers associate the publication with a specific, limited facet of their lives or work. If the core readers value the publication for a wide variety of reasons, it is probably special-audience.

For big-circulation magazines, the circulation test works pretty well, but the advertising test falls down. When a publication achieves a very large circulation, advertisers tend to buy by the numbers, whether it is special-audience or special-interest.

Implications for editorial

As is evident from the *Omni* example, the obvious consequence of the difference in a special-audience publication's editorial approach is its greater flexibility in editorial forms. Special-audience publications frequently range from serious essays to fiction and cartoons. Special-interest publications are more limited in their editorial techniques, depending on the interest served.

For the same reason, there is little room for highly personal editing in the special-interest magazine, while there can be a great deal of opportunity for such editing in a special-audience publication—simply because the editing is more people-oriented than subject-oriented. The *Saturday Review of Literature* was a special-interest weekly edited by committee. As Norman Cousins' personal vehicle it became the special-audience *Saturday Review*. Herb Mayes's *McCall's*, Arnold Gingrich's *Esquire*, Harold Ross's *The New Yorker* were all special-audience magazines.

Finally, as mentioned in the interview, it is easier to keep ahead of a special interest than of a special audience. By easier, we do not mean less expensive. (Experts and specialists don't come cheap.) We mean it is more difficult to find or develop editors with the necessary rapport and highly honed instincts.

Special-interest publications can be edited by committee, but special-audience magazines almost always need a dominating editor in chief. Great special-audience editors edit from the gut and know what is right instinctively. *Cosmopolitan*'s Helen Gurley Brown ignores readership research and makes a practice of never reading reader correspondence.

Implications for circulation

Special-interest publications tend to have larger core audiences in relation to their total circulations than do special-audience magazines. This is because the special-interest reader's attitude toward the magazine usually reflects his attitude toward the special interest. A model-railway buff's enthusiasm for *Model Railroader* will wax and wane with interest in the hobby. Since a subscription to the magazine is a further commitment to the special interest, new subscribers tend to become committed readers almost at once.

Special-audience magazines usually have to win reader commitment more gradually. A woman may subscribe to *McCall's* for its recipes, and might be exposed to the magazine for months, before she grows into an inveterate through-the-book reader.

Distinguishing between special-audience and special-interest can be of tremendous help in circulation strategy.

Very seldom does a special-interest magazine convert an accidental or fringe reader into a dedicated or core reader. Appeals to fringe prospects are a mistake (unless the magazine is priced to profit from initial sales). A special-audience publication, on the other hand, frequently converts fringe readers into core readers. In fact, exposing fringe readers to the magazine is often the principal technique for developing core readers.

For a special-interest publication, therefore, to whom you mail the promotion piece is more important then what the piece says or looks like. The basic task is to find prime prospects. Convincing them that the publication serves that interest is comparatively easy. The union of reader and magazine is a marriage of convenience. For a special-audience publication, the union is a love match. First acquaintance, then courtship is required. Usually, it is not too difficult to find prospects. But the copy and graphics of the mailing piece demand a lot of attention.

For similar reasons it is easier to establish the special-interest publication than the special-audience publication on the newsstands.

Can promotion convince readers to adopt a special interest they do not have? It may be possible in theory, but in practice it is a terribly expensive and ineffective way to build an audience.

Implications for advertising

Serious advertisers judge media by the efficiency with which it reaches their prospects. Techniques for determining that efficiency fall into three categories:

1. Common sense: "Anyone interested in this magazine has to be interested in my advertising message." Pleasure boat manufacturers don't need demographic data to advertise in *Yachting*.

2. Demographic analysis: "The age, sex, income, education, marital status of the average reader means a high percentage of this audience will be interested in my message." It makes sense to advertise a pleasure boat in *Town & Country*.

3. Testing: "I'll run my ad and see how many people respond to my message." The boat dealer repeats an ad in *Chicago* because the last ad brought 57 people to the showroom.

The ability to make the buying judgment on the basis of common sense is the great advantage most special-interest magazines have over special-audience publications—provided there is a special advertising market corresponding to the magazine's special interest. As Don Wall points out, you can run into serious problems if your special interest does not relate to a worthwhile advertising market. There are probably as many people who play the piano in this country as there are people who play the guitar, but you won't find a piano magazine as fat with ads as Jim Crockett's *Guitar Player*.

When a special-interest magazine's reader appeal covers all the prospects of an advertising category but also attracts many non-prospects, the publisher should ask whether the publishing venture was misconceived. Were *Hockey News* dependent for all or most of its revenue from ads, it would make sense to change the editorial focus and circulation procurement to exclude hockey watchers and restrict readership to the players who buy hockey equipment. But more than 75% of *Hockey News*'s revenue comes from circulation.

It is usually impractical to support a limited circulation special-interest publication on advertising revenue unless the special-interest is directly related to a rich advertising market. If there is no such market, the magazine had better depend on circulation revenue, as the *Harvard Business Review* does; develop a big circulation, as *Psychology Today* tried to do; or change to a special-audience publication, as *50 Plus* did. The limited-circulation special-audience magazine, incidentally, succeeds in advertising only so far as the limits on its audience improves its demographics.

There are few special interests wide enough for big circulation with corresponding advertising categories. Among the few are fashion, beauty, home care, and baby care.

Some notes on business papers

By definition and numbers, business papers and professional magazines are limited-circulation publications. Since most industrial marketing tends to be targeted by industries, most business papers are special-audience, and job-category or job-title analysis takes the place of demographic analysis.

Although many special-interest business papers have controlled circulation, e.g., *Muffler Digest* and *Modern Office Procedures*, controlled circulation is fundamentally a special-audience technique. With a pre-selected audience, it is natural to edit for the audience rather than to the subject. Thus controlled-circulation books tend to become special-audience even when they were launched to fill a special-interest need. *Marketing & Media Decisions*, formerly *Media Decisions*, is an example.

From the advertising sales view, the better a business paper can prove it is a special-interest publication, the easier it should be to sell advertisers with products or services dependent on that interest.

MANAGEMENT REVIEW

Check List for Audience vs. Interest Implications

I. Decide whether your publication is . .
A. __ big-circulation (potential readers total at least 5% of the adult population).

or __ limited-circulation (potential readers deliberately limited to a population segment of under 5%).

B. __ special-audience, i.e.,
   • editing is more audience-directed than subject-directed.
   • your core readers feel the publication adds to many different aspects of their lives.
   • yours is a limited-circulation publication supported by ad revenue from many categories of advertisers.

or __ special-interest, i.e.,
   • editing is more subject-directed than audience directed.
   • your core readers associate the publication with a specific, limited facet of their lives.
   • yours is a limited-circulation publication with revenue predominantly from one ad category.

II. Evaluate your editorial.
A. For special-audience publications:
   1. Do you exploit the full range of possible editorial forms?
   2. Are you making the most of the personal editorial editorial approach?

    3. How successful are you in anticipating your audience's needs?

    4. Is there a dominant editorial decision maker, or does editorial suffer from committee editing?

B. For special-interest publications:

    1. Are you careful to avoid editorial features that do not contribute to the special interest?

    2. Are editorial decisions disciplined enough not to indulge personal likes at the expense of the special interest?

    3. Is the publication really tuned in to current and future developments in its special interest?

    4. Is there enough input, both objective and thorough, from staff members and other experts to keep coverage of the special interest?

III. Evaluate the circulation program.

A. For special-audience publications:

    1. Do promotions succeed in getting readers to try the publication?

    2. Does the magazine use enough trial and no-risk offers?

    3. Do trial subscriptions run long enough to convert the reader?

    4. Is there enough promotion to make single-copy sales work for a special-audience publication?

B. For special-interest publications:

    1. Are promotions restricted to people with the special-interest?

    2. Do the promotions sell the publication's contribution to the special interest, rather than waste time selling the special interest itself?

    3. Do circulation offers, cover and subscription prices take advantage of the special-interest prospect's readiness to make a commitment?

    4. Is the single-copy sales program geared to the special interest in terms of outlets, covers and promotion?

IV. Evaluate the advertising-sales program (if advertising does or should supply the bulk of your magazine revenue).

A. For special-audience publications:

    1. Can the magazine reach big circulation soon enough to compete in the numbers race?

    2. If no, does limited circulation improve demographics sufficiently to make the magazine competitive?

B. For special-interest publications:

    1. Is there an advertising market directly related to the special editorial interest?

2. If yes, (a) is that market large enough to provide the advertising revenue the magazine needs?

(b) does sales exploit the ''common sense technique'' in selling space?

(c) are editorial and promotion careful not to cultivate readers who do not contribute to profits?

3. If no, (a) can the magazine reach big circulation soon enough to compete in the numbers race?

or (b) can the magazine switch to circulation for its principal source of revenue?

or (c) can the magazine become a special-audience publication with superior demographics?

CHAPTER THREE

Are Editors Entertainers or Educators?

Featuring an Interview with
James B. Horton
President of Working Woman

Magazines have been called "the great educational medium." Yet, with the exception of small, very specialized publications, people read magazines mainly to pass the time. No matter how practical a magazine may be, it will never get and hold a mass audience unless it is entertaining.

It is easy to observe that even the most serious publications are enjoyed by the people who read them, and that something can be learned from the most frivolous entertainment vehicles. The hard question to answer is just what is the proper balance between entertainment and education in each particular case.

We chose Jim Horton for the following interview because we were intrigued by a statement he had made on another occasion: that the most important recent trend in magazine publishing was the move from entertainment to education. It was his opinion that the magazine medium, which was once predominantly an entertainment medium, had now become predominantly an educational medium.

Jim Horton is a magazine generalist in the best sense of the term. But, if we had to define his speciality, we would say it is magazine marketing. He is an expert in analyzing magazine markets and developing publications to fit them.

Jim began his career by selling space. In 1950, fresh from earning his B.A. at Columbia University, he took a sales job in the advertising department of *The Wall Street Journal*. Shortly after, he joined the Robert T. Kenyon Company, a sales organization representing European newspapers.

In 1955, Jim joined Curtis Publishing as a salesman for *American Home*. Management recognized his ability to see more than surface sales opportunities and, in 1958, promoted him to manager of research & sales development for that magazine. Two years later he was appointed manager of sales administration for all the Curtis magazines and, in 1963, he was made director of development & assistant to the president of the Curtis Publishing Company.

In 1964, in the midst of the troublesome period when Joseph Culligan was president of Curtis Publishing, Jim left to become director of print media relations at Young & Rubicam. Four years later he went back to magazines as publisher of *Atlas*, and in the following year, 1969, he became vice president and general manager for magazines at CRM Inc., publisher of *Psychology Today* and *Intellectual Digest*.

Jim remained at CRM after it was sold to Boise Cascade, but left when Boise Cascade sold it to Ziff-Davis Publishing. There followed a series of short adventures: working with Dr. Jonas Salk on a health magazine that never secured financing (1973-1974), as general manager of Dow Jones's *National Observer* (1975-1976), and as group vice president of Playboy Enterprises (1976-1978).

Then, in 1978, Dale Lang, founder of Media Networks, bought out the bankrupt *Working Woman*, and asked Jim to be its publisher and chief executive. Jim recently relinquished the publisher title, but remains president and chief executive officer.

INTERVIEW

Q: You once said the role of magazines in our society has shifted from entertainment to education. Does that mean entertainment magazines are finished?
A: No. As educational magazines like *National Geographic* and *Scientific American* were successful in the heyday of entertainment magazines, so there will always be room for magazines published to entertain.

Education and entertainment

Q: Don't all magazines have to be somewhat entertaining?
A: By entertainment media, I mean media used predominantly to kill time.

Q: The way most people use television?
A: There's a real parallel between television's role today and the role of the *Saturday Evening Post* in the '30s. I remember the *Saturday Evening Post* would arrive, and my aunt would lock herself in her room for about four hours to read it. She was killing time.

Q: That sounds as if she considered what she was doing more important than killing time.
A: I don't use "killing time" pejoratively. Killing time is important. Everybody needs relaxation.

Q: Is the function of a magazine like People *to entertain? Or does it inform, maybe even educate?*
A: It informs, but I don't think it educates. Few readers come away from it with concepts that give them a better understanding of their world.

Q: So information can entertain, as in gossip. But can't education also be entertaining?
A: A scientist may read *Scientific American* for entertainment, and good teachers make education exciting.

Q: We have to distinguish by motive. If the reader wants the information because he enjoys gathering it, it's entertainment. If he wants it for use of self-improvement, it's education.

Education and knowledge

A: Peter Drucker was one of our advisers at *Psychology Today*. He holds that the body of knowledge is growing so rapidly that we awake each morning knowing less proportionately than we knew the day before. Our grandfathers may have been able to go to school and live off that knowledge for the rest of their lives. We can't. We have to learn continually, just to keep up.

Q: That should be a boon for magazines.
A: It is. Dan Yankelovich did a study showing that *Psychology Today* was teaching psychology to more people than all the schools put together. Magazines are great educational instruments, less expensive and more available than classes, easier to keep updated and current than books.

Education and instruction

Q: Isn't there another, preliminary distinction: how-to magazines? We can hardly call instruction on applying makeup education, but it's not entertainment either.
A: But even how-to magazines add educational elements. A woman reading how to apply makeup is also interested in what it does to her skin. The public is constantly becoming better educated, forcing magazines to shift to dealing with concepts, ideas, judgment.

Q: There are certainly more people with an education, but are they really better educated? Ability to read doesn't guarantee an interest in education. In medieval times, the relatively few people who could read used that ability more preciously.
A: Then one man could know all there was to know. Galileo could be in the forefront of every science. That is impossible today. Look at the university journals, hundreds of them in every imaginable field.

Q: But the universities themselves have changed. The medieval universities were dedicated almost 100% to education. How-to was left to the guilds. Today's universities are more concerned with how-to than why.
A: One of the greatest confusions in education today is in deciding why we educate. Are we educating to produce doctors, lawyers and accountants? Or are we educating to produce educated people? It's quite different.

Education and value systems

Q: Do more readers look for entertainment, instruction or education in justifying their reading?
A: It's not so much useful vs. pleasant, as relevant vs. irrelevant. They are interested in relevance both in entertainment and pursuit of knowledge: what relates to their lifestyle, their value system. When I was publisher of *Psychology Today*, someone sent us an article on shamanism, the belief in spirits responsive only to witch doctors. The editors turned it into an article on the Grand Shaman

of 1600 Pennsylvania Avenue. It drew parallels between shamanistic ritual and the place of the presidency in our society. The article achieved much greater reader acceptance not because it was more entertaining, or more educational, but because it had been related to readers' lifestyles and value systems.

Q: You're talking about the first law of journalism: relate the information to the reader's interests.
A: That's also the first law of education. I had a great teacher who taught us Homer's *Odyssey*. He taught it to us not as the story of a man in ancient times, but as an allegory of our own lives. He made Homer exciting. I once attended a meeting of scholars to discuss the Vietnam War. Margaret Mead saw the war as a continuation of the tribal rivalries that had plagued the country for centuries. To Herbert Marcuse it was a phase in the worldwide people's revolution. One historian saw it as a replay of the American Civil War, with the industrialized North seeking to control the resources of the agricultural South. Another looked at it as a continuation of colonialism. What fascinated me was not how they disagreed, but how each brought some meaning and sense out of the chaos of facts. I think magazines have a similar function.

Education and problem solving

Q: Academics have a way of considering their job done once they have classified information. They're more interested in qualifying facts than in solving problems. Don't readers expect magazines to go further?
A: The responsibility of academics is not to solve problems, but to give future leaders the intellectual tools for solving problems. It's much the same for magazines. Editors shouldn't be envisioned as sitting on high, revealing truth to the uninformed.

Q: Would readers be happy if Working Woman *offered no solutions for the problems facing women who work?*
A: Our job is not to solve readers' problems, but to provide insights, concepts they can use in solving their problems. Even in our case histories, the solution of the problem is not as significant as the insights or concepts that can be drawn from the case.

Education and belonging

Q: For many readers, isn't sharing the problem almost as important as learning a principle?
A: Magazines do many things for readers. A major one is making readers feel better about themelves. We tell our readers it's okay to be a working woman. The ability to do that explains a lot of the success of *Reader's Digest, Cosmopolitan* and *Working Woman.*

Q: That brings us to another point: the importance of a sense of belonging.
A: *Psychology Today* editor George Harris (now at *American Health*) used to say the best model for magazines was the community weekly which wrote about the people who read it. But community is much more than geography. Many communities are national: the publishing community or chess-playing community.

Education and advertising

Q: How does the educational function impact magazines in selling space to advertisers?
A: Advertisers should analyze a magazine's educational approach, the reader concern on which the editors focus. At Young & Rubicam we created a series of ads with women standing in their kitchens in scuba gear, with skis, and so on. They went over big with John Mack Carter, then editor of *Ladies' Home Journal.* He saw *LHJ* as a magazine for busy women anxious to get cooking and housekeeping out of the way so that they could go out and do fun things. But Gerry Rhoads, then at *Woman's Day*, said our ads would insult her readers, for she edited *Woman's Day* for women who like to use their hands, who were proud of cooking and housekeeping. A Lloyd Hall analysis of both books showed a more-or-less identical coverage of housekeeping subjects. But the guts of what each magazine was, the editorial foci, were quite different, a difference that is measured by none of the services.

Q: Yet extremely important to advertisers.
A: Absolutely. You've got to read the magazines. There are big differences between the home-service books. *Better Homes & Gardens* is very much a practical here-and-now magazine. Other home books are wish or dream books. They involve readers in a different way. Both approaches are valid, but one can be better for a particular advertiser. A handy-man product in *Better Homes & Gardens*; a luxury item in *Architectural Digest*.

Education and circulation promotion

Q: How important is all this to circulation promotion?
A: Very. There are super-slick writers of direct-mail packages who prefer to sell what they think will draw rather than the magazine. Or they'll describe the magazine's subject matter. Neither is good promotion in the long run. Circulation promotion should tell readers how they'll benefit from reading the magazine, how its insight will affect their lives, their problems. Sometimes editors don't understand this. I remember an editor at *Intellectual Digest* being upset by a promotion suggesting people should read the magazine to be the life of the party, one-up intellectually over their peers. He wanted copy on new ideas as the cutting edge of society, on being renaissance men—all true, but not telling readers how they would benefit.

Q: Working Woman *was in pretty sad shape when you took over. It's in great shape now. Did what we've been talking about have any bearing on the change?*
A: A lot. We narrowed the basic editorial idea, focusing it. The founding editors came out of *Family Circle.* They wanted to address all the working women in the U.S., create another 10-million circulation magazine. The fact that people work does not make them a magazine audience. They have to see their problems in a certain way. They have to want a certain type of education. We found that women who are moving up in the business world have a real information need. They are the people we can help. If I were to get another 500,000 circulation, and they were all women who worked, but were dying to get married and quit work, I'd be in trouble. Our readers' median age is 32-33. They're women who want to work, career women.

Q: Are you reaching your circulation plateau?
A: We're currently moving our rate base up to 575,000, and I am sure we'll go higher. But we won't broaden our focus to do it. We'll grow because the number of career-oriented women is growing.

ANALYSIS

Reader Goals and Magazine Means

According to Jim Horton, the function of magazines in our society has shifted from entertainment to education. He gives two reasons for this. First, the entertainment function has been usurped by other media, principally television. Second, the need for education has grown with the tremendous growth in the body of man's knowledge.

Everything Jim says is borne out by experience. If we search *Standard Rate & Data*'s consumer magazine edition, we find that since 1970 more than 50 important magazines have been launched and are still publishing. (At least ten more have been started since, but are not old enough to be labeled successes.) Of the 50, only six can be said to have entertainment as their primary function: *Games, Hustler, Oui, People Weekly, Soap Opera Digest and Us.*

There are others, like *Country Music, Omni, Playgirl, Soldier of Fortune, Travel & Leisure, W,* and even *Smithsonian* and *Life,* that are used by many readers primarily for entertainment, but which are clearly not edited primarily to entertain. In fact, *Playgirl,* which could have been designated an entertainment magazine when it was launched in 1973, survived by making the entertainment function secondary to service.

From another angle, consider the 19 U.S. magazines that have been publishing for more than a century: *Atlantic, Capper's Weekly, Christian Herald, Episcopalian, Graduate Woman, Grit, Harper's Bazaar, Harper's, The Living Church, McCall's, The Nation, New York Times Magazine, Popular Science, Presbyterian Survey, Saturday Evening Post, Scientific American, Thoroughbred Record* and *Town & Country.* Even though some of these were once read primarily for entertainment, none of them is now. And those publications to whom entertainment was most important—*Saturday Evening Post, Grit, Capper's Weekly*—are considerably less important than they once were.

Needham, Harper & Steers ceo Paul Harper calls our decade the "contradictory '80s," since we are experiencing "a colossal polarization of people's tastes and values." He describes the two poles as "earth values" (basic, practical, useful) and "feather values" (flighty, sensational, exotic, self-gratifying). Both poles offer marketing opportunity for media—including magazines. But some media, such as television, will find greater opportunities in feather values, while others, e.g., magazines, will find more opportunities in earth value.

The entertainment/instruction balance

As is clear in the interview with Jim Horton, a magazine need not be an entertainment magazine to entertain. In fact, the best teachers make learning entertaining. Although all editors should try to be entertaining, they should know how important the entertainment factor is to their magazine. Being entertaining is far more important to *Mad Magazine* or *National Lampoon* than to *Scientific American* or even *Omni*.

What determines the difference, the degree of importance? The values or desires of the magazine's reader market. For the purposes of this analysis we can reduce all motivation to pleasure (an end in itself) or usefulness (a means to other ends). Most readers are motivated by both pleasure and use. But some look primarily for pleasure, others primarily for use.

There are three levels of usefulness in editorial: 1) what is useful for the intellect, helping us to understand; 2) what is useful in developing taste, helping us to judge or evaluate; and 3) what is useful in perfecting skills, helping us to do something. As a general rule, the more editorial is targeted at the intellect, the less entertaining it has to be, the less readers who want that type of editorial will expect to be entertained.

In other words, the entertainment/instruction or fun/work balance tends to shift away from entertainment or fun, and move toward instruction or work, as the editorial target approaches the intellectual.

Thus the intellectual approach of *U.S. News & World Report* depends less on entertainment than the taste-oriented *Architectural Digest*, which in turn does not require as many entertainment values as the skill-sharpening *Good House-keeping*.

Note that we are speaking only of minimum requirements for marketing the editorial product, not about absolute or ideal editorial goals. It is possible to be exquisitely entertaining while appealing directly to the intellect. But that requires uncommon genius. Shakespeare, Dickens and other great writers managed to entertain as they increased understanding and developed taste. But for every great book sold as entertainment, a hundred potboilers have achieved equal or greater financial success. For every Santayana and William James among philosophers, there are a hundred who contribute to the thought but not the pleasure of their readers.

Entertainment and the need for fringe readers

There is one external factor that can disrupt our concept. The more important the useful goal is to the readers, the less entertainment is required to make it palatable. An educational or instructional magazine with 100% hard-core readers has no need to entertain. Thus specialized how-to magazines, like *Family Handyman* or *Horse Care*, can neglect entertainment, while mass how-to magazines, like *Self* or *Family Circle*, cannot.

This fact, however, has a very important economic consequence. Many magazines cannot afford to operate with only a hard-core readership. Those for whom the editorial is indispensable are too few or too poor to provide the income (from advertising, circulation or a combination) required to run the magazine. Such publications depend on fringe readers to exist, and the more entertaining a magazine becomes, the easier it is to attract fringe readers.

This is a principal reason why, over the years, *The New Yorker* has been so much more successful than *Harper's* or *Atlantic; National Geographic* more so than *Natural History* or *Sierra; Time* and *Newsweek* more than *U.S. News & World Report. The New Yorker* built strong entertainment value with cartoons and fillers, *National Geographic* with pictures, *Time* and *Newsweek* with human interest.

Another important factor can help magazines like *The New Yorker* and *National Geographic* with fringe readers: prestige value and/or the fringe reader's self-esteem. Many readers keep subscribing to these magazines, not because they read them, but because they want others to see they get them, or want to convince themselves they are going to read them. Magazines targeted at taste or intellect, of course, can generate this kind of appeal much more easily than those targeted at skill or pure entertainment.

Converting fringe readers to core readers

Good editors see the need for the sugar-coating of entertainment, but never let it interfere with or replace the central purpose of the publication. In fact, the great goal of sugar-coating is to attract fun readers who may eventually become serious readers.

There are magazines whose success can be traced to outside forces that increased the number of potential core readers. *Runner's World* would never have reached 400,000 circulation if running and physical fitness had not become a national craze. But, as publisher Bob Anderson says in Chapter 19, *Runner's World* also played a part in increasing that market by making the magazine's editorial relevant to more people.

Jim Horton speaks of gaining reader acceptance by making editorial matter more relevant to the lifestyle and value systems of readers. Marathon running was once relevant only to potential winners. *Runner's World* made the subject relevant to many more by making finishing, not winning, a goal in running marathons.

The ability to make a magazine's editorial relevant to more people, without diluting its focus, is the secret to great editing. Relevance is superior to entertainment primarily because it builds core readers, while entertainment attracts fringe readers. And the former are more lasting and valuable than the latter.

Four ways to be more relevant

A magazine is in focus when it fully satisfies the expectations of its core readers. These readers expect certain types of subject matter. But people do not read for subject matter; they read to fill needs. Hence any subject that fills the need will satisfy their expectations, and no subject will violate those expectations if the editors make it relevant.

There are an infinite number of ways to make information or ideas relevant to an audience, but most of them can be reduced to four: private-relevance, person-relevance, party-relevance and place-relevance.

Private-relevance makes a topic important because it directly concerns the reader as an individual. When *Cosmopolitan* ran an article on phone-answering devices, it pointed out how a machine can end the uncertainty of whether the man in a woman's life tried to phone her.

Person-relevance gives a topic importance by using it to add knowledge about someone in whom the reader is interested—usually a public figure, since the same person must be of interest to many readers. *Psychology Today* turned a piece on shamanism into an article on the President.

Party-relevance relates the subject to the group, appealing to the reader's sense of belonging. Readers of *Black Enterprise* (or *50 Plus*) are more interested in the achievements of black businessmen (or elder citizens) than in those of white businessmen (or younger citizens), even when there is no difference in the lesson or information to be learned.

Place-relevance makes something more important by bringing it closer to home geographically. The readers of *San Diego* find more appeal in stories on that city than they would in similar stories about other cities.

Practical applications

Once a publisher has determined how important entertainment is to his or her publications, several conclusions can be drawn from the foregoing, conclusions that affect editorial, advertising sales and circulation promotion.

1. A magazine's need for editorial flair, i.e., editors with genius, is determined less by its editorial target than by the number of fringe readers it requires. Core readers are attracted by subject-matter, fringe readers by presentation. This, of course, is balanced by the fact that magazines with large circulation usually are in a position to afford more talented editors.

2. Entertainment and prestige values give advertisers numbers, not attention. One way for a magazine to overcome a lack of entertainment value and a loss of fringe circulation is to reduce its circulation guarantee and raise its cpm. Advertisers to whom attention is more important than numbers will accept this.

3. Circulation promotion must be closely coordinated with editorial policy. Nothing can kill a magazine faster than an editorial department concerned only with core readers combined with a circulation department acquiring lots of fringe readers. There is real danger in hiring circulation-promotion experts with more flair and genius than your editors. It is vital to make sure that editorial and circulation people are equally talented, that they understand and respect each other, and that they agree on what is best for the magazine as a whole.

MANAGEMENT REVIEW

Check List for Editorial Fun/Work Balance

I. Indicate your publication's primary editorial target.
_____Pleasure: entertaining readers.
_____Skill: teaching readers how to do things.
_____Taste: teaching readers how to evaluate or appreciate.
_____Intellect: helping readers to understand.

II. Indicate the proportion of fringe readers your publication needs.
_____A very high proportion (e.g., over 45%).

_____A moderately high proportion (30%-45%).
_____A small but significant proportion (10%-29%)
_____A negligible proportion (under 10%).

III. Determine the need for entertainment in your publication by target and audence.

A) _____If pleasure is the target, entertainment is always paramount and essential.

B) _____If skill is the target, and the proportion of fringe readers needs is:
_____Very high, entertainment is crucial.
_____Moderately high, entertainment is vital.
_____Significant, entertainment is important.
_____Negligible, entertainment is unimportant.

C) _____If taste or intellect is the target, prestige or self-esteem values can substitute for entertainment values so that, if the proportion of fringe readers needed is:
_____Very high, entertainment is vital.
_____Moderately high, entertainment is important.
_____Significant, entertainment is helpful.
_____Negligible, entertainment is unimportant.

IV. Evaluate your publication's success in achieving necessasry entertainment values.

A) _____Very successful.

B) _____Could stand improvement.

C) _____Fails seriously.

V. If improvement is indicated, select a course of action.

A) _____Increase and improve your publication's entertainment values by doing one or more of the following:
_____Developing awareness and ability in your editorial staff.
_____Hiring additional or different editorial people.
_____Increasing the editorial budget to purchase more entertaining material.

B) _____Decrease your publication's dependence on entertainment by doing one or more of the following:
1) _____Making it possible to reduce circulation and eliminate fringe readers

_____by cutbacks in operating costs.

_____by charging readers more.

_____by charging advertisers more.

2) _____Retaining circulation levels but increasing the proportion of core readers

_____by making the editorial more relevant to more people.

_____by changing circulation-promotion techniques.

3) _____Repositioning the publication to make it less dependent on entertainment.

CHAPTER FOUR

Business vs. Consumer Editing —How Different?

Featuring an Interview with
Joel Harnett
President of Media Horizons

It used to be said that business publications had to settle for editors who could not make the grade on consumer magazines. It never was true, and it is being said less and less.

Editors have jumped from business publications to consumer magazines, and from consumer magazines to business papers. Herb Mayes was editor of *American Druggist* long before he became editor of *McCall's*. Jim Brady, former editor of *Harper's Bazaar*, is now on the staff of *Advertising Age*.

Is business editing a totally different profession than consumer editing? Or is there no difference beyond the subject matter?

To find the answer we interviewed Joel Harnett, president of Media Horizons. We chose Joel because, after working almost two decades with *Look* magazine, he went into business publishing—giving him ample experience in dealing with both consumer and business editors and, more important, in dealing with the marketing of both consumer and business magazines.

Joel Harnett is a graduate of the University of Richmond and a major in the Army Reserve. He began his career in publishing at the age of 25, when he joined *Look* magazine's promotion department. He spent 19 years with *Look*, and was vice president of marketing in charge of research and promotion when he resigned, in 1969, to found Media Horizons.

Media Horizons started with two radio stations, WGNY and WFMN in Orange County, New York. But the company soon purchased United Business Publications, a small publisher of business magazines, among them *Audio-Visual Communications, Industrial Photography* and *Laboratory Management*.

Today Media Horizons owns 10 magazines. Many of the additions are the direct result of Joel's ability to recognize and open a market niche and create a magazine to fill it. Among his most successful launches were *Videography* and *Marketing Communications* (both in 1976) and Media Horizon's only consumer affiliate, *Phoenix Home/Garden*.

Joel's interests have always been very cosmopolitan. He was chairman of the City Club of New York, ran for mayor of New York (in 1977), helped launch Marketing Communications Executives International, once wrote *Look*'s annual multimedia shows, and is credited with inventing the use of Zip Codes for demographic editions of mass magazines.

INTERVIEW

Q: What do you consider the principal difference between consumer and business publications?
A: Style, manner of presentation. Even when it's very specialized, like a hobby magazine, the consumer publication needs more flair, more graphic excitement, more attention-getting and attention-holding devices.

Q: Because there's no external need to read a consumer magazine, whereas there is for a business paper?
A: Even when readers are so involved in a hobby that they feel they must read about it, it's not the same as obtaining information you need to earn your living.

Editorial differences

Q: Are business-paper sources closer to the readership than sources for consumer-magazine editorial?
A: Often, not always, business sources are also readers of the publication. This

is less likely with consumers, who usually rely on the magazine for expertise they do not have. This also influences the type of people you write about and how you write about them. Business readers are interested in success or failure, what the subject did. Consumer readers are interested in personality and glamour as well as information. Subjects are more likely to be stars, intriguing personalities, cultural phenomena, or startling new developments.

Q: Does this mean you need a different type of editor?
A: I think so, and that's why it is difficult, often impossible, for a business-paper operation to move into consumer publishing. Expert trade-paper editors know their industry well, know the people who make news, and can go right to the jugular in getting the facts and interpreting what's happening. Such knowledge is not enough for consumer editors. In fact, knowledge in consumer magazines is often less important than presentation. You read more superficial stories in consumer magazines. Consumer editors need style, a flair for presenting ideas and information creatively, qualities that are seldom found even among the most knowledgeable and expert trade-paper editors.

Q: Would you say consumer magazines tend more to generate editorial excitement from within?
A: Its excitement is that of a creative production, often a team effort of art director, writer and editor.

Q: What about developing a leadership position? To make a consumer magazine stand out in its market you can be more creative, hire better writers, develop a unique personality for the magazine. Can you become the leader in a business-paper field in the same way?
A: There's no rule. A strong publisher helps in the business field, someone around whom a magazine seems to coalesce, someone the industry recognizes as a leader. Business-paper publishers should make it their life to know the industry and care about it. That's essential for leadership—to know what has to be covered and how it has to be covered, the kind of circulation you need, the precise service you can give to all advertisers, and how much money is required to do it all.

Q: Is it easier to challenge the leader in a business field than in a consumer field?
A: It depends on the field. Because industry fields are easy to define, trade papers are an easy-entry business—monthlies more than weeklies. Our company was one of the first to publish a video trade magazine. We now have five or six competitors. The hotter the industry the more competition. To an extent, it's true in consumer fields. But consumer magazine economics get tougher all the time.

The markets are too large or too dispersed to be captured without a major investment. There are easier opportunities in trade publishing.

Differences in selling space

Q: An important objective of business-paper advertising is to generate leads for industrial sales. Such leads mean far less in consumer advertising.
A: That's very important for trade books. There are industries, like consumer media, that don't want direct response to their ads. But most industries not only want response, but use it to evaluate media.

Q: Hence bingo cards are more common in trade papers.
A: Not all business papers have them, but most do. And they can be very powerful tools. We own trade papers that generate 50,000 to 100,000 responses. At *Look*— with seven million circulation— it took something really out of the ordinary to come close to that.

Q: Is this because trade papers are better read?
A: The trade paper is a channel of communication for the industry it serves. It creates a live network of people attentive to their industry. If the magazine is on target, its readers will be very responsive to each other and to the advertisers. Hence response is a very important indicator of a trade paper's vitality.

Q: Is this in part because most business-paper ads are primary ads, about the same subjects as the editorial?
A: Ads unrelated to the editorial usually can't afford to use business papers. The cpm is too high, and the editorial environment is not helpful.

Q: Yet business papers have tried to sell as a group, or use other techniques to get consumer advertising.
A: And it doesn't usually work. It can work for speciality consumer books, where the numbers are big, like the old Ziff-Davis magazines and Petersen networks. In trade papers cpms are higher and it's not as easy sell. Trade papers have tried card mailings, and mail-order consumer items. But that's an attempt to ride the trade paper's high response rate.

Differences in circulation practices

Q: Isn't it puzzling that newsletters concentrate on the business field so that they can charge high prices for subscriptions, yet so many trade papers rely on free circulation? If the editorial is so much part of the readers' lives, why won't they pay for it?

A: It's numbers. You can make money on a newsletter with relatively small circulation, but it's very hard to do that with a magazine's high production costs. So you have to rely on advertising, and that requires circulation coverage. If your circulation is paid, competitors can always lower their subscription prices, or give their magazines away to get better coverage.

Q: If a trade paper is really read, it's read for business reasons and it's not hard to get the business to pay for it. If you have to give away the magazine to get coverage, chances are it isn't being read. Why is it that advertisers don't come to that conclusion?

A: Only newsletters can be so specialized or so provocative that their limited audiences cannot get along without them. Magazines, with much larger audiences and many more pages, cannot be that specialized. Since they depend on advertising, they also can't be as provocative. Nor can a magazine be as timely or concentrated as a newsletter. Executives read a business paper because it carries a lot of information that concerns them, but most of it is information they can get elsewhere, often without much effort. You cannot charge them a high price for that, particularly when other publications, with similar material, give it away free.

Q: Competition leads to free circulation?

A: Competition makes it very difficult to build a package people are willing to pay for. Our company has one ABC business publication, *Videography*. It's preeminent in its field. Everyone who came after us has free circulation. We've managed to hold the lead position and remain paid because of vigorous editorial and superior coverage. But we're talking about a $15 subscription, not $100 or $200. If we charged $100, our circulation would soon be too small to sell advertising.

Q: Isn't it usually easier for a business paper to compile a list covering the desired audience than it is for a consumer magazine?

A: In most fields, yes. But it's harder in some than in others. It can be very difficult in areas of emerging technology, before a field is clearly defined. For most of our top publications we had to develop our own lists—and continually update them. But it's usually easier than building an audience for a consumer book.

Q: What about ease in compiling prospect lists?
A: It depends on how specialized the magazine is. It's much easier to get a list of beauty parlors than a list of people who use beauty parlors. And with consumer magazines, a big problem is how many readers are enough? The answer is easy for most business papers, while for consumer magazines it requires a complicated formula involving publishing economics and marketing strategy.

Q: Is it easier for business papers to get renewals?
A: It depends. An emerging field will have a lot of turnover. People aren't sure what your magazine is, or what they want. It takes a year or more to find the audience, and then, if a magazine is on target, the percentage of renewals will jump way up.

Q: Don't business papers need higher market-penetration and, therefore, higher renewal percentages?
A: Yes. Their universe is better known, more limited, and high renewal is essential to maintain competitive coverage of the critical mass of industry readers and leaders.

Q: But audited free-circulation books have to obtain periodic written requests, which for all practical purposes is like soliciting renewals.
A: But still easier to get than bona fide paid subscriptions.

Q: Are there fewer fringe readers in business-paper audiences than there are in consumer-magazine audiences?
A: There should be, because the publications deal with their business. There's little point to reading them otherwise. Consumer magazines are more likely to have many readers who pick up issues only occasionally, and don't mind missing an issue altogether. It's entertainment for them.

Q: Isn't part of it, too, that consumer magazines have more need to constantly feel their way and try to expand their reader universe?
A: That's changing. More and more consumer books are raising newsstand prices and cutting back on circulation, going after a smaller, more easily defined audience, e.g., *House & Garden, Sports Afield*. The economics of publishing today make it less and less feasible to maintain peripheral circulation. One of the reasons for the success of Hearst Magazines is that they've understood that. They make money from circulation.

Q: Would you say the more circumscribed a consumer magazine's audience, the closer it is to a business paper?

A: A key element in publishing for a community, whether business or consumer, is that the smaller, more homogeneous the community you serve, the easier it is to get close to that community and become important to it. There are many ways to do that, and publishers should explore them all: books, newsletters, research, trade shows and conferences. Our basic business is not publishing. It's communications. We should serve the total communications needs of a particular group. This is easier to do in a trade field than in most consumer fields. But consumer magazines can do it.

ANALYSIS

Distinguishing Magazine Types by Needs Served

There are several standard ways of classifying magazines when studying the different requirements for marketing and managing them. We can speak of mass vs. class, based on reader demographics. There are general-interest magazines and specialized magazines, and specialized magazines can be special-interest or special-audience (see chapter 2). Finally, there are the two categories that concern us here: consumer and business.

All these classifications, including the last, are easier to distinguish in theory than in practice. Is *National Geographic* a mass or class magazine? Is *Reader's Digest* of general interest— or does it specialize in self-improvement? Is *Scientific American* a magazine of special-interest or special-audience? Are *Spectrum*, edited for engineers, and *Diversion*, edited for doctors, consumer or business publications?

Irvin Borowsky, the savvy chief of North American Publishing, distinguishes between consumer and business magazines chiefly in terms of risk. Consumer publishing offers more chance to make it big, and more chance to lose lots of money. ("Starting a Consumer Magazine," *FOLIO*, February 1982). Trade papers are safer because establishing circulation is easier. But this, too, is relative. Joel Harnett points out that circumstances can make business circulation very difficult.

A marketing classification

If we take a marketing approach, viewing each magazine as a service filling a need, we arrive at a more useful classification, one that can help in evaluating management alternatives.

Magazines can be needed in three ways:

(1) Essentially. The magazine provides the only way to do something. For most readers in the computer industry *Computerworld* fills an essential need. *Guitar Player* may be essential to advertise a new type of guitar.

(2) Preferentially. Objectives can be attained in other ways, but the magazine is the preferred way. Readers can get similar information elsewhere, but prefer to get it from *Health*. An advertiser prefers to use *Better Homes & Gardens*, though other media reach his prospects.

(3) For gratification. The magazine is used because the use itself provides satisfaction. This is the reader appeal of entertainment magazines like *National Lampoon*. It can be the advertiser appeal for magazines read by an advertiser's peers. e.g. *Playbill, Business Week* or *Fortune*.

When we speak of the differences in editing (and managing and marketing) business papers vs. consumer magazines, we are usually—but not always—describing the differences between publications serving essential needs and those filling preferential or gratification needs.

It is the contention of this chapter that for editing, managing and marketing, it is more advantageous to concentrate on the type of need a publication fills rather than whether it is a business paper or a consumer magazine.

Serving readers essentially

Joel Harnett's principal distinction between consumer and business publishing is that consumer magazines need more flair, graphic excitement, attention-getting and attention-holding devices. When the reader need is essential, such devices are nice but irrelevant. The *New England Journal of Medicine* is frequently a joy to read, but the doctors who read it would have to read it even if it were hard labor. When a business paper covers industry news, most executives in its field consider it essential. They need to know what is going on, and will read even when presentation is lackluster and graphics humdrum.

As Joel Harnett points out, most industries have several competing publications. In theory, once two magazines cover the same field, the need for either becomes preferential. In reality, business readers seldom trust one publication to cover everything, and consider it essential to page through several.

One reason why *Business Week, Forbes* and *Fortune* are often referred to as consumer publications is that their need for most readers is preferential. Very few executives feel they have to keep up with everything going on in the entire business world. Researchers Trewhella/Cohen/Arbuckle (working for Cahners Publishing) found that 88% of decision makers in 25 industries read at least one of the top four trade magazines, but only 73% read one or more of the five top general business publications.

Editorial competition can take place in two areas: matter and form. If the basic thrust of the magazine is to fill an essential need, matter is far more important than form. The best editors for such publications are the ones who really know their industries and work hard at getting the facts. Nancy McMillan, editor of *Boston Business Journal*, says it's her job ''to find reporters who know how to pick the brains of the experts.'' No good editor neglects presentation and graphics, but in this kind of magazine they are definitely secondary.

Many consumer magazines come as close to serving essential needs as any business publication. For most of their readers *Byte, Custom Bike, Guitar Player, Racing Digest* and *Rodeo News* fill an essential need. Here, too, matter is more important than form.

When a magazine serves an essential need, it is usually much easier to determine its editorial goals and there is far less danger of getting bogged down in positioning problems. Essential needs tend to be clearcut, easy to define—for readers and editors. The less a magazine's success depends on presentation or style, the less it is subject to constantly-changing, hard-to-pin-down popular taste.

Serving readers preferentially

A magazine serving preferential needs does not have the reader's sense of obligation working for it. Readers are drawn to the magazine because its material is useful or good for them, but they pick and choose, reading only what catches their fancy.

Editors, writers, and art directors on such publications must be more skilled, more creative. When they use authorities for columns and articles, they either engage experts with a flair for writing, or provide a lot of help in presentation and choice of subject.

Because a high degree of creativity is required, such magazines have the advantage of being able to manage with a lot of material that does not require extensive research. Articles in competing publications differ less in what they say than in how they say it, whether it is *Venture* vs. *Inc.* on cash flow, or *Savvy* vs. *Cosmopolitan* on skin care.

There are two major disadvantages for preferential magazines. The very fact that editors do not need original material encourages insubstantial fluff, and the pressure for creative forms leads the less talented to lean on formulae. Ideas that work are repeated over and over. Hence the interminable procession of women's-magazine covers with pretty faces looking directly at the reader.

Serving readers for gratification

A magazine serving gratification needs depends entirely on how much pleasure readers get out of reading it (*National Lampoon*), looking at it (*Club*), or using it (*Jackpot*). Just as a candy stand and a restaurant both serve the pleasure of eating, so magazines can gratify either by the entertaining things they assemble (*Games, Cheri*) or by the entertaining manner of presentation (*Mad Magazine, National Lampoon*).

But the success of such publications always rests on how much pleasure they give the readers, which depends on creative ability, whether in choosing models and photographs for a men's sophisticate, or in deciding which games are too easy and which too hard for an audience of puzzle buffs.

Today, opportunities for magazines directed at gratification are far fewer than they used to be, due to competition from other media. On one level, television devours huge chunks of entertainment time; on another, the economics of soft-cover publishing enables books to compete directly against magazines. Moreover, since the power to gratify dulls quickly with repetition, gratification magazines survive either by high circulation turnover or by constant editorial renewal. Hence the ups and downs in *National Lampoon*'s success.

Serving advertisers essentially

Magazines serve their advertising markets also on the three levels of essential need, preferential need, and gratification need. The best example of a magazine serving an advertiser essentially is the magazine which is the only medium reaching the advertiser's primary market. There is no way a marketer of a new guitar accessory can reach primary prospects effectively outside the pages of *Guitar Player*, or the marketer of a new aerosol component, outside of *Aerosol Age*.

One reason why business papers are far more likely to serve advertisers essentially is the lack of other media covering specific business markets. Cable television may eventually change this but, today, most business books have no significant competition for their advertising market except direct mail and other business papers.

It is very easy to sell an advertiser who has an essential need for your magazine. But sole coverage is not enough. The advertiser must have a need to advertise. Karl Engel may have seen all medical media as essential advertisers when he started *Medical Advertising News*. But do medical media have to advertise? They have managed without a medium for years. Launching a magazine for essential advertisers is too easy for the field to be empty at this late date.

Serving advertisers preferentially

For the great majority of advertisers, most magazines are preferential—highly useful for marketing-communications but not individually essential. For preferential magazines success depends as much on how they sell as on what they sell, and buying decisions are determined by a multitude of incidental factors, often subjective.

Because ad directors of preferential media depend so much on sales skill, they often forget that preferential media still depend on ability to fill an advertiser's real needs. They begin to think they can sell anything, and waste time and money trying to sell categories that do not belong in their publications.

Serving advertisers for gratification

It is doubtful that any national magazine could generate sufficient cash flow just by filling the gratification needs of advertisers. But, for many magazines, such advertising provides a substantial supplement to regular advertising revenue. Advertising space bought for gratification takes five forms: vanity advertising to satisfy the ego of the advertiser, morale advertising to satisfy the ego of the advertiser's salespeople or employees, donor advertising to satisfy charitable instincts, token advertising to satisfy an opinion, and legal notices to satisfy the law.

In each form the decision to buy the space is more important than the advertisement itself. Hence very little creative energy is expended on such ads, and they can easily be an affront to the reader. They also tend to turn off regular advertisers and to develop a type of selling that is more hindrance than help in the business world. But there are exceptions. Gratification advertising played an important role in launching *Ms., Black Enterprise* and *Equal Opportunity.*

Needs are seldom simple

Human needs are almost always complex. The reader who has an essential need for your publication may also be using it to satisfy preferential and even gratification needs. The advertiser whom you know has an essential need to buy space in your publication may see it more as a preferential need, and may spend more if he also finds gratification in the purchase.

But in almost every case one need dominates, and the successful editor, as well as publisher, ad director, or circulation manager will direct strategy at the dominant need without losing sight of the secondary needs. Here is where editing business papers often differs from editing consumer magazines, and why publishers who diversify often run into trouble. The thing to remember is that two business books can sometimes differ more than a business and consumer book. What matters is the nature of the need on which a magazine is focused.

MANAGEMENT REVIEW

Check List to Evaluate by Type of Need

I. Classify your publication by determining how its primary readers need it:
_____Essentially. (They feel they cannot achieve their objectives without it.)
_____Preferentially. (They prefer using it, though it isn't the only way to achieve their objectives.)
_____For gratification. (They use it for the satisfaction they get from its use.)

II. Evaluate how your publication serves its readers:

A. To fill an essential reader need, the publication should:

____emphasize matter or content more than form or presentation.

____choose editors whose knowledge of the field is more important than their creative ability.

____put budget emphasis on fact-gathering rather than production and non-essential graphics.

____change editorial focus to anticipate the audience's changing information needs.

B. To fill a preferential reader need, the publication should:

____emphasize form or presentation more than matter or content.

____choose editors with high creative skills.

____put budget emphasis on production values and graphics.

____change editorial focus to anticipate the audience's changing tastes.

C. To fill a reader need for gratification, the publication should:

____emphasize entertainment before usefulness.

____choose editors who understand the audience's entertainment values and how to meet them.

____put budget emphasis on creating or gathering material to meet those values.

____change editorial focus to anticipate the audience's changing tastes.

III. Classify your publication by determining how its primary advertisers need it:

____Essentially. (They feel they cannot achieve their objectives without it.)

____Preferentially. (They prefer using it, though it isn't the only way to achieve their objectives.)

____For gratification. (They use it for the satisfaction they get from its use.)

IV. Evaluate how the publication serves its advertisers:

A. To fill an essential advertiser need, the publication should:

____provide as complete coverage as possible of the market the advertiser wants to reach.

____appeal to an audience to whom a sufficient number of advertisers really need to advertise.

____avoid audiences which advertisers can reach effectively through other media.

____make the space-buyer's convenience the core of the space-selling program.

B. To fill a preferential advertiser need, the publication should:

_____maintain a sales program that reaches all the space-buying influences.

_____develop personal relationships with the key people making the buying decisions.

_____provide data that makes it easy for space-buyers to justify choosing the publication.

_____establish some area where the publication can be proved to be the best medium, and make that fact the core of your space-selling program.

C. To fill an advertiser's need for gratification, the publication should:

_____in vanity or token advertising: appeal to the real reason covertly, while overtly providing reasons to justify the ad.

_____in morale, donor or legal advertising: stress the dual effectiveness of the ad.

CHAPTER FIVE

How Editorial Works for Advertising

Featuring an Interview with
Gilbert W. Chapman, Jr.
President of Diversion Publications

Most editors would like to go about their business and forget that advertising exists. But, in most cases, it is advertising that pays the editor's salary, and advertising that makes the magazine possible. Few magazines have died because editorial pages could not be filled. Many have died from a lack of advertising pages.

But, though advertising may finance the magazine, editorial makes it an advertising medium. Take the editorial matter out, and magazines would become catalogs, and catalogs with much smaller, less-interested audiences. In that sense, magazine editorial works for the advertisers.

But how precisely? Do editors have to worry about advertisers as well as readers? Are they serving readers or advertisers? Can they serve both?

In no area of publishing do feelings run stronger or publication policies differ more widely. And there is no subject in the magazine business where it is harder to achieve a consensus.

In fact, careful readers of the following interview and the analysis that follows will see that even here disagreement is evident.

We chose Gil Chapman for this interview because of his extensive experience with publications that differed widely in the relationship of their editorial to the advertising they carried. Gil has been publisher of business magazines, where editorial and advertising were so closely related it was sometimes hard to tell where one began and the other ended. He was president of *Esquire*, where there was no connection at all between the editorial matter and the ads. And he is now publisher and president of *Diversion*, which is mailed only to doctors, relies heavily on ads of interest only to doctors, but carries editorial in no way related to those ads.

Gil graduated from Yale in 1956. His first job was assistant to Jack Cominsky, publisher of the *Saturday Review*. In 1957, he moved to McGraw-Hill publications as a sales trainee.

Gil spent 12 years at McGraw-Hill, rising to publisher of "Force 5," the company's short-lived experiment in having a single centralized publishing operation for five related magazines (*Factory, Product Engineering, Industrial Distribution, American Machinist* and *Purchasing Week*). In 1971, McGraw-Hill sold the first three of those publications to Morgan-Grampian, an English company which hired Gil as chief operating officer of its U.S. operation.

In 1975, Gil took the big leap back into consumer magazines, and accepted the presidency of Esquire Inc.'s magazine division. In 1978, after Esquire Inc. sold *Esquire* magazine, Gil left to assume his present job as publisher-president of *Diversion*.

INTERVIEW

Q: Diversion is a very unique publication. Who had the original idea, and how was it started?
A: *Diversion* was launched in April 1973. The idea was developed by Johnson & Johnson, and Max Geffen published the magazine for them as a joint venture. It was then, as it is now, a controlled-circulation travel and leisure magazine for physicians. The original premise was that the only pharmaceutical ads carried in *Diversion* came from Johnson & Johnson subsidiaries. The magazine's outside revenue came from consumer advertisers interested in reaching doctors, a market with incredibly high demographics. Apparently the plan did not generate the revenue Johnson & Johnson expected. The magazine was sold to a group of private investors in April of 1976.

Q: The magazine did poorly in the first 18 months after the new management took over. What was the problem?

A: The new management's first big change was to open *Diversion* to all ethical drug advertisers. In the medical market, it was like starting a brand new magazine. It took 18 months for *Diversion* to gain full acceptance among pharmaceutical advertisers. Then it took off: 363 ad pages in 1977, 1,204 in 1978 and approximately 1,800 in 1979.*

Q: What proportion will be professional vs. consumer?
A: About 88% pharmaceutical; 12% consumer.

Editorial thrust vs. advertising thrust

Q: In theory, Diversion *shouldn't work. Editorial aims at the doctor's leisure, the ads at the doctor's work.*
A: I don't think the doctor turns the pages in *Diversion* saying to himself, "leisure, work, leisure, work." I think he says what the reader of any magazine says: "Editorial, advertising, editorial, advertising."

Q: Some time ago Business Week *had an advertising promotion campaign based on the theme, "There are two sides to every businessman: the business side and the consumer side." I don't think it worked.*
A: I disagree. Many magazines could live handsomely on *Business Week*'s consumer billings. Of course, its cpm is too high for many consumer advertisers. The great portion of their advertising will always be from the business sector. The same situation exists for *Diversion.*

Q: If a doctor's leisure magazine works for pharmaceutical ads, why don't medical books carry more consumer ads?
A: The great majority of medical books are addressed to special medical disciplines. They have very small circulation and very high cpms, too high to compete for consumer ads. Broader-based doctors' publications do compete. *Medical Economics* recently hired a former *Newsweek* salesman to sell consumer advertising.

Q: How much is a magazine like Travel & Leisure *in direct competition for your reader market?*

**Diversion's advertising pages now run over 2,500 a year.

A: The editorial thrust of the two magazines is, of course, similar. Where a doctor receives both *Travel & Lesiure* and *Diversion*, we are in direct competition for that doctor's time and attention. But it is highly unlikely that audience duplication is significant.

Q: How much is it in direct competition for your ad market?
A: Almost all of our consumer advertisers have a separate appropriation in their ad budgets to reach doctors. They probably would not switch money out of *Travel & Leisure* to go into *Diversion*, and certainly not vice versa.

Q: Do consumer advertisers hold it against you that your circulation is not paid?
A: A few advertisers we think logical for *Diversion* have a flat rule not to use non-paid magazines. The most notable is Cadillac. But overall it is not a problem.

How editorial helps the ad

Q: Is there any research on how Diversion *sells drugs vs. purely medical magazines?*
A: The pharmaceutical companies do an incredible amount of research in the marketing area. They probably have such data but it is not made available to us. The amount of space we are running certainly indicates that they think we do a good job in getting doctors to their ads.

Q: How do you think editorial environment affects reader response to advertising?
A: I think editorial gets the reader to the ad. Once he is there, his response is the same, no matter what the editorial environment. Do I think a Mercedes ad would get the same response in a pulp magazine as in *Smithsonian*? My answer is no. But it's because the editorial of the pulp does not attract prospective Mercedes buyers, whereas the *Smithsonian*'s editorial does.

Q: A magazine's effectiveness as an ad medium can be evaluated on three levels: (1) how many prospects does the issue reach, (2) how successful is the issue in bringing the particular ad to the prospects' attention, and (3) how effective is the magazine in predisposing the prospects to accept the ad's message. The rest is up to the advertisement itself. Do you agree?
A: Not entirely. I think after (1) and (2), it's up to the ad itself. I don't think it's editorial's job to predispose the reader to accept any given ad's message or to buy a specific product. Editorial's job is to get the reader to the ad. After that, the ad has to do the selling. Of course, if the ad has been preceded by three pages of editorial puffing the product in the ad, the reader may well be predisposed to buy, but that doesn't and shouldn't happen very often.

Q: Don't you think a doctor is more disposed to respond to an ad for an analgesic that appears in The New England Journal of Medicine *than in* Diversion?
A: If your question is, "Do I believe that the heavier the clinical orientation of the magazine, the more likely the reader is to believe the claims in its pharmaceutical advertising?", my answer is no—just as I don't believe that a reader of a Mercedes ad in *Car & Driver* is more likely to purchase that Mercedes than if he had read the identical ad in *The New Yorker*.

Q: You were president of Esquire Inc.'s magazine publishing division. How did Esquire*'s audience differ from* Diversion*'s? Weren't there many doctors who read* Esquire?
A: As with any general consumer magazine, *Esquire*'s audience demographics are much, much lower than *Diversion*'s. The many doctors who read *Esquire* are a very small percent of its total audience, far fewer than ours.

Q: And you believe that the same doctor seeing an ad on a new tranquilizer would be just as affected by it if he saw it in Esquire *as if he saw it in* Diversion?
A: Yes. In reaching a given doctor who reads both magazines with equal intensity, the ad would be equally effective in either. But obviously that tranquilizer advertiser is not going to advertise in *Esquire*; he has no interest in paying to reach the great bulk of *Esquire*'s readers who are not doctors.

Editorial and the buying decision

Q: Let's look even more closely, by examining each of the five levels on which advertising affects the buyer's decision-making process: attention, interest, evaluation, trial, decision, confirmation (or re-evaluation after purchase). On which of these five levels is the editorial environment most important?
A: Editorial should only affect the first step: attention. Editorial's obligation to the advertisers is to get the reader's eyes on his ad. It definitely should not move the reader down the decision path for one product over another competing product.

Q: What of religious or ethnic publications? Don't the readers' feelings about the editorial somehow rub off on the advertisers who support that publication with their ads? Pat Carbine once said that certain advertisers bought space in Ms. Magazine *as a statement that they supported the women's movement.*
A: If an advertiser feels that he can benefit by linking his image, product or service to a magazine's editorial thrust, he had better do it in his ad copy. Just being there is not enough. A *Ms.* reader who is inclined to do business with companies

that support the women's movement will not automatically assume such support because an ad appears in *Ms.* The ad itself must get that idea across.

Features vs. total editorial

Q: Look at the editorial environment another way: the entire editorial approach of a magazine vs. the particular article or feature. Which is more important?
A: The entire editorial approach is much more important to the advertiser. That's what gets the reader into the magazine issue after issue. It's what builds "through the issue" readership.

Q: If an ad for a new tranquilizer has the option of appearing in the middle of an article on dermatitis or in the middle of an article on Caribbean cruises, where will it be more effective?
A: Which will attract more readers able to prescribe the tranquilizer? That's where the ad will be most effective.

Q: Many publications feature special sections, and many advertisers buy space on the condition that their ads appear in such sections. The food pages in a women's magazine, for instance.
A: Precisely. The advertisers want to be in that section because its editorial is more likely to attract the readers at whom the food advertising is directed.

The irritation factor

Q: Isn't there an irritation factor damaging to the advertiser when a doctor picks up a magazine to relax and finds ads relating to work?
A: No, I don't think so. As with any magazine, if the subject of the ad interests the reader, he will read it. If not, he will pass over it.

Q: Are there certain consumer advertisers who don't want their products advertised among a lot of pharmaceutical ads—even to doctors?
A:There are some who fuss about it. But because we are the most efficient way of reaching the physicians market, we don't lose much space because of it.

Missed opportunities?

Q: Time *magazine has a doctors' edition. Is that direct competition for* Diversion? *Does* Time *carry a lot of pharmaceutical ads?*
A: *Time*'s doctors' edition has a circulation of about 150,000. As far as I know, they don't carry any pharmaceutical ads, and I cannot recall our consumer salespeople ever mentioning *Time* as a competitor for business. Their cpm is about $10 higher than ours.

Q: Your background was not in the medical field. How about Diversion*'s advertising sales personnel?*
A: Our three pharmaceutical space salespersons all have backgrounds in pharmaceutical advertising, two on the agency side and the other with medical magazines.

Q: Does the one who previously sold for medical magazines have to change the sales approach for Diversion?
A: No radical change is required. However, due to the non-clinical nature of our editorial, our salespeople must be prepared to answer questions similar to the ones you have posed.

Q: Has anyone thought of putting out another Diversion, *with basically the same editorial, for dentists, or engineers, or lawyers? Something like MBA Publications does, but on a larger scale?*
A: We have discussed it often. But with the possible exception of dentists, there is not a large enough advertising base to make the concept viable.

ANALYSIS

Three Levels of Editorial Aid to Advertising

As Chapman emphasizes, the primary function of the editorial-advertising relation is to bring the ad to the attention of sufficient numbers of the right people. We analyze this function first, and then move on to the possible secondary functions: interest and persuasion.

Attention: Getting the ad to the prospects

There are six different ways in which editorial can deliver potential reader attention:

1. Attraction of the editorial package. This is the most fundamental level on which editorial works for advertising. It attracts the right people to subscribe to, purchase, and/or pick up the magazine. Media buyers concerned with cpm, reach and frequency seldom go beyond this level.

We are talking of psychological, not physical delivery. The direct cause of *Diversion*'s advertising success is not that it is delivered free to 180,000 doctors, but that Steve Birnbaum's editorial package interests them.

Under this head we note an important distinction seldom exploited by media buyers. Some types of editorial encourage reach. The light, quickly-read editorial of *People, Us* and *TV Guide* fosters multiple readership. Other types of editorial promote frequency. The in-depth, authoritative articles in *Harper's* and *Scientific American* encourage the initial reader to pick up those magazines again and again. There are editorial packages that successfully achieve both reach and frequency, such as *National Geographic, The New Yorker* and probably *Reader's Digest*. Among business papers this difference can be very explicit. One trade paper puts a route list on its cover. Another sells binders to hold the issue for repeated reference.

2. Getting readers to individual ads. Once editorial persuades readers to pick up the magazine, can it also get them to open the page that has the ad? The most effective way editors do this is by developing what Chapman calls "through the issue" readership. If the magazine gets 90% of its readers to look at 100% of its pages, 90% of the readers are guaranteed to see each ad. Editors use specific devices to ensure through-the-book readership, e.g., *The New Yorker's* cartoons and *Reader's Digest's* fillers.

There are other ways editorial can guarantee attention from more readers for particular ads. The most frequently used is position. Starch Inra Hooper president Jay Wilson claims an average 60% more readers will note an ad on the back cover than the average run-of-magazine ad, while inside covers earn an extra 30%. The relative value of inside positions (front, back, middle of book) are difficult to determine. Wilson claims no noticeable difference.

Editors' recognition that position can increase noted scores for advertisers is one reason why the editorial well is disappearing, and why many art directors resign themselves to designing left-hand caption pages, leaving right-hand pages for advertisers.

3. Getting selected readers to see the ad. The reason many magazines have special-interest sections is to catch the attention of prime prospects for certain advertisers. Food advertisers want space in the food section of *McCall's*; travel advertisers, in the travel pages of *Glamour*.

Magazines employ the same lure with seasonal or one-shot features. Consumer and business papers use upcoming stories to sell extra space. Special issues and supplements work the same way. (See Chapter 12.)

4. The editorial alert. Direct editorial mention to bring an ad to the reader's attention is done infrequently, primarily because it is difficult to do without discriminating against other advertisers, secondarily because many editors feel it looks mercenary. But it has been, and can be done with taste: to welcome a new advertiser or category; to recognize a reader opportunity; or just as straight news (done by *New York Times* columnist Phil Dougherty). A more common way to alert readers is an advertisers' index or a reader-service directory.

5. Advertising as an editorial feature. All advertising should benefit the reader, but ad sections and featured ads can take on the appeal of editorial offerings. Classified advertising is the most easily recognized example of this means of attention getting. Once the presence and quality of a classified section is established, it becomes an integral part of the editorial package and can even attract its own audience. *The Wall Street Journal* uses this technique with "Employment Mart," *Popular Photography* with its mail-order section, *Hudson Valley* with a "Pull-Out Restaurant Guide."

Although it is more common in newspapers, major magazine advertisers, particularly retailers, have learned that by buying space regularly, especially when coupled with a specific position in the book, they can train the readers to look for the ad.

6. The distraction factor. This is the most subtle way editorial can affect the attention given to an ad. Although little, if any, research has been done in this area, it makes sense that the more concentration an editorial feature requires, the less likely the reader is to notice adjacent ads. Similarly, an ad would suffer from placement directly opposite attention-getting editorial graphics. There are good business reasons why we find no ads in the middle of *Penthouse* pictorials, despite the high "readership" of those pages.

Theoretically the best place for an ad should be at the end of an article, where the reader is ready to think of something else. Hence, also, the trend to more short features and fillers. Dipping in and out of a periodical not only increases ad exposure, but provides more opportunities for attention.

Do editorial carryovers increase or decrease attention to ads? Undoubtedly they provide more opportunities to place ads adjacent to editorial. They also occasion more paging through the magazine. But do readers notice the ads while they are hunting for continuation of an article (particularly when regional inserts make page numbers so hard to find)? This is another area that needs research.

Interest: Facilitating involvement in the ad

Editorial can and should increase interest in the ads, depending on the type of magazine. It achieves this directly, indirectly, or by penetrating the reader's zone of concerns.

1. Direct cultivation of interest. Book, movie and restaurant reviews increase interest in ads all the time. In fact, most advertisers are willing to risk unfavorable reviews, and many are convinced that even an unfavorable review increases interest in the ad. New-product columns and consumer reports are among other methods of stimulating interest in specific advertised products or services. Can one imagine a travel article on Jamaica that would not increase interest in the ads placed by Air Jamaica or the Jamaican Tourist Board? Is it pure coincidence that an Israel story in *Travel Agent* is accompanied by five ads on tours or charters to Israel?

2. Indirect cultivation of interest. This happens whenever an article interests readers in a particular advertising category. A piece on buying a car not only attracts prospective car buyers (attention) but develops interest in reading the automobile ads.

3. Penetrating the reader's zone of concerns. Each individual has a zone of concerns that is a central force for focusing interest. A fundamental technique in advertising is to associate a product or service with one of the reader's concerns. The goal of a well-positioned publication is to (a) find a really widespread concern, (b) appeal to it, (c) relate editorial subjects to it, and (d) simultaneously widen and deepen it.

The deeper the editorial thrust penetrates the reader's zones of concerns, the more likely it is that readers will associate the ads with their concerns. A publication's success in penetrating one reader's zone of concerns does not guarantee all its ads a free ride into that zone. Ads totally unrelated to editorial seldom benefit.

Persuasion: Facilitating acceptance of the ad

Once an ad has won attention and interest, it is ready for step three: persuasion. Can editorial help here? Editorial can facilitate acceptance of the ad's message by positive endorsement, by negative endorsement, by association, and by not interfering in the persuasion process.

1. Positive endorsement. A magazine can recommend a specific product or service by name. As Chapman says, an ad preceded by pages of editorial praising the product can predispose the reader to buy. Editors do not sacrifice their integrity by honestly evaluating products of interest to readers. Nor do we know of an advertising medium that refuses ads for products praised by editors.

2. Negative endorsement. A magazine states or implies that nothing is wrong with what's advertised, either explicitly, as *Good Housekeeping* does with its Seal of Approval; or implicitly, as most magazines do that are dedicated to specific value attitudes. Advertisers have used *Good Housekeeping* because they value its Seal as a persuasive device. They have also placed ads in *Christian Century* and *Ms.* for an implicit "seal of approval."

3. Persuasion by association. The differences between persuasion by association, negative endorsement and penetrating the zone of concerns are subtle but real. Advertisers buy space in *The New Yorker, Town & Country, Vogue* because the "class" aura of those magazines rubs off on the product. To benefit from a "with-it" aura, record marketers buy space in *Creem* and *National Lampoon.*

4. Not interfering in the persuasive process. Each way editorial can add to an ad's persuasiveness it can also detract from it. A direct condemnation of the product can hurt the persuasive power of the ad. So can indirect disparagement. An article on the ten best restaurants can hurt an ad for the eleventh best. Finally, association with clashing editorial can destroy or neutralize the persuasive force of an ad. Airlines pull ads when they expect a story on a crash. Advertisers do not want food ads facing closeups of famine victims.

Some editorial packages have an image-damaging aura for many advertisers—a reason why many marketers will not use publications like *True Story* and *The Star*.

Some practical conclusions

The foregoing analysis leads to seven useful conclusions for publishers who depend on advertising revenue:

1. Editorial has to help advertising, at least to the extent of attracting sufficient genuine prospects for the advertisers' messages. This is true whether a reader need or an advertiser need occasioned the publication's founding. The ultimate goals of the editorial, circulation and advertising departments are identical.

2. There is nothing wrong with a conscious effort to help advertisers via editorial. But it can be dangerous. Editorial prostitution, or compromising readers' interests to help advertisers, ultimately hurts the advertiser.

3. There should be more attempts to research response to advertising in differing editorial environments. The Starch Inra Hooper study of primary audience is a feeble step in the right direction. But it could do more harm than good if it persuades media buyers to concentrate on how magazines are acquired rather than how they are read.

4. Ad managers should recognize that space in their magazine is not of equal value to every advertiser. An understanding of the different levels of benefit should help (a) target sales presentations, (b) distinguish between primary and secondary prospects, (c) recognize the sales opportunities in upcoming editorial. The same analysis can indicate when an advertiser should be discouraged from buying space. Ads that will not work hurt the medium.

5. Relative value of the editorial to the advertiser should be reflected in pricing when practical. More publishers should distinguish between secondary and primary ad values in their rate structures. Position is not the only advantage for which advertisers should pay premiums.

6. Editorial changes directed at helping one class of advertisers more than other classes must be handled with great caution. Adding material to attract a special class of readers for a special group of advertisers can ruin through-the-book readership.

7. And most important of all: The norm for what is the right kind and amount of help editorial should give advertising will differ with each publication, and must be decided by each publisher. What works for *1,001 Decorating Ideas* may not work for *Today's Living*. What is expected in magazines like *Meeting News* and *Meetings & Expositions* might create an uproar in *Business Week* or *Personnel Journal*.

MANAGEMENT REVIEW

Check List for Evaluating Editorial Aid to Ads

I. Determine effectiveness of editorial in guaranteeing attention for advertisements.

A. Attraction of the editorial package.
- What proportion of your target audience reads the magazine each month (average per issue)? _____%
- What proportion of those readers are prime prospects for the majority of your advertisers? _____%

B. Getting readers to actually see each ad.
- What proportion of readers are through-the-book readers (see almost every ad)? _____%
- What percentage of total advertisers have requested special positions in the past year? _____%

C. Getting selected readers to see particular ads.
- What percentage of total ads were positioned to be near special editorials? _____%
- What percentage of total ads were sold on the basis of special editorials? _____%

D. The editorial alert.
- What percentage of issues published in past year mentioned one or more ads or advertisers editorially? _____%
- What proportion of total readers used your reader service directory, advertiser index, or reader service cards? _____%

E. Advertising as an editorial feature.
- What proportion of total readers use your classified or similarly departmentalized ad section? _____%
- What percentage of total ads are placed on a regular basis with a request for ''usual'' position? _____%

F. The distraction factor.
- What percentage of editorial pages can be considered to compete unnecessarily with certain ads for attention? _____%

II. Decide how well editorial succeeds in encouraging interest in the advertisements.

A. Direct cultivation of interest.
- What percentage of products of services advertised in your magazine this year were reviewed or referred to editorially? _____%

B. Indirect cultivation of interest.
- What proportion of your publication's principal advertising categories were given editorial treatment in the past year? _____%

C. Penetrating the reader's zone of concerns.
- What percent of the year's total number of ads were related to your editorial thrust? _____%

III. Evaluate editorial's contribution to the relative persuasiveness of the advertisements.

A. Positive endorsement.
- What proportion of the different products and services advertised in the past year were directly endorsed editorially? _____%

B. Negative endorsement.
- What proportion of your readers would hold it against your publication if they were deceived by an advertisement in the publication?_____%
- What percent of your total advertiser prospects were explicitly refused or purposely turned down by the magazine in the past year?_____%

C. Persuasion by association.
- What proportion of your advertisers were influenced by desire to associate their products or services or companies with your publication's image when they decided to buy advertising space? _____%

D. Not interfering with the persuasion process.
- What percent of actual and prospective advertisers have complained about your editorial? _____%
- What percent of actual and prospective advertisers are worried about your publication having an image problem? _____%

PART TWO

The Theory of Successful Editing

To analyze precisely what an editor is doing when he or she creates a magazine, we look at the fundamental editorial function from four angles. Two concentrate on the internal process of creating a magazine, two on how the magazine and its editor should respond to what is going on in the world of magazines all around us.

Chapter 6, with Ed Grunwald, considers the magazine's internal construction. What turns a potpourri of articles, columns and features into a magazine? "Editorial Focus—What It Is and How to Achieve It" analyzes the function of putting a magazine together so that it works as a magazine.

Then, in Chapter 7, we join John Mack Carter to look at the same project from outside. What makes one magazine superior to another? "Establishing a Unique Editorial Franchise" considers what the editor must do to construct an editorial package that can compete successfully against other media.

Thirdly, in Chapter 8, we return to magazine introspection, but now we look at the magazine as a progressive phenomenon—a series of ever-changing issues. With Henry A. Grunwald we discuss "Why and How You Must Keep Ahead of Your Readers."

Finally, Chapter 9 considers how the magazine as an evolving series of issues can and should relate to other media. It uses them as a source of new ideas to constantly recreate itself. With Osborn Elliott, we learn "How to Imitate Other Editors Creatively."

CHAPTER SIX

Editorial Focus—What It Is and How to Achieve It

Featuring an Interview with
Edgar A. Grunwald

Former Editor in Chief of Purchasing Week

The primary function of a magazine editor is selection. Readers buy a magazine because they have confidence that the editor will give them a selection of material that they will want. Magazines are neither miniature libraries nor encyclopedias. Editors are expected to do a lot more than put a lot of random reading matter in some kind of order. Readers pay the editor to make judgments as to what they should read.

Hence the first thing an editor has to understand is precisely what turns a lot of editorial matter into a magazine, what is the principle behind editorial selection. Writing on one subject is not enough. Neither is unity of style, or putting a lot of subjects into some kind of logical order.

We use the term ''editorial focus'' to describe the deciding element that makes a magazine work. To explore precisely what is meant by editorial focus we interviewed the most down-to-earth editorial genius we could find, Ed Grunwald, former editor in chief of *Purchasing Week*, advisor to numerous editors of business publications, and for years the editor-writer of the newsletter for editors issued by the American Business Press.

Ed got his first editorial job in 1932, on the long-dead advertising magazine *Tide*. He had a bachelor degree in classical languages from the University of Chicago and had done graduate work at Columbia University.

Ed spent three years at *Tide*, and worked his way up to associate editor. Then, in 1935, he joined the staff of *Variety*, the show business bible. There, in addition to many other duties, he edited the *Variety Radio Directory*.

In 1941, he was offered a job as marketing editor for McGraw-Hill's *Business Week*. His editorial work was interrupted by World War II, in which he served as a medical corpsman, earning five battle stars and the Bronze Star Medal. Then, back to *Business Week*, where he was promoted to managing editor in 1945.

Ed was managing editor of *Business Week* for ten years, until 1959, when he became chief editor for *Purchasing Week*, another McGraw-Hill publication. He ran *Purchasing Week* for 13 years, until it was sold in 1972.

Ed's last two years before retirement were spent as assistant to the president of McGraw-Hill. Since retirement, Ed has been a consultant to numerous business publishers in the United States, Canada and England.

Ed's experience on the wide-ranging *Business Week* and the narrow-range *Purchasing Week* makes him a natural expert with whom to discuss the nature of editorial focus.

INTERVIEW

Q: Can a magazine's editorial be too specialized?
A: Definitely, when it becomes so specialized that it reduces reader and advertising potential beyond what's needed to support the book. This happens in the medical field all the time. There are over 300 publications in that field. A lot of them are so specialized they live on the ragged edge of profitability.

Q: How about editorial being too general?
A: The same thing in reverse: a publication without sufficient focus. Probably the classic example was Huntington Hartford's *Show*. It was supposed to compete with *The New Yorker*. But *Show* never had any focus. An editor can't tell the reader, "Here's a pile of stuff; pick out what you want." A good example of how to do it correctly is *Cosmopolitan*. It appeals to an audience whose lifestyle has changed. Its focus is continued reassurance that the new lifestyle, though different from the old, is the right thing.

Defining Focus

Q: Do you have norms for selecting material? Can it appeal to only 20% of the audience? Only 10%?
A: You can't set percentages. All such a norm would do would be to reduce readers' choices in the magazine. My rule is to give the readers as much choice as possible.

Q: But how do you keep the focus? There must be subjects that don't belong in the magazine.
A: You shouldn't go outside your field. There's always enough material within your field to fill a magazine and then some. But you can't measure audience interest in percentages. In practice you try to give the reader as much choice as possible within your focus.

Q: Does this mean you edit for your core readers and avoid putting in material to please fringe readers?
A: Even the core has to have a choice. It's better to be a supermarket than a mom-and-pop store.

Q: How much choice can you give? When Sports Illustrated *does a feature on swimsuits, is it still in focus?*
A: The editors evidently think so. Such decisions must involve everyone: circulation, advertising, management. If *Sports Illustrated*'s editors introduced a column on gardening, the advertising department would laugh them down. As for swimsuits, I'm sure the ad people said, ''That makes a lot of sense.'' When adding new subjects, there should be some sensible relationship to the field you're already in. This is a matter of business as well as editorial judgment. Does the new element make sense for the magazine as a whole?

Q: But how do you know the reader won't say, ''What the hell is this doing here?'' Even if he doesn't choose to read the piece, he shouldn't feel that it spoils his magazine.
A: You have to know your readers. That's why magazines need knowledgeable editors.

Q: Are such judgments easier for some magazines?
A: I think so. *Purchasing Week*, like most business papers, had a closed universe. We knew there were about 100,000 purchasing agents and we reached them all. It was easy to edit for them. We talked to these people. We knew they wanted information on five basic subjects: prices, products, vendors, availability of mer-

chandise, and new purchasing techniques. Even when there was a shift in interests, it happened slowly and it was easy to spot it and respond to it.

Q: Purchasing agents pay income tax, why didn't you give them articles on how to fill out the tax forms?
A: Because this is not why they want the magazine. You don't spend time on a magazine on the chance that there will be something about income taxes in it. Some of the world's best bridge players were purchasing agents. But they didn't pick up *Purchasing Week* to peruse articles on bridge. You edit to the basic purpose readers have when they choose to read your magazine.

Q: Isn't it the same thing that makes a consumer magazine successful? A magazine stands for something in the reader's mind, and it's dangerous to violate that.
A: When readers pick up a magazine, they expect a specific payout. If the magazine contains material that does not conform with what they expect, it's out of focus. Focus both determines what the readers expect and is a response to their expectations.

Exceptions prove the rule

Q: As Purchasing Week *editor, did you consider the magazine to be special-interest, on purchasing, or special-audience, for purchasing agents?*
A: It was a special-interest book on purchasing.

Q: You never tried to broaden the subject matter to include other interests of purchasing agents?
A: I've never thought that a good idea. It dilutes the focus of your book.

Q: Didn't McGraw-Hill experiment with a general interest executive insert in all their magazines?
A: They did, and it didn't work—partially for internal reasons: constant argument over the size of each magazine's cut. It was basically an advertising project, not an editorial proposition.

Q: Why doesn't the "Personal Business" section in the back of Business Week *dilute the magazine's focus? We know it is one of the best-read parts of the magazine. Would you recommend extending it?*
A: I'm not going to second guess the editor of *Business Week*. Lou Young knows what he's doing. But I doubt he would extend "Personal Business" to other

parts of the magazine. In other sections it would ruin the focus of *Business Week*. It doesn't do so now because its point is that it's an extra attraction.

Q: How much extra attraction can you put in a magazine before it hurts its focus? "Personal Business" is two pages. Could it be six?
A: I can't answer that. The fact is that two pages have been successful, and that's what they've stayed with. Remember, it is not the purpose of *Business Week* to be a personal adviser in that sense.

Q: If it's not its purpose, why is it a good idea to do a little of it? And what's a little?
A: It's a good idea since it's successful, and a little is what's successful.

Q: What was their thinking when they started it?
A: I know because I started it. My purpose was twofold—first, to give some attention to aspects of a businessman's life which were not self-evident in the rest of the magazine; second, to step up the pace of the back of the magazine. A magazine should not trail off at the end.

Q: Why did you decide on two pages and not four?
A: For mechanical reasons. The column is printed on special paper which wraps through the book: two pages in front and two pages in back. I couldn't change it in back without causing problems in front.

Adjusting or changing focus

Q: To improve a magazine's readership one can attract additional readers (widen the base), get current readers to read more of the magazine (deepen the base), or get different readers interested in reading the magazine (shift the base). How would editorial techniques differ for each?
A: To widen the reader base you add new material that's going to attract new readers. To shift the base, you do the same thing, only more so. To get present readers to read more, you first see whether you can improve the quality of what you've been doing, and then decide whether more material for your regular readers will help.

Q: When you add new subjects, don't you risk alienating old readers?
A: You've got to face the fact that you're trying to shift the audience base. Adding is the only alternative. But you can't add totally incompatible subjects.

Q: The new subject has to interest the old audience?
A: It may not be as interesting to the old audience as the old subjects, but it should stay somewhere within range. If *Sports Illustrated* wanted to broaden its reader base, it certainly would not wander off into gardening or sewing. There has to be some relevance to the book's focus.

Focus and advertising

Q: Since expectation determines focus, couldn't two magazines have exactly the same audience, and each still have an entirely different focus?
A: It happens all the time. Thus *Medical Economics* has a focus altogether different from the focus of the *Journal of the American Medical Association*, though I'm sure most of their readers are the same doctors.

Q: Yet a lot of the ads are identical. How much difference does the focus make to the advertisers?
A: The norm for editorial doesn't apply to advertising in the same way. People have been trained to accept advertising in media as pertinent information, even though it is irrelevant to the subject at hand. Yet I believe the editorial focus has some effect on the advertising. I suspect there are certain reader expectations, regarding the context in which ads are placed, which make them more interested in an ad for a high-priced camera in a camera magazine, or in an ad for computers in a computer magazine, than in the same ads in a general magazine.

Q: If you saw an ad for a book in a religious magazine, you would presume the book was, at least, not offensive to the religion.
A: Right. But advertisers are more concerned about how the magazine is read and who the readers are. That's the first step. And this goes back to focus. A magazine that fulfills the expectations of its readers attracts more readers, guaranteeing more exposure for the ads. From the magazine's point of view, there's another thing to consider: Advertising can add greatly to a magazine's readership. It's estimated that 30% to 50% of the average business paper's readership is contributed by the ads. The same is true for many consumer magazines, such as photographic, science or hobby books.

Q: Certainly an underrated asset.
A: And once this chicken-and-egg process starts, it works two ways: the editorial helps the advertiser, and the ads help the publication. Ad agencies consider *The New Yorker* a superior buy because the ads generate high reader interest. A

very substantial part of the reading time *The New Yorker* gets is devoted to the ads. In fact, *The New Yorker* has run a promotional campaign to that effect.

Q: In the trade, paging through a magazine for the ads is called ''The New Yorker phenomenon.''
A: My point is that this convoluted process is the key to print. The editor's focus creates an audience suitable for the advertiser, who then helps the magazine, not only financially, but by contributing to reader interest. It's a unique phenomenon of print media, with no parallel in television.

ANALYSIS

Maintaining Editorial Focus

When one critic writes that a magazine is on target, another that it is perfectly positioned, and a third that it has a distinct personality, they are all saying that its editorial is in focus.

But what is meant by this focus? Precisely how do editors keep magazines on target, position them, give them distinct personalities? Clay Felker's *Esquire* and Gruner+Jahr's *Geo* proved that more is required than maintaining high editorial standards; Walter Annenberg's *Panorama* and *Reader's Digest's Families*, that it does not suffice merely to concentrate on a single subject.

A magazine's editorial is in focus when it fully satisfies the expectations of its audience. Ed Grunwald says, ''You edit to the basic purpose the readers have when they choose to read your magazine.'' A magazine succeeds by fulfilling this promise made to its readers: This is the kind of magazine you want and, though you do not know what will be in the next issue, we promise it will fulfill your expectations.

Does this mean that all we have to do to stay in focus is to publish material of interest to our target audience? Unfortunately, no. At least 60% of all new-magazine failures can be traced to publishers who believed it was enough to select a definable group of potential readers and design an editorial package appealing to their common interests.

The reason such an approach does not work is that when readers select a magazine they choose form as much as content. They choose not just information or entertainment, but the provider of the entertainment. They want a relationship which will provide information or entertainment in a certain way.

Form should not be confused with format. The imprint of the personalities of DeWitt and Lila Wallace on the form of *Reader's Digest* goes far beyond condensation and variety. Although *Newsweek*'s format is basically the same as *Time*'s, readers relate differently to the two weeklies. Nor does form mean attitude, politics or philosophy. As *Time* executive editor Jason McManus explains: the "difference between the two magazines (*Time* and *Newsweek*) . . . is one of personalities . . . not of one being liberal and one being conservative." Although readers expect both magazines to fill the same general need, it is done differently enough to make a difference to many readers as to which one they want to read regularly.

Consider what is happening among women's magazines today. The big general women's books, in particular *Ladies' Home Journal* and *McCall's*, are experiencing difficulty, while new women's books, such as *New Woman, Self, Savvy* and *Working Woman*, are prospering. Yet the new books carry basically the same subject matter as the old. The difference is in focus, which is determined not by subject but by form.

Achieving focus

In *Solving Publishing's Toughest Problems*, (FOLIO, 1982), Norman Cousins said: "There are two theories of editing. One is that an editor should engage market research to find out what readers want to read. The other is that an editor must edit to please himself or herself. If there are enough people who share his or her tastes, the latter method is apt to be more successful."

Most editors rely on instincts and personal tastes to keep their magazines in focus. They have developed a knowledge of their audience, whether by gut feeling based on personal experience (*Cosmopolitan*'s Helen Gurley Brown), or by intellectual rapport confirmed by personal contact (*Saturday Review*'s Norman Cousins), or by personal observation supplemented by reader research (*Self*'s Phyllis Star Wilson). But this knowledge is always filtered through their own personalities. Their editorial judgments are seldom, if ever, based solely on research or reader response.

This is more art than science, which means that editorial focus is always somehow the product of a single creative mind. Not that magazines cannot be edited by committee. Cinema is an art, and most great movies were created by committees. But here too, a single personality must dominate the creative process, usually the director's. So it is with magazines, whether the dominator is overwhelming (Bob Guccione at *Omni*) or subtle (Jim Michaels at *Forbes*).

As with art, establishing editorial focus is never a matter of pure logic. Emotions, personal biases, likes and dislikes, help to create the final result: the form or character which is the basis of the personal relationship between reader and magazine.

Even very specialized magazines like *Games, Guitar Player* or *Stores* have distinct characters. We see this clearly when we compare direct competitors, e.g., *Car & Driver* and *Motor Trend, Giftware Business* and *Giftware News,* or *Outdoor Life* and *Sports Afield.*

As Cousins observes, there have to be enough people who share the editor's tastes. Light (topic) and lens (editor) are not enough to achieve focus; the object (audience) must also be in proper range. Hence, establishing that a large enough group of potential readers exists is not the same as finding out whether there is an audience for your magazine. Research can guarantee you that there are enough prospective readers with a need for certain kinds of reading matter, but it can give you only hints as to whether they will choose your magazine as the way to get it.

Like a radio station, achieving focus requires a strong signal (editorial matter the audience wants and needs), a distinctive wavelength (editorial form, created by the editor's personality), but, most important, an audience tuned into that wavelength.

Focus and subject matter

Once we recognize that editorial focus lies in fulfilling reader expectations, it is easier to understand Ed Grunwald's advice to "try to give the reader as much choice as possible within your focus," and how some magazines remain in focus with an enormous range of subject matter. *Reader's Digest* and *The New Yorker* can offer almost any topic without violating reader expectations. But they could not publish any article. Readers expect the range of subjects, but they expect them in the *Reader's Digest* or *New Yorker* manner.

Our definition also explains why Grunwald insists you cannot measure audience interest in percentages. In some magazines, readers expect wide choice, and are satisfied if each issue gives them one or two articles they want to read. Magazines like *National Geographic, Scientific American* and the *New England Journal of Medicine* are not meant to be read cover to cover.

Because expectations rather than subject matter determine focus, it is possible for *Business Week* to introduce a special feature like "Personal Business." A limited change of pace need not violate expectations, and may even become a part of what is expected.

Focus and leadership

Though a great variety of subject matter is possible within reader expectations, editors, as Grunwald points out, cannot tell the reader, "Here's a pile of stuff; pick out what you want." A critical element in reader expectations is the conviction that the magazine will be a guide in choosing what to read. This editorial leadership is essential to maintaining focus.

Leadership implies more than choosing for others. It involves securing their trust. Readers may not expect to read everything in a magazine, or even to be pleased with everything, but they must have sufficient confidence in its editorial judgment to convince them that it helps them. This can be as simple as confidence that program listings in *On Cable* are accurate or that one will find an adequate number of challenging puzzles in each issue of *Games*.

The leadership in editorial focus requires ability to foresee what readers will want before they are aware of it themselves. Human beings, and human audiences, are continually changing. A magazine that remains in focus fills needs as they arise, not before, not after.

This requires not only perceptiveness on the part of the editor, but a certain amount of risk taking and enormous self-confidence. It also explains why good editors never allow readership studies to make judgments for them. Yesterday's results may indicate a trend's general direction, but they cannot show what will happen tomorrow.

The importance of leadership also provides another insight: Successful magazines can experiment and innovate with far less risk than new publications or publications that are out of focus. The more successful a magazine becomes, the more confidence readers have in its editorial judgment and, therefore, the more willing they are to accept the new and different. A new magazine, or a magazine out of focus, cannot rely on this reservoir of trust and good will.

Focus and change

Since editorial focus exists in the fulfilling of expectations, change is not a problem for a magazine that consistently maintains focus. As expectations change, so will the focus—automatically.

Only magazines that are out of focus require major adjustment to get back on target, i.e., conscious repositioning. Helen Gurley Brown made revolutionary changes in *Cosmopolitan* when she took over in 1965. She has been making changes ever since, but they have been evolutionary and hardly noticed. The difference, again, is reader expectation. The 1965 changes were unexpected for old *Cosmopolitan* readers, while today's changes are what current readers expect.

A magazine in focus changes subject matter as the interests of its audience change. It does not change its basic service. If electric cars became a major concern of mechanics, *Motor* would not be changing its focus by increasing its coverage of electric motors. In fact, it would have to do it to remain in focus. Switching from repairing cars to selling cars, however, would be a major change in focus. It would be offering a new service, generating a new set of expectations.

There are cases where the subject matter and/or point of view are difficult to separate from the service. This is true of well-defined special-interest publications (*Popular Photography, Polo, Skiing*) and of opinion magazines initially identified with a political position or philosophic point of view (*Commentary, National Review, New Republic*). Such magazines usually live or die as interest in their subject matter lives or dies. This is a prime reason why Martin Peretz, after he becomes the owner of the *New Republic*, had difficulty retaining focus as he abandoned traditional liberal positions.

An interesting phenomenon of focus and change is the way some magazines can evolve into entirely new positions without the tumult or revolution of sudden repositioning.

Gentleman's Quarterly is an outstanding example of this, and it also exemplifies what we have said about the ease with which readers of sharply focused publications accept experimentation and innovation. *GQ* first established itself as a mentor and arbiter of fashion in men's clothing. Once it had earned enormous reader confidence on that level, it was able to expand far beyond clothing to become a mentor and arbiter of total male lifestyle.

Focus and advertising

That editorial focus has a bearing on advertising is very evident in the history of *GQ*. The gradual expansion of its service from clothes to lifestyle made an enormous difference to advertisers. Although circulation rose dramatically (200,000 to 400,000), it hardly explains the increase in advertising—especially in advertising outside the clothing field. What made the difference had to be the growing evidence of the readers' confidence in *GQ*'s leadership.

Fairchild Publication's *"W"* is a similar case. At its launching in 1971, few magazine publishers recognized the requirements for success in its editorial (largely reprints from *Women's Wear Daily*), frequency (biweekly) or format (newspaper)—especially for a publication aimed at the affluent. But, from the very beginning, *"W"* was sharply focused. Publisher John Fairchild knew how to fulfill the expectations of the very select group for whom he was publishing. The result: enormous confidence in everything *"W"* printed, including the advertising. It took *"W"* less than four years to become profitable.

MANAGEMENT REVIEW

Check List for Evaluating a Magazine's Focus

I. **Rate your publication's focus in relation to what you know about its target readers.**
   A. How distinctive do readers consider your publication vs. others on similar subjects?

   Practical tests:
   - Is your publication asked for by name at single-copy outlets?
   - Does price (higher than your competition's) have little effect on circulation?

   Rating: Very_____   Somewhat_____   Not at all_____

   B. How much is your audience in tune with your publication's "form"?

   Practical tests:
   - What is its share of its reader market?
   - Do you get a high percentage of cancellations on soft offers?

   Rating: Very_____   Somewhat_____   Not at all_____

   C. How frequently do readers find something unexpected but delightful in your publications?

   Practical tests:
   - Are such surprises frequent (say once each issue)?
   - Is subscriber mail about such surprises abundant and favorable?

   Rating: Very_____   Somewhat_____   Not at all_____

   D. How much has your publication changed in the last several years without readers noticing it?

   Practical tests:
   - Compare current issues with three, five and ten years ago.
   - Has the average age of your readers remained constant (not grown older)?

   Rating: Very_____   Somewhat_____   Not at all_____

II. **Rate your publication's focus in relation to what you know about your editorial staff.**
   A. How much is the publication's form or character the product of a single creative mind?

   Practical tests:
   - Is the editor confident and definitely in charge?

- Would replacing the editor be a serious problem?

Rating: Very_____   Somewhat_____   Not at all_____

B. How successful is each issue in providing variety with consistency of manner?

    Practical tests:

- Over a year's issues, is it clear the editors have no problem in finding appropriate interesting topics?
- Select articles on different subjects from three issues and ask several people to tell whether all three came from the same magazine.

Ratings: Very_____   Somewhat_____   Not at all_____

C. How wisely does the editor use readership research?

    Practical tests:

- Is it used more to analyze past mistakes than to select future articles?
- Does the editor avoid imitating features that got high readership scores?

Rating: Very_____   Somewhat_____   Not at all_____

D. How willing is the editor to experiment?

    Practical tests:

- Are the editor and the editorial staff receptive to and enthusiastic about new ideas?
- Is the editor confident of favorable reader response, or is it a cause for worry?

Rating: Very_____   Somewhat_____   Not at all_____

CHAPTER SEVEN

Establishing a Unique Editorial Franchise

Featuring an Interview with
John Mack Carter
Editor of Good Housekeeping

What happens when the editors of three different magazines are in pursuit of the same audience with more or less the same subject matter? If each of these editors succeeds in maintaining editorial focus, will the three resulting magazines be so much alike it will be hard to distinguish between them?

What, on the other hand, would happen if the same editor was successively editor in chief of each of these magazines? Would that guarantee sameness?

These questions are interesting because answering them should help to refine the idea of editorial focus. The most valuable thing an editor can do for any magazine is to establish a unique editorial franchise.

We knew of only one editor who could answer the above questions: John Mack Carter, who edited successively *McCall's, Ladies' Home Journal* and *Good Housekeeping*, three magazines as similar as magazines can be in audience and subject matter.

John Mack Carter has been editor of *Good Housekeeping* for more than ten years. When he accepted the job, in 1975, it was commonly observed in the trade that he would turn *Good Housekeeping* into another *Ladies' Home Journal*. That could not have been more wrong, which is why we chose him for this interview.

John started his publishing career in 1945, as a reporter for the *Ledger & Times* in Murray, Kentucky. He was not there very long. He had to move on to college. In 1948, he graduated from the University of Missouri with a Bachelor of Journalism degree. A year later he got his M.A. and his first job on a magazine, as assistant editor of Meredith's *Better Homes & Gardens*.

In 1951, he left Meredith for three years in the Navy where he achieved the rank of lieutenant, j.g. Upon return to civilian life, he joined *Household* in Topeka, Kansas, as managing editor. He spent five years there, rising to editor. In 1958, he left to become executive editor of *Together*. The following year he moved to *American Home* as editor.

In 1961, Herb Mayes, looking for a successor to edit *McCall's*, hired John with the title of executive editor. John got the editor title the following year, and remained at the helm of *McCall's* until 1965, when Ed Downe of Downe Communications hired him away to edit *Ladies' Home Journal*. There John rose to president and then chairman of the publishing division.

In 1973, John purchased the troubled *American Home* from Downe Communications and returned to it as publisher, editor and owner. The adventure was short lived, ending in 1975, when Hearst Corp. offered him the editorship of *Good Housekeeping* on terms too good to refuse.

INTERVIEW

Q: Good Housekeeping, Ladies' Home Journal *and* McCall's *are lumped together in many people's minds.* Family Circle *and* Woman's Day *are very close. Do you consider this a problem in establishing your reader franchise?*
A: It is a problem. You can neither develop a core audience nor win new readers without somehow being distinguished from your competitors.

Q: Is it a problem with advertisers?
A: The bulk of advertising is purchased by people who lump the women's magazines together. Men, who have done most of the buying, often do not read the women's magazines and therefore aren't equipped to distinguish between them. So they buy according to the lowest cpm. This means that even with a superior product you have to fight continually to avoid being dragged down to competing on a pure costs basis.

Making the editorial point of view unique

Q: You were editor of each of the three big women's magazines. How did you see each as different?

A: I saw *McCall's* as a more sophisticated magazine. There were size differences in those days—680 lines on *McCall's* and the *Journal*; standard size on *Good Housekeeping*. Guided by Herb Mayes, I took advantage of that size to develop a sense of elegance through good design and lavish color. We used the display potential of the large page to its fullest, so that the magazine became a visual happening. At *LHJ* I stressed contemporary treatment, what was happening—not so much in service areas as in terms of celebrities and a literate *People* magazine approach. *People* is a photographic version of a major part of the *Journal*. There were a lot of first-person stories, news-making stories and inside stories about the famous. At *Good Housekeeping* I've re-emphasized the service pages. I want to fully justify the magazine's reputation by having strong service material and more pages devoted to food and beauty, making use of our research facilities to provide more solid information, having more scope.

Q: Don't Family Circle *and* Woman's Day *challenge* Good Housekeeping *in this area?*

A: I don't believe they are viewed by the reader in the same way. They have built their appeal on the easy pickup at the checkout counter, the automatic "So what; it's only 49 cents."

Q: Since you became editor, have you made any changes specifically to make readers and advertisers think Good Housekeeping *is unique?*

A: On almost every page there has been change. But I haven't done anything solely to make *Good Housekeeping* different. I have done these things to make the magazine more distinctive, and if that has caused people to see us as different from other magazines it is because distinctiveness inherently sets one apart. A major change has been a much more authoritative approach to health subjects. Another change is the journalistic use of mechanical engineers, chemists, home economists and experts in other fields who have been working in the Good Housekeeping Institute, mainly doing research on advertised products. I am now using them widely on research for editorial material.

The impact of media promotion and ads carried

Q: Did you do any external things, outside editorial, to help differentiate the product? I am thinking of the current promotion campaign.

A: My part in that campaign was merely to influence. We recognized that one of the problems we had to overcome was our stereotyped image, the assumption by young people in advertising agencies that our audience was old, tired and opposed to change. The media campaign talked about a whole new breed of women in the marketplace, not just in *Good Housekeeping*'s audience. The new breed is more questioning, younger, tougher. The sheer fact that *Good Houskeeping* was interested in women as tough customers drew a lot of attention. It also drew recognition to the fact that *Good Housekeeping*'s rapport with and reputation among consumers could be useful to advertisers in winning over that tough customer. Simultaneously the publisher decided to revive another unique weapon in the magazine's arsenal, the *Good Housekeeping* Seal.

Q: Don't you think the advertising a magazine carries plays a part in forming its image?

A: That is true. We turn down many ads. There are whole categories we don't accept, such as cigarettes and hard liquor. This has helped our image.

Q: At McCall's *you were looking for a stylish, high-class image. Certain types of schlock advertising went directly against the image you were trying to create. Did you take a stand against such ads?*

A: No. Editing a magazine and selling advertising space are different operations. An editor chooses what runs in the magazine. When you're selling advertising, you don't pick the advertiser, he picks you. You may work hard on preferred categories, but others tend to come in. There will always be some advertising which runs against the character of the magazine.

Q: Don't you think a magazine, in the long run, cuts its own throat by not trying to control that problem?

A: Agreed. And it's possible to influence advertisers. *McCall's*, for example, influenced advertisers to change the style of their advertising. A number, especially in beauty and fashion, acknowledged that they were influenced by the *McCall's* approach.

Q: Chances are the advertising will do its job better if it works the way the magazine works.

A: I don't know how much proof we have for that, but I certainly subscribe to the theory.

Specifying reader and advertiser needs

Q: When a marketer selects a product market in the development of a new product, he starts by isolating a consumer need. What's the need Good Housekeeping *fills?*
A: Our magazine is edited toward today's woman's needs: how to cope with the opportunities as well as the responsibilities involved in having a home and family, in having interests outside the home, in reacting to the changes taking place in society.

Q: If I asked the same question when you were editor of LHJ, *would you have said something different?*
A: I would not have put as much emphasis on management, the fiscal-management, home-management aspects.

Q: What is the unique need Good Housekeeping *fills for the advertiser?*
A: *Good Houskeeping* adds an element of confidence—in the advertiser's claims, in the product advertised. Any magazine gives the product and ad an added value. I believe *Good Housekeeping* does this in a superior way because of the confidence created by the *Good Houskeeping* Seal and our tough advertising standards.

Q: How about the difference between Ladies' Home Journal *and* McCall's *for the advertiser? When you edited them, did they fulfill distinct needs for the advertiser?*
A: Advertisers benefit from the type of reader responsiveness produced by the magazine's editorial. In *McCall's* there was flair, an element of sophistication in terms of design and editorial approach. On the *Journal* there was far more of the "You-and-I" approach, involving the reader through deliberate stimulation of two-way communication. The *Journal* established an advertising environment that was more friend-to-friend, while *McCall's* was more intellectual, more an appeal of style.

Q: Are you saying that a product of style, like Chanel, for instance, should advertise in McCall's *rather than in* Good Housekeeping?
A: I was talking about *McCall's* editorial environment in 1963, 15 years ago. Today's *McCall's* is not the same. There no longer exists a mass women's magazine with the same kind of grace.

Q: Is there any advertising category that belongs more in Ladies' Home Journal *than in* Good Housekeeping?
A: Outside of liquor and cigarettes, none I can think of.

Communicating the image internally

Q: You feel you have a clear idea of what Good Housekeeping *should be. How do you communicate that idea to your editorial staff?*
A: Largely by two-way communication, my response to staff suggestions and ideas. At every meeting I remind my staff that I want all their ideas, not just enough to fill an issue. I particularly ask them for ideas about departments other than their own. I get memos from most of the editors which include clips from newspapers, ideas on how to treat certain subjects, what they would like to see in other sections. I frequently use a suggestion as the occasion to instruct, to explain the magazine. Besides informal meetings to discuss trends, we hold a regular meeting for the entire staff when each issue comes out to review it and see what could be improved.

Q: How do you communicate your idea of Good Housekeeping *to the promotion and advertising departments?*
A: Communication to those departments is almost entirely to help them understand the editorial viewpoint and reader attitudes. This is done at an every-issue meeting of the entire advertising and promotion departments at which various editors and I review contents.

The final arbiter of image

Q: Who decides precisely what a magazine should be? Is it the editor? Or is it top management?
A: No good top management can afford to relinquish the right to determine the basic purpose of its magazine. Magazines that have a schism between top management and editor don't survive. There must be agreement, with each recognizing his particular function. Bad management often involves itself in execution, but ignores the policy question of what the magazine should be. The insecure editor will fail to understand or accommodate himself to management policy; he says he knows what the magazine ought to be, without recognizing that this has to be an ownership decision.

Q: If management's role is policy and the editor's execution, how does management make sure that the editor is making the right decisions—without becoming editors themselves?
A: Management has to discipline itself, to establish norms (frequently based on

industry expectations) to measure success or failure. The mistake that is made too often is that management judges the elements that go into making the magazine, instead of the whole magazine or, better, the results of the magazine. Management must have sufficient patience with and faith in the editor to wait for results. I don't mean that occasional guidance or suggestions aren't in order. But final management judgment must wait for results: advertiser response and reader response, i.e., sales.

Q: You can clock the horse as often as you wish, but you don't know you have a winner until after the race.
A: That's it.

ANALYSIS

Securing a Unique Position in Your Markets

Marketing theorists distinguish three types of competitive situations:

1. Pure competition—when there are many suppliers and their products are considered more or less identical by buyers, e.g., writing paper, gasoline.

2. Oligopolistic competition—when the competing products are viewed by buyers as more or less identical, but the competition is dominated by a few companies, e.g., cola drinks, automobiles.

3. Monopolistic competition—when one company manages to differentiate its product so that, in the eyes of the buyers, it is the only product of its kind.

The skin books were as near to pure competition as magazines can get until *Playboy* established a monopolistic position for itself by bringing class and intellectualism to a field where both were unknown. When Bob Guccione brought *Penthouse* to America, he positioned it initially on the basis of oligopolistic competition—the tortoise was racing the rabbit alone. His purpose: to differentiate his product negatively, by classifying it with *Playboy* against all the other skin books. Once that was achieved, he worked toward establishing more a monopolistic position with readers by becoming more daring than *Playboy*, concerned with sex as sex vs. *Playboy*'s view of sex as part of Hugh Hefner's vision of the good life. (Note that when *Gallery*, tried to differentiate itself from its older competitors, it decided it was less voyeuristic.)

Competition on two levels

Magazines that carry advertising serve two markets: readers and advertisers. A publication can enjoy a monopoly situation in one of these markets while being oligopolistically competitive in the other. Thus Guccione could settle for oligopolistic competition in his advertising market while working toward monopoly in his reader market. In fact, monopoly is both easier to achieve and more important in the reader market than it is in the advertising market.

Readers like to think that the magazine they buy is a one-and-only. The strength of the reader's instinct to give a magazine monopoly allegiance can be seen in the case of *TV Guide*, which enjoys a reader loyalty far beyond what can be explained by its editorial (common to many other television listings with the exception of the articles in its wraparound). This does not mean that there are no readers who consider competitive magazines as more or less equal. Just as there will always be people who shop to buy fruit and don't care whether it is apples or oranges, so there will always be readers who want a home-service magazine and don't care whether they get *Woman's Day* or *Family Circle*, and those who want a newsmagazine, and don't care whether it is *Time* or *Newsweek*. We can call such customers fringe readers (as opposed to core readers). Core readers always consider the magazine unique. Fringe readers seldom do.

While readers tend to encourage monopoly, the advertising market tends to encourage oligopoly. Space buyers prefer to group publications, to consider several magazines as more or less equal. A far higher proportion of space buyers consider *Time* and *Newsweek* identical for advertising purposes than the proportion of subscribers who consider the two magazines the same for reading purposes.

No place is this distinction clearer than in the trade-paper field. The best-read journals are successful because they fill a peculiar reader need better than any other publication. If the reader wants news in the advertising business he reads *Advertising Age*; if he wants analysis, *Marketing & Media Decisions*. In the supermarket field, it is *Supermarket News* for news, *Progressive Grocer* for analysis. The media buyer, however, considers *Advertising Age* and *Marketing & Media Decisions, Supermarket News* and *Progressive Grocer*, respectively, to be equals—and ends up buying both for his clients, or whichever costs less per thousand.

The space buyer's inclination to judge competitive magazines with comparable demographics (or job titles) and cost-per-thousand as equal for advertising purposes traps many publishers. They define advertiser need as merely the need to reach a specific audience at the lowest cost, and totally disregard the vital advertising values of editorial environment and reader involvement—with tragic consequences for both readers and advertisers.

How is monopoly achieved?

Monopoly is achieved by either filling a need that no one else is filling, or by filling a need better than anyone else is filling it.

In either case, you must first define the need your publication aims to fill. And that means that the need must be both clear and specific. When the New York Times Company launched *Us* magazine, management insisted that the need it filled was different from that filled by *People Weekly*. But the need was not defined clearly enough to be understood by most people outside the magazine and, judging from reports from ex-staffers and the turnover in personnel, the staff's understanding was no better. Magazine management is frequently afraid to be specific about the need to be filled, due to the fear that this would relinquish part of the market to a competitor. Thus *Los Angeles Magazine* and *California* have been on a head-on collision course, when both would probably be better off if each concentrated on what it does best and were more specific about the need it is trying to fill.

The less specific and the broader your definition of the need, the more competition you are likely to have and the more you must depend on doing the job better than anyone else. Trade publications and other special-interest magazines can frequently survive with third-rate editorial and graphics because they have no competition in the limited area they serve (or the competition is as bad or worse than they are). The problem John Mack Carter faces is very difficult precisely because *Good Housekeeping*, *Ladies' Home Journal* and *McCall's* are such broad-purpose books. If *Cosmopolitan* and *Ms.* stand out from the big three, it is not because they fill the needs of modern women with superior editorial resources and skills, but because they are aimed at more specific needs.

Somewhere along the line, the publisher has to decide which route his publication must take. The broader the target market, the more money, perseverance and, yes, editorial genius is needed to make money. And, incidentally, the more chance you have of ending up in a business with great cash flow and small return on investment. The narrower the target market, the easier it is to become the big fish in a small pond, e.g., GPI Publications's *Guitar Player* or its *Contemporary Keyboard*. Of course, your pond can be a trap if it is overstocked with fish, as happened a number of years ago among publications addressed to the computer industry and appears to be happening again with publications on personal computers.

Once the differentiating element is clear and specific in your own head, how do you make sure it is clear to the reader and advertiser marketplace?

Selling your difference to the reader

There is little doubt that a magazine must be its own primary promotion. If your readers cannot tell your publication from others in the field, you will never convince them with external promotion. Either your are not communicating with your editor or you need a new editor. It is worth noting here that it is easier for an editor when the need to be filled is special rather than general. Editors, like all artists, work best when their objectives are clearly defined and the limits of their medium are easily recognized. It was much easier for Bob Anderson to decide what did not belong in *Runner's World* than it was for Bill Davis's parade of editors to decide what did not belong in *Us*.

Not only is the magazine itself the primary promotion to readers, in many respects it is the only effective promotion. You cannot sell a magazine over a long period of time by telling readers what the magazine wants to do. Promises may get you a few up-front subscription and single-copy trial pickups, but promises too often build expectation above the level you can fulfill. It is better to describe what the product is—what is in the current or upcoming issues, as *Reader's Digest* and *TV Guide* have done for years. If the differentiating characteristics of the magazine are not evident in the type of article it features, you have a problem that goes far beyond your promotion.

Can graphics help to establish your magazine as different from your competitor's? They can make your product look different, but looks can be of surprisingly secondary concern to readers. When Doris Shaw became editor in chief of *House Beautiful* several years ago, one of the first things she did was to bring in Henry Wolf Productions to redo the graphics. We presume both she and Mr. Wolf had enough sense to realize that graphics could serve only to enhance editorial improvement. Editorial, not graphics, was the primary reason for her being replaced less than a year later. Of course, graphics can be very close to the purpose of the magazine. As Carter points out, when he edited *McCall's* (under Herb Mayes), graphics were at the heart of the difference. There was a need for presenting women's interests as a "visual happening" and *McCall's* met that need. Graphics played a similarly important function in *Life* and *Look* as originally conceived and, to a lesser extent, in today's *People*. Graphics, then, can differentiate your magazine either by assisting the editorial to fill the target need or by directly filling the target need.

Telling the advertiser

Communicating the differentiating elements to the advertising industry is more complex. It almost seems as if space buyers do not want to know. It is so much easier to consider five magazines as equal in everything that computer analysis cannot measure. Thus when *EDN Electronic Business* put out a "Comparison of Market Coverage and Efficiency Among Major Electronic Publications" and failed to list *IEEE Spectrum*, the latter's publisher immediately issued "A Comparison of Market Coverage and Efficiency Among All Major Electronic Publications" with *IEEE Spectrum* included. The habits of space buyers have forced most publishers to prefer that their magazines be best (even second-best) in their class to being the only one of its kind.

Despite the prevalence of computer analysis, independent judgment has not vanished. No magazine has ever succeeded on the basis of "the numbers" alone. Although it is difficult to convince the media buyer that you have a monopoly position for the advertiser, it can be done. *Playboy* managed it for many years. So do *The New Yorker, Parents* and *National Geographic.*

Can promotion help convince advertisers that your magazine is special? Carter indicates one of the best techniques: Relate advertiser need to reader need. His "tough customer" defines the advertiser's need so as to dovetail it with the reader need *Good Housekeeping* is geared to fill. The key to successful selling of your differential is defining it in terms of need. Once the need is clear, recognition of your product's ability to fill that need follows with little effort.

Convincing your staff

Defining the need rather than the means of filling it is also the key to internal management. As Carter states, management has to discipline itself not to interfere with the decisions of the editor, but to wait until the results come out.

What is left unsaid is what management does to point the editor in the right direction. Management must define the need and let the editor decide how the magazine fills it. In many instances, it may be the editor who actually defines the need. But it is still management who decides whether the need, as defined, is the business of the company or not. Thus Helen Gurley Brown recognized and defined the need *Cosmopolitan* brilliantly fills, but Hearst management had to accept her view and provide the authority needed to do the job.

The same formula holds for managing the circulation department. Defining the reader need can provide the critical element in persuading circulation-promotion personnel to concentrate on soliciting core readers vs. fringe readers. A clear definition of the need the magazine fills not only gives the creative people something to say, but makes it much easier to identify prime prospects. Better prospects mean higher response rates and higher renewal percentages. Higher subscription rates become more feasible. Most important, the circulation department will be reinforcing the magazine's monopoly position, not fighting it.

A clear definition of both reader and advertiser needs can also be your most effective tool in managing the ad department. To convince space buyers that you have a monopoly on the advertising market you serve, you must first convince your salespeople. This can be surprisingly difficult because space salespeople tend to reflect the attitudes of space buyers. That is why there is so much negative selling, particularly among business-paper salesmen. Nothing makes positive selling easier than a well-defined need and a clear idea of how your publication fills that need.

MANAGEMENT REVIEW

Check List for Competitive Positioning
(To be applied to one publication at a time)

I. What is your competitive situation
   A. In the reader market
   _____ Pure?
   _____ Oligopolistic?
   _____ Monopolistic?
   B. In the advertiser market
   _____ Pure?
   _____ Oligopolistic?
   _____ Monopolistic?

II. Is the reader need your publication is meant to fill
   _____ Clear to almost everyone?
   _____ Clear to some?
   _____ Clear to relatively few or unclear?

III. Is the reader need your publication is meant to fill

_____ Very specialized?

_____ Broadly specialized?

_____ General, or a group of needs?

IV. Is the advertiser need your publication is meant to fill

_____ Clear to almost everyone?

_____ Clear to some?

_____ Clear to few or unclear?

V. Is the advertiser need your publication is meant to fill

_____ Very specialized?

_____ Broadly specialized?

_____ Not really special?

VI. To improve your competitive position should you

A. Clarify the definition of the reader need

_____ 1. With the staff?

_____ 2. With readers?

_____ 3. With advertisers?

B. Clarify the definition of the advertiser need

_____ 1. With the staff?

_____ 2. With advertisers?

C. _____ Target the publication at a more specific reader need?

D. _____ Target the publication at a more specific advertiser need?

E. _____ Make changes to improve the way your publication fills the reader need?

F. _____ Make changes to improve the way your publication fills the advertiser need?

VII. Has management voiced an explicit policy decision on

A. _____ Reader need?

B. _____ Advertiser need?

VIII. Can you improve the understanding and acceptance of management policy regarding reader need by

_____ The editor?

_____ The editorial staff?

_____ The head of advertising sales?
_____ The advertising sales personnel?
_____ The circulation department?
_____ The promotion department?
_____ Your advertising agency?

IX. **Can you improve the understanding and acceptance of management policy regarding advertiser need by**
_____ The editorial department?
_____ The head of advertising sales?
_____ The advertising sales personnel?
_____ The circulation director?
_____ The promotion department?
_____ Your advertising agency?

X. **For a specific review, evaluate your publication's recent performance from 0 to 100%:**
A. Is the reader need, as you see it
_____ Filled by the editorial features in the latest issue? _____%
_____ Recognized by the ads in the latest issue? _____%
_____ Appealed to in the last circulation promotion? _____%
_____ Appealed to in the current renewal series? _____%
_____ Exploited in the most recent advertising promotion campaign? _____%
_____ Used by the advertising sales force? _____%
B. Is the advertiser need as you see it
_____ Confirmed by the type of advertising carried in the latest issue? _____%
_____ Making sense in the light of the last issue's editorial matter? _____%
_____ Embodied in the latest advertising promotion campaign? _____%
_____ Used by the current space salesforce? _____%
_____ Helped by the demographics of the current readership? _____%
_____ Being considered in the choice of lists for the latest circulation promotion? _____%

CHAPTER EIGHT

Why and How You Must Keep Ahead of Your Readers

Featuring an Interview with Henry A. Grunwald

Editor in Chief of Time Inc.

So far, we have looked at editorial focus as establishing something, making the editorial package fit the market, and making it distinctive enough to stand out from competitive editorial packages. But magazines are not static. They are living things that change from issue to issue.

Just how do editors retain focus while constantly changing? And, remember, it is not just the magazine that is changing. So are the readers. Not only does each issue reach new readers, but the old readers are also changing. So it is not enough to achieve focus, or to figure out how your magazine can be unique. You must constantly refocus it to keep ahead of your readers.

To learn more about this most crucial function of editing we interviewed Henry Anatole Grunwald, Time Inc.'s editor in chief. He is the executive with final responsibility for the editorial excellence of *Discover, Fortune, Life, Money, People Weekly, Sports Illustrated* and *Time*—seven very different and constantly changing editorial products.

Henry Grunwald arrived in this country from Austria when he was 17 years old. Five years later, in 1944, he graduated Phi Beta Kappa from New York University, a philosophy major and editor of the college newspaper. While in college, Henry worked for *Time* magazine as a copy boy. But after graduation he joined a labor newspaper as a reporter.

But he still had his eye on *Time* and, in July 1945, the magazine accepted him as a writer-on-trial. By November he was assigned to the foreign news department. Six years later he had written 30 cover stories and become the youngest senior editor in *Time*'s history.

In 1966, Henry was appointed assistant managing editor of *Time*. Two years later he became managing editor, a job which, at Time Inc., is the equivalent of being the magazine's editor.

Henry's innovations, during the years he was *Time*'s managing editor (1968-1979), included several new editorial departments (The Environment, Energy, and Behavior & The Sexes), the adoption of writers' by-lines, the introduction of special issues, and a complete overhaul of the magazine's graphics.

In 1979, Henry was chosen to be Hedley Donovan's successor as editor in chief for all Time Inc. publications, the job he holds today.

INTERVIEW

Q: Who has final responsibility at Time Inc. to see that each magazine keeps up with the times?
A: By definition, as editor in chief, I have final responsibility for everything editorial. But the operational responsibility falls on each managing editor.

Q: What is most important in keeping editors up to date: instinct, awareness, reader feedback or reader research?
A: The first two, and they are closely related. Awareness is the biggest responsibility an editor has, and the way he develops instinct. Reader feedback is not unimportant, but you can't edit by listening to suggestions from readers. That also goes for research.

Q: Has Time Inc. any kind of formal program to keep editors current?
A: A formal program would be artificial. But we do a lot to promote awareness. Choosing what should be printed is the biggest job an editor has. It's more important than his ability to edit copy, even than ability to get along with his staff. We work at developing this awareness all the time. The nearest thing to a formal program is the lunch, usually weekly, at which I meet with the managing editors to talk about a lot of things: politics, the economy, foreign affairs, etc.

Q: Do you prepare an agenda?

A: Almost never. I usually have one or two topics in mind, but it's pretty casual. I don't mention it as a major instrument to develop awareness, just as an example of our constant communication, exchange of ideas, etc. There's reading too. I've always felt there must be a kind of serendipity in an editor's reading. If you read only the things that are directly pertinent to the work, you miss a lot. You have to read all over. You may find ideas, sense trends in fiction, for instance.

Techniques for keeping current

Q: How important is travel in keeping editors current?

A: Very important. I've never been on a trip where I haven't picked up new story ideas or angles. Unfortunately our managing editors are very busy, and probably don't get out enough.

Q: Are seminars and conventions much help?

A: It depends on the meeting. We do quite a bit of this sort of thing. Every couple of years we collaborate with some university, and take a group of editors to a two-day seminar on some broad field. We have an ongoing program at Duke University where writers and editors spend a whole month studying. We have conferences on specific issues with legislators. Last year's was on antitrust.

Q: Do the editors do much on their own, e.g., having lunch or getting on the phone with an expert?

A: They do a lot of that. We frequently have scientists or politicians in for lunch with one or more editors.

Q: Do you ever engage someone from outside or from another part of the company to tear an issue apart—just to stir things up, get everybody perking?

A: It is a very important part of my own job to critique issues or parts of issues. Also to praise, when that's indicated. We haven't had outsiders do this, though it may not be a bad idea.

Q: What's important is not really the criticism but the response of the staff, the intellectual stimulation.

A: Occasionally we'll pack off the staff for a couple of days' in-depth look at the magazine. When I became managing editor of *Time*, I held such consciousness-raising sessions. All kinds of ideas, some very far out, came up. It was very useful. Seeds of ideas survived to be used as much as five years later. But we didn't have an outsider come in and tell us what's wrong with *Time*. The nearest we came to that was when I hired a grammarian to write a critique of *Time*'s use of language.

Q: Can the ad department help in updating editors?
A: It can, but it's dangerous. Ad people have a different perspective. They aren't in close contact with readers. Yet they can't be ignored. There was a time when the word in advertising circles was that *Newsweek* was hot, while *Time* had become dull. When something like that happens, you may think it's unfair, but you had better know about it. Use your judgment as to the validity. I certainly took notice of that talk, and was influenced by it, though I can't say that I made specific changes in response to it. Mostly it confirmed changes I had already decided to make. On the other hand, it can be dangerous to take seriously every report about an advertiser who criticized the magazine while turning down a salesman.

Q: How about the circulation people?
A: I think circulation people can tell you a lot. They certainly can give you the flavor, the reputation of a magazine among readers, and they can tell you whether they have to spend too much money to get new subscribers.

Listening to the readers

Q: How about reader contact? Is watching correspondence left to the discretion of the editors?
A: Entirely. But I think you would find a consensus among our editors that you should not pay too much attention to reader correspondence. Every magazine in this company receives a regular mail report. We have a large letters department which answers every letter. Editors receive a regular summary: the number of letters and a breakdown by subject matter. *Time*, for example, had an overwhelmingly negative flood of mail on our choice of Khomeini as ''man of the year.''

Q: How much does reader reaction influence the editors?
A: I don't say that editors should ignore reader mail, but you cannot edit a magazine by its mail. I anticipated the reaction to Khomeini. We went ahead without hesitation. An editor must do what he thinks best. Besides, letters are not a good indicator of how readers feel. The active letter-writer is unusual, not typical.

Q: How valid are renewals as an indicator?

A: Very important. We have a tradition in this company of keeping the editorial and financial sides quite separate. But it would be idiotic not to have some contact. If there is a serious problem with newsstand sales or renewals, the editor hears about it, and attends sessions at which the staff tries to analyze it.

Q: Do you feel newsstand sales are more apt to reflect a specific element in the editorial package, like the cover subject, whereas renewals are more apt to reflect the constant pattern of the total editorial package? Are some editors more strongly influenced by what happens on the newsstands than others?

A: Yes, to both questions. For a magazine like *People*, which depends predominantly on single-copy sales, how a subject moves on the stands is extremely important. *People*'s managing editor pays a lot of attention to that. *Time* is also interested in newsstand sales, but is predominantly a subscription magazine. Also, its primary obligation is to the news. We may know that a certain politician on the cover will not sell as many copies as a television star. Yet we do it.

Q: Do the editors use reader research very often?

A: Not often, though there are variations within Time Inc. There's a longstanding tradition at *Time* to distrust reader research, while *People*'s first managing editor, Dick Stolley, was very interested in focus groups. Dick found them useful, though they didn't profoundly change what he did in the magazine. *Money* has occasionally commissioned reader research, but has paid relatively little attention to it. One study said the book-review section was the poorest read department, but it's still there.

Q: Do individual editors talk to individual readers?

A: A lot. I do it deliberately when I travel or socialize. I want to hear what people have to say about the new *Life* or the new *Fortune*. Again, you put it in perspective. You don't necessarily go back to the office and do something right away.

The art of staying ahead

Q: They say an editor has to know what the reader wants before the reader does. Do you interpret that literally?

A: It depends on the magazine. With *Time*, when there's a news development, such as the current rise of Islam as an influence in world politics, it doesn't take clairvoyance to know readers need more about Islam. But you do try to anticipate what is likely to be ahead, judging from the early indicators and symptoms, and sometimes you must give readers what you think they should read. On publications not tied to news, you still have to watch the world to learn what will interest readers, but you, as editor, are somewhat freer to invent the agenda.

Q: Can you pretest ideas before you use them?
A: On a going magazine, there's no way to pretest ideas except by talking to colleagues and other people. With new magazines or magazine concepts, where there's a huge investment involved, we pretest by direct-mail and other methods. But that's not practical for new departments or cover stories. Besides, the reader doesn't really know what he wants until he sees it.

Q: Herb Mayes once said that every issue should have a surprise for the reader. Doesn't that mean knowing what the reader wants before he does?
A: Yes. Surprises are good and necessary. To become predictable is always a danger. Readers shouldn't know ahead of time precisely how the magazine will cover a subject. On the other hand, there is something comforting in knowing what to expect, that you will get what you bought the magazine for. The editor has to achieve a balance. The object of the editor should be to stretch the reader's mind, but not so much as to make the reader uncomfortable. Thus the importance of knowing one's readers. That's not to be confused with the data publishers gather for advertisers: average age, income, etc. Such information can be useful, but the knowledge the editor needs has to be much more impressionistic. A good editor understands his readers to the point of identifying with them. Hence his final norm is to make sure he is not bored by his own magazine.

Q: We've said that special-interest magazines are much easier to keep updated than special-audience magazines.
A: You're absolutely right. For a special-interest magazine, say on photography, new developments in the field come to you almost automatically. But with a special-audience magazine, *Esquire* for instance, news events may point the way, but generally, trends are harder to spot.

Q: Part of every audience likes change and part always resists change. How do you please both?
A: By making changes gradually. But you can't always do it. In the design change at *Time*, for instance, there was no way to sneak up on it. We had to do it and get it over with. But generally, change should be very gradual. In fact, before you change you should first consider whether it's change you need or whether what you're doing currently is being done incorrectly. Sometimes change is just a way of escape.

Q: Was the change in Fortune*'s size and frequency really done to keep up with reader's needs?*

A: There were two reasons for the change. One, frankly, was a business reason: to offer advertisers greater frequency. But that alone would not have been a sufficient reason. There was also the feeling that many people found *Fortune* too cumbersome, the articles too long, the magazine difficult to carry around. The new format and frequency have already proved an advertising success and, despite some early uncertainty, the latest information shows that the readers definitely welcome them too.

ANALYSIS

A Matter of Leadership

Magazine publishing is built on expectation. Readers put down good money because they expect publishers to give them what they want in the future.

Like all living things, audiences change constantly. The woman who buys a one-year subscription to *Science '85* today will not have exactly the same reader needs when she receives *Science '86*. New readers and attrition will make changes in the magazine's entire audience even greater. Even periodicals with 100% audience turnover every few years, like *Scholastic* or *Modern Bride*, cannot afford to repeat issues. The need they fill may remain generically the same, but specifics will change with the times.

The publisher's goal is to synchronize changes in the magazine with changes in the audience. That is what is really meant by keeping editors current. Nothing kills a magazine faster than an audience that moves in one direction, while the editorial moves in another—or stands still.

Theoretically a magazine can stay in step with its readers either by following or by leading. Practically, only leading works.

Whether a magazine is published to inform, inspire or entertain, it has to assume a position of leadership. Readers look to their magazines as guides, counsellors, teachers. This is true even of publications like *Mad Magazine* or *The National Lampoon*, which seem to aim at little more than to lead readers from laugh to laugh.

Magazines master change by leading readers in a direction they are willing to go. Willingness is essential. This is why Henry Grunwald recommends that change be achieved gradually. Abrupt change finished off both the old *Saturday Evening Post* and *American Home*.

Thus leadership implies rapport with one's followers. Leaders always move in new directions, but never leave their followers behind (as *Crawdaddy* did when it became *Feature*, and the *Saturday Review* did when it tried to become four magazines).

To measure success in leadership is easy. If you march at the right rate in the right direction, the number of your followers increases. When your leadership wanes, so does your following.

To successfully keep ahead of its readers, i.e., to be their leader, a publication needs knowledge, foresight, judgment, understanding and charisma.

Knowledge and foresight: Stay ahead of your subject

A magazine should have a knowledge of its field superior to that of most of its readers. It should be intimate with the field's sources for both background and news.

To monitor knowledge-requirements for leadership, editors should first make sure the field is clearly defined in their own minds and those of their staffs', and then, penalize error and ignorance. Lastly, editors should guard against knowledge excesses—mental fatigue, mind set, waning curiosity and pride of learning—which lure an editor into writing for his or her peers to the neglect of less sophisticated readers.

But knowledge is not enough. To lead a magazine, you must go beyond knowing what is and be able to see what will be. Ability to look into the future enables a publication to keep ahead of its readers, to see where it is taking them. Thus *Playboy*'s Hugh Hefner opened an editorial office in California because "the West Coast is in many ways a clue to the future."

Every magazine is not an *Omni* or a *Next*, but every periodical has to interpret the significance beyond the facts. This requires knowing the influential people in its field well enough to factor in the impact of their personalities on the flow of events. Hence Grunwald's emphasis on personal contact with newsmakers.

In evaluating themselves as forecasters, editors must beware of two extremes: future phobia, in which the editor considers change a threat rather than a challenge; and power hunger, where the prophet feels destined to make events transpire in accordance with his or her vision. Closely allied to the first are editors who excuse themselves from the obligation to predict the future by claiming "objectivity." Related to the second are editors who allow pet theories to color their interpretation of what will happen.

Judgment and understanding: Stay ahead of your audience

Grunwald points out the need to stretch the reader's mind, but not so much as to make him uncomfortable. It takes exquisitely tuned judgment to teach without tiring, to entertain without boring, to coax without compelling, to excite without irritating.

Publishers looking for signs of failure in judgment should watch for editorial narcissism and exhibitionism. Both undermine judgment by putting personal needs before readers' needs. Much more easily overlooked are the "business-minded" editors who put pleasing the publisher or fellow executives ahead of readers' needs.

Good judgment is possible only if the editors understand their readers. As Grunwald says, audience data helps, but what is really needed is much more impressionistic. Research provides data. Editors need insight.

Essential to understanding one's readers is respect—and affection. This protects editors from forcing personal preconceptions on readers, as well as providing readers ground for rooting faith and trust. The difference between *Playboy* and previous skin books was largely that Hugh Hefner respected his readers. The genius of *Reader's Digest* founders DeWitt and Lila Wallace lay in their solicitude. They always had a parent-child relationship with their readers. Such an attitude prevents formula editing or the tendency of editors to rely too much on what worked in the past. One reason for *Psychology Today*'s problems when Ziff-Davis owned it, was its reluctance to change the formula that skyrocketed the magazine to success in the late '60s.

Charisma and inner vision: the magic element

Charisma, the magic of leadership that arouses popular loyalty and enthusiasm, is found in magazines as well as individuals. Like all magic, it defies explanation. It arises partially from being in the right place at the right time (proper market positioning can help make it happen), and there are specific recognizable conditions needed for it to happen: strength, patience, charm, contagious enthusiasm and inner vision. A classic example of these conditions, when occurring at the right place and time, resulting in charisma is found in the Rodale publications, *Prevention* and *Organic Farming*. Both founder Jerome Rodale and his son Robert had the strength of conviction. They had the patience not to sur-render on the one hand, and not to descend into stridency on the other. Their contagious enthusiasm—over two generations—is evident and remarkable. The publications, ugly at first look, have charm in that their appearance confirms their message: back to basic simplicity.

In humans, inner vision is more easily sensed than defined. In magazines, it is closely connected to editorial focus, or the clear realization of a reader need and how the publication fills it. This inner vision can be found in publications as diverse as *Cosmopolitan* and *Guitar Player*. It can be felt in work-a-day business papers like the *National Underwriter* or *Air Force Magazine*. There is a quality that holds each of these publications together, that gives the reader the feeling that each knows what it is doing and where it is going.

Though charisma is hard to define, its counterfeits are easy to recog-nize. A magazine (or editor) plagued by self-examination, self-explanation, or self-admiration definitely lacks the goal-obsession required for leadership (a phenome-non that may account for the decline of Bill Buckley's *National Review*). Stub-bornness and defensiveness under criticism indicate a lack of strength and patience irreconcilable with charisma. The ''Bert Parks complex,'' where enthusiasm is habitual rather than spontaneous, is another sign, and may partly explain the decline in popularity of the ''fan books.''

Techniques for sustaining leadership

The qualities of leadership do not just happen. They have to be constantly nourished. Editors and other publishing executives have to cultivate contacts for the information and inspiration which are the raw material for knowledge, fore-sight, judgment, understanding and charisma. It is up to the editor to see that opportunities for such contacts exist and are used, i.e., that each key staffer cultivates constant contact with sources, fellow staffers and readers.

Indirect sources can be almost as important as direct sources for nourishing both foresight and charisma. Editors need to know the makers and shakers in their field. Hence the importance of outside contacts, travel, participation in con-ventions and other public events.

For the same reason, it is important for editors to meet advertisers who are also trying to influence the magazine's readers. What they do today can help editors understand how readers will think tomorrow.

In many fields, recognition and cultivation by advertisers are both instru-ment and yardstick of the magazine's charisma, as embodied in editor or publisher. Advertisers consider editors like *Golf Digest*'s Nick Seitz and *Traffic World*'s Joe Scheleen to be leaders in their industries.

The need for contact and interaction with fellow staffers cannot be overestimated. Editors cannot be expected to lead readers if they cannot lead their staffers. One of the reasons McCall Corporation's *Your Place* failed, while Conde Nast's *Self* is a winner, is that *Self* editor Phyllis Wilson took the lead in the internal struggle to determine editorial focus.

Editors have to be catalysts for other executives' decisions, including those of circulation, advertising sales, production and overall management. Hence the need for what Grunwald calls "consciousness-raising sessions" and what management consultants call "open planning"—for department heads to spend two or three days together, away from the office, discussing the magazine's "survival."

Finally, there is the all-important contact with readers. No one can talk intelligently if he does not first listen. Even controlled-circulation publications must listen to readers, a need that can easily be overlooked if the publication is not audited, carries no bingo cards or other response mechanism, and if there is no struggle to monitor reader reaction.

The principal reader contact is through the publication itself. Editors must learn to interpret renewals, subscription-promotion results, single-copy returns, response on BPA qualification cards, service complaints and other circulation data. An editor who does not know the significance of first renewal-notice response versus total renewal-series response is not listening. Reader correspondence is also important, but less an indicator of what readers think than a barometer of what excites them.

Reader research has its place. But most editors discount it, primarily because what they need to know most is least responsive to this type of measurement. The biggest danger is that "scientific" methodology and high cost may give research results importance beyond their value. An editor hooked on research can do a lot of damage. It was scary to hear *Realities* publisher Paul Jacquet say: "We don't presume to know what our readers want, so each month we survey 1,500 of them to find out."

It is very difficult for a magazine's management to organize a program for personal contact between staffers and readers. Such contact is essential, but usually has to be left to the initiative of the individual editor or department head.

The objective is not to reach a representative sample or collect scientifically reliable data. The purpose is to "get inside the reader's skin," to develop the insights and instincts that make foresight, understanding and inner vision possible. At best the publisher can ordain that editors circulate at shows, conventions and other places where readers congregate, and encourage them to develop habits like former *Saturday Review* editor Norman Cousins's after-hours phone calls to subscribers. The need for personal contact with readers was one reason why *Good Housekeeping*'s Latin American edition failed until it was franchised to locals under the title *Buenhogar*.

MANAGEMENT REVIEW

Check List for Leadership

I. Evaluate your periodical's leadership qualities.

  A. Knowledge. Is it evident from the publication:

    1. That you, your staff and the readers agree on the definition of the field?   Yes_____ No_____

    2. That its editors' general knowledge of the field is superior to that of most readers?   Yes_____ No_____

    3. That your staff can ask intelligent questions on areas of specialization?   Yes_____ No_____

    4. That there is real concern for accuracy and thoroughness?   Yes_____ No_____

    5. That the editors welcome and constantly look for new ideas and developments?   Yes_____ No_____

    6. That it is written to help readers, not impress them or others?   Yes_____ No_____

  B. Foresight. Does each issue:

    1. Have information or news that is exclusive, having appeared nowhere else?   Yes_____ No_____

    2. Present topics or treatments of wide interest to the readership in a unique way?   Yes_____ No_____

    3. Indicate that the editors are using personal contacts with the field's influential people?   Yes_____ No_____

    4. Interpret events, developments without hesitation, apology, or prejudice?   Yes_____ No_____

  C. Judgment. Can you honestly say the publication:

    1. Teaches without tiring?   Yes_____ No_____

    2. Entertains without boring?   Yes_____ No_____

    3. Coaxes without compelling?   Yes_____ No_____

    4. Excites without irritating?   Yes_____ No_____

    5. Is always edited for the readers, never for the staff or management?
                                  Yes_____ No_____

D. Understanding. Does the publication indicate:
    1. That the editors have respect and affection for the readers?
                                  Yes_____ No_____

    2. That reader rapport is based on more than editors can learn from reader research?   Yes_____ No_____

    3. That changes to meet reader tastes are made subtly but regularly?
                                  Yes_____ No_____

E. Charisma:
    1. Is reader enthusiasm and loyalty as good as you would like it to be?
                                  Yes_____ No_____

    2. Are your editorial positions as strong as they could be?
                                  Yes_____ No_____

    3. Is the editorial approach as patient as it should be, neither discouraged nor strident?   Yes_____ No_____

    4. Is the publication as charming as it could be
      a. In editorial style?   Yes_____ No_____
      b. In editorial approach?   Yes_____ No_____
      c. Graphically?   Yes_____ No_____
      d. In format?   Yes_____ No_____

    5. Is the editorial infused with an enthusiasm that is both spontaneous and contagious?   Yes_____ No_____

    6. Has the publication an inner vision to give it unity and purpose?
                                  Yes_____ No_____

II. Review the techniques used to sustain leadership.
A. Contact with sources. Do editors, other executives:
    1. Have adequate contact with all the direct sources for information in the field?   Yes_____ No_____

    2. Make sufficient effort to meet and cultivate the field's influential people?
                                  Yes_____ No_____

    3. Have budgets and schedules which encourage such contacts?
                                  Yes_____ No_____

    4. Meet advertisers to learn what they are doing and thinking?
                                  Yes_____ No_____

B. Staff interaction. Does management provide for:
   1. A position of leadership for the editor among non-editorial department heads? Yes_____ No_____
   2. Open-planning sessions, where department heads can discuss the publication's "survival"? Yes_____ No_____
   3. Discussion of editorial ideas with the staffers in non-editorial departments? Yes_____ No_____
C. Reader contact. Do executives, especially editors:
   1. Know how to interpret reader attitudes from circulation data?
      Yes_____ No_____
   2. Watch reader correspondence without giving it more importance than it deserves? Yes_____ No_____
   3. Have a healthy attitude toward reader research, using it but not depending on it? Yes_____ No_____
   4. Habitually look for opportunities to meet readers personally?
      Yes_____ No_____

CHAPTER NINE

How to Imitate Other Editors Creatively

Featuring an Interview with
Osborn Elliott
Dean of the Graduate School of Journalism at Columbia University

It has been said that "great editors innovate, while lesser editors imitate." It is an adage that massages an editor's ego and has a nice ring to it, but nothing could be further from the truth.

Since no editor works in a vacuum, every editor has to be influenced by the work of other editors, what other magazines have done and are doing. In fact, one of the most fundamental characteristics of genius—whether in a scientist, artist or editor—is the ability to stand on the shoulders of others, both predecessors and contemporaries.

We think some form of imitation is essential in every creative act, and editing is definitely a creative act.

To talk about this neglected but important element of editing, we called on Oz Elliott, the dean of Columbia's Graduate School of Journalism, whose career included more than 15 years in top spots at *Newsweek* and six years on the editorial staff of *Time*. Since *Newsweek* was started as an imitation of *Time*, Oz seemed the perfect editor with whom to discuss imitation as it relates to magazine editing.

Oz Elliott graduated from Harvard in 1944. After service in the Navy during World War II, he joined the *Journal of Commerce* as a reporter. Three years later, he moved to *Time* magazine as a contributing editor. In 1952, after three years as contributing editor, he became associate editor.

Oz left *Time* in 1955 to become senior business editor for *Newsweek*. Four years later *Newsweek* promoted him to managing editor—and in 1961, six years after joining the company, he became *Newsweek*'s editor.

For the next 15 years Oz served *Newsweek* as president, vice chairman, editor in chief and chairman. He left in 1976 to become New York City's Deputy Mayor for Economic Development.

In 1979, Oz became dean of the Graduate School of Journalism at Columbia University. He is also author of *The World of Oz*, published by Viking in 1980.

INTERVIEW

Q: When you were editor of Newsweek, *did you ever deliberately copy or adapt something* Time *had done?*
A: I worked at *Time* for six and a half years before I went to *Newsweek*, in 1955, as editor of the business section. *Newsweek*, of course, started as a kind of imitation of *Time*, ten years after *Time* was founded. But from the beginning, *Newsweek* tried to carve out a distinct identity, what Rosser Reeves used to call a "unique selling proposition." From the start, *Newsweek* emphasized that it separated fact from opinion—a direct dig at *Time*'s insinuation of opinion into its news columns. *Newsweek* had columns of opinion by people like Raymond Moley and George Jean Nathan.

Imitating a magazine idea

Q: Did Newsweek *try to undersell* Time *in any way?*
A: I honestly don't know. When I got to *Newsweek* in 1955, it stood, in advertising and circulation, somewhere between *U.S. News* and *Time*. I was shocked to find that *Newsweek*'s business people were slipping into the mistaken response of aiming their guns at *U.S. News* rather than *Time*. I thought it rather discouraging to look down rather than up. But the editors' attitude was entirely different.

Q: How?
A: John Denson, who became editor just about when I came to *Newsweek* and was editor for the next six years, undertook a very dramatic campaign to make

Newsweek more exciting. He aimed his guns at *Time*. He went after exclusives, which *Time*, due to the way it was edited, did not know how to handle. A former *Time* managing editor used to say that *Time* with an exclusive was like a whore with a baby—"we don't know what to do with it." John Denson knew what to do with it: slam it on the cover, promote the hell out of it, and show it around the block saying, "Look, folks, we have an exclusive." *Newsweek*, under Denson acquired an image as the newsmagazine with the exclusives.

Q: In saying the business side aimed more at U.S. News *than at* Time, *are you including circulation promotion?*
A: That was certainly my impression.

Q: Yet Newsweek *never had* Time's *resources.*
A: When Phil Graham of the *Washington Post* purchased *Newsweek* in 1961, he opened a whole new era for the magazine. He made a lot of money available to me, as the new editor, and gave us complete freedom to do what we wanted to do.

Q: And what was that?
A: During the '60s, *Newsweek* broke the mold of the newsmagazine as it had existed. We profited from the fact that *Time* was asleep at the switch during the early '60s. *Time* was not at the cutting edge of the important social movements that seized that decade, whereas *Newsweek* saw their significance very early. Civil rights is a good example. We were the first to wed the old art of journalism to the new pseudo-science of opinion polling by combining reportage of the movement with public-opinion analysis by Lou Harris. The result: our blockbuster cover story on Black America in the summer of 1963. It was a major breakthrough for *Newsweek*, announcing to the world that this magazine was important and was exploring new journalistic approaches.

Q: If I remember correctly, you did an outstanding job on the assassination of President Kennedy.
A: For the first time under the new management, *Newsweek* was head to head with *Time* on a really historic story. *Time* made the mistake of putting Lyndon Johnson on the cover instead of Jack Kennedy. *Newsweek*'s publisher's page ran an excerpt from Walt Whitman's poem, "When Lilacs Last in the Dooryard Bloom'd"—*Time*'s self-adulatory publisher's letter noted that it had lost its number-one subscriber. The story broke on Friday. *Newsweek* closed on Saturday. We had to tear the whole magazine apart, fly reporters and photographers to Washington, Dallas, Hyannis and so forth. But we turned out almost twice as much copy on the event as *Time* did, and the quality was as impressive as

the quantity. A great many people who usually read only one of the magazines, read both that week, and there was no doubt *Newsweek* did the better job.

Imitating techniques

Q: You've emphasized the effort to be different. Were there occasions when Time *did something too good not to imitate?*
A: People often say, "Why do *Newsweek* and *Time* so often have the same cover stories?" Usually, they don't.

Q: I'd like to avoid that. There is only one "news," and since you both cover all the news, you are bound to come up with the same lead stories occasionally. I don't consider that imitation. What about techniques, e.g., departments, which have changed over the years in both magazines. Weren't there instances when Time *introduced a department and then you started a similar one?*
A: You could say *Time* introduced the whole system of departmentalizing the news. To that degree, *Newsweek* directly copied *Time*'s Business, Foreign Affairs, National Affairs sections, etc. I suspect that there was at least one department we copied in the area of life and leisure. *Time* also copied us. The *Time* "Essay" was, in a way, a copy of *Newsweek*'s signed columns, but it also encouraged us to do more of the same. One of the major departures we took during the '60s was the use of by-lines. After long deliberation, we finally decided to let reviewers sign their pieces. When we finally did it, we didn't announce it to the readers until six weeks after it was done, and then, in a rather backhanded manner. Eventually by-lines were extended to all departments, and *Time* followed suit.

How to imitate successfully

Q: If you're editing a magazine and you see a good idea someplace else, you would be a fool if you did not consider trying something like it. Are there norms for imitating? Is it important, for instance, to disguise the fact?
A: I think it's self-defeating to steal directly—and self-demeaning among your peers in the trade.

Q: Perhaps we worry too much about our peers, and not enough about our audience.
A: The best judgments made about magazines are still by fellow editors, so I would very much avoid a direct copying of another editor's idea.

Q: Yet many new magazines start as direct steals.
A: Yes, but like *Newsweek*, if they are to succeed, they have to establish their own identity.

Q: Are you saying the important thing is to transform the idea, give it an identity of its own, even though you may have gotten it from someplace else?
A: I think it is better to get your own ideas, but if someone else's idea is so good that you are compelled to use it, you should reshape it. It would certainly go against my grain to copy directly. In the case of the Modern Living section begun by *Time*, we spotted it as a good idea because we saw a new need and interest in living styles and changing trends. So we made it our own.

Q: Do you think U.S. News & World Report *would be better if it imitated more* Time *and* Newsweek *techniques, such as the special departments?*
A: Yes. I've always found it a terribly dull magazine. But, as I read in current ads, they're making that their unique selling proposition.

Q: What about Business Week?
A: That's a very successful example of an idea that was, in part, borrowed, but to a large extent shaped to new and special purposes.

Functional vs. personal editing

Q: Do you think functional editors tend to imitate competitors more than personal editors do?
A: Tell me what you mean by functional editing.

Q: Where the magazine itself (or its owner) closely defines what the magazine is supposed to do. I contrast this with personal editing, where the style and content is determined more by the tastes and interests of the editor. The Saturday Review *is a good example of how personal editing can change a magazine. It changed from a book-review weekly to a magazine that covered the totality of editor Norman Cousins' interests. Is there more of a tendency in functional editing to imitate?*
A: On a magazine like *Newsweek*, there's a combination of the functional editing process and the personal editing process. The function is to distribute information on a broad range of subjects, but the approach reflects the personality of the editor or a group of editors. Thus, while *Newsweek* covers the same subjects as *Time*, I think it tends to cover them in a less cold, less impersonal manner. The approach is more personal.

Q: I thought Time *was supposed to be opinionated while* Newsweek *separated fact from opinion?*

A: The old slogan of separating fact from opinion really became outdated as *Newsweek* became more analytical, more personal in its approach. Even in covering the news, the editing process requires personal judgment. An example: in the spring of 1972, I selected a cover on acupuncture. The subject happened to fascinate me, and we had a very dramatic picture of a lovely woman's face with needles in her cheeks. That issue, except for the Kennedy assassination issue, became the biggest newsstand seller in our history. Most cover decisions are personal hunches, unless a catastrophic news event forces your choice.

Advantages and dangers

Q: An advantage of using someone else's idea is that you already know it worked, whereas with your own idea, you don't know whether it will work until you do it.

A: That's a terribly boring way to edit.

Q: Admittedly, but there is a tendency for business departments to want to edit that way.

A: Fortunately, there was never any pressure at *Newsweek* from the business side. That's how it should be. If an editor makes too many wrong decisions, he should be replaced. I also think it is a terrible mistake to try to edit to demographics, to try to second guess some average reader with 3.5 years of college, 2.3 children, and an income of $23,400 a year. The only way to edit is to edit to your own interests.

Q: What are some of the dangers you see in imitation?

A: Because one publisher has an idea that works for him, doesn't mean that stealing it will turn out to be a good thing for you. Witness *Us* magazine vs. *People*.

Q: One could cite the "skin books." Imitators are falling all over each other, most trying to duplicate the success Penthouse *achieved by following* Playboy.

A: Are they all trying to be king of the mountain?

Q: At the top, it's strictly between Playboy *and* Penthouse. *But many people feel they can make a lot of money in third, fourth or fifth place.*

A: There were *Life* and *Look* back in the '30s. *Look* was an imitator of *Life*, although they claimed they weren't. But there was a market for two picture magazines for a long time. They both made the mistake of trying to compete with television, trying to sustain comparatively large audiences.

ANALYSIS

Imitation: Tool of Creativity

Editors who boast that they avoid all input from peers or competitors are either fools or hypocrites. The creative mind cannot function in a vacuum. New ideas are not only seeded by previous ideas, but grow best in soil made rich by the humus of other people's ideas.

Creativity, of course, is not exclusive to editors. Everyone involved in the development of a publication must be creative. Yet no place is it as essential to understand the tools of creativity as in publication management. It is essential both for one's own use and to make sure these tools are available and properly used by one's staff.

As a tool of creativity, imitation must be handled with extreme caution. Without some sort of imitation no creativity is possible, yet an over-dependence on imitation kills creativity. Successful magazine editing is impossible unless the editor can distinguish between imitation used to stimulate creativity and imitation used as a substitute for creativity.

Imitating a publication's concept

The easiest way to learn how imitation works for publishing is to consider the most fundamental form of imitation in the magazine business: adopting another publication's publishing concept. As Oz Elliott points out, *Newsweek* imitated *Time; Look, Life; Penthouse, Playboy;* and *Us, People.* The biggest advantage in such imitation is that the precursor has already tested the market and proved that a responsive reader need exists. The risk, of course, is that the innovator may have already saturated the market. Even when there is room for more than one publication, it requires extraordinary resources, skill, and luck to dislodge the leader sufficiently to preempt a profitable share of the market.

This brings us face to face with a basic principle: The secret of successful imitation is in adaptation, in making the copy different from the model. Note that Elliott discusses *Newsweek*'s imitation of *Time* entirely by describing what was done to make *Newsweek* different. No publisher ever succeeded by duplicating another publisher's operation without making any changes.

This is why our analysis of the various forms imitation can take is largely an analysis of various points of departure. There are five ways in which a publisher can imitate another publication's basic concept:

1. Copying. The imitator follows the original so closely that, if the logo were changed, the new magazine could pass for another issue of the original publication. Because the product is a copy, the newcomer has to rely entirely on selling (circulation and advertising) to successfully compete against the original. This works only when the imitator is able to outgun the model with definitely superior firepower—a larger and better sales staff, significantly more advertising and promotion. The New York Times Company gave up on *Us* because, while the editors produced nothing more than a copy of *People*, the company was unwilling to spend the kind of money required to outgun Time Inc.

2. Excelling. The imitator fulfills the same basic need (reader, advertiser, or both) as the original, but does it better. Rudolph Murdoch launched the *Star* to fill the same needs as the *National Enquirer*, but better. (He also banked on heavier sales firepower.) Generoso Pope has managed to keep the *Enquirer* in front by copying Murdoch's improvements (color, for instance). Hugh Hefner's *Playboy* succeeded by defying sexual taboos and making discreet nudity respectable. Bob Guccione's *Penthouse* excelled *Playboy* by carrying that defiance a step further with indiscreet nudity.

3. Refining. The imitator analyzes the innovator's success, isolates the most desirable segment of the market, and repositions the publishing concept not only to appeal exclusively to the desirable segment, but in so doing, to enlarge it. *People* is an imitation of the basic concept of the *National Enquirer* and the fan books, but Time Inc. repositioned it to attract an audience with more appeal to advertisers. Henry Luce saw the value of attracting the top of the business hierarchy when he created *Fortune*, 13 years after the founding of *Forbes*. He used the same strategy with *Sports Illustrated* vs. *Sport* and *Sporting News*.

4. Segmenting. This has similarities to refining, but more closely resembles what package-good manufacturers call market segmentation. You produce a specialized magazine for a segment of the other magazine's market. *Business Week* imitated *Time* for the audience especially interested in business. This technique has been used again and again in the business-paper field. *Datamation, Computer Design* and *Computerworld* were followed by specialized EDP periodicals like *Mini-Micro Systems, Byte* and *Computer Retailing*.

5. Transplanting. The imitator lifts the basic publishing concept that has been successful in one market and transfers it to an altogether different market. Many of the more recent city magazines are imitations of success in other cities. *Playgirl* and the now dead *Viva* transplanted the *Playboy/Penthouse* concept from the male to a female market. *Jewish Living* tried to transplant the *New York Magazine* concept to an ethnic market.

Red-flag areas

These five techniques are all surrounded by dangers. The greatest—especially common in copying, excelling and refining—is to adopt someone else's concept with no clear idea of how you are going to be different. It is not enough to be resolved to "do it better." Not even copying or excelling can be achieved by muddling through. The essential strategy for making your publication stand out from the original must be in place before you start.

The closer your imitation, the greater the need for financial resources to equal or outweigh those of your competitor. To put it another way, the smaller your spiritual resources (market-oriented original ideas for adaptation), the greater your material resources must be (to buy talent, publicity, promotion—and to survive long-term initial losses).

One problem is that imitation without innovation automatically makes your publication out of date. If your model is successful, it is changing from issue to issue, and your imitated changes will always be at least one issue behind.

The least creative way to compete is to undersell. In magazine publishing, it is usually also the least effective way. Long-run support of readers and advertisers rests heavily on an image of superiority, and a lower price never contributes to a higher image.

Finally, there is the risk of introducing changes just to be different. Differences that provide the imitator with no marketing edge usually hurt more than they help. Creative imitation requires discovering points of departure, adaptations that make the imitation superior in filling particular marketing needs. *Paris Hebdo* was a failure because it transplanted the concept of the U.S. city magazine without adapting it to the peculiarities of the Parisian market.

Imitating techniqes

Even when a periodical's concept is 100% original, it will be influenced by other publications. In our industry, copying of editorial, sales, production and promotion techniques is common to the point of suffocating creativity. This is especially true among many second-generation executives—the men and women who take over after the founders are gone.

Here, again, successful imitation is in the adaptation. The sharper the editorial focus of a publication, the easier it is to purposefully adapt imitated ideas. When success blurs the focus, i.e., when the audience gets so large that staffers are tempted to follow it rather than lead, it becomes increasingly difficult to make the borrowed idea one's own. This is the principal reason why *Good Housekeeping*, *Ladies' Home Journal* and *McCall's* are so similar today; why it is almost impossible to distinguish *Family Circle* from *Woman's Day*, or *Penthouse* from *Playboy*.

There are significant advantages in using the ideas others have used successfully. Such ideas have been pretested. Since they have been proven and exist in a form outsiders can study, they are easier to explain to one's staff—and easier to sell to one's boss.

There is nothing wrong with exploiting any of these advantages, provided one uses the greatest advantage of all: an idea already applied to a concrete situation. Such an idea provides a firmer footing for a point of departure than one that is still floating around in the abstract.

The skill required for this kind of imitation has two sides: 1) the ability to recognize a good idea, and 2) the ability to adapt it.

The first is a matter of craft. Executives who cannot tell a good idea from a bad one are in the wrong job.

The second is a matter of marketing. Two publications, no matter how closely competitive, cannot have identical marketing needs. The creative spark in imitation results from striking somebody else's idea against the unique needs of your market. If your publication has the resources to provide tinder for that spark, you will ignite a successful adaptation.

One way to strike the idea against your marketing situation is to consider the previously described forms of imitation.

Can you afford merely to copy the idea? This is usually hopeless unless you operate from a position of great power. The king can make a subject's innovation a national custom just by adopting it. A publication that really leads the field bestows honor on an idea by using it.

A better way to borrow an idea without really changing it is to excel in the use of it. This can be done by superior skill or superior resources. A graphic innovation can be improved by your art director's talent or by some characteristic of your magazine. For example, your magazine can use full color whereas the originator had to use black & white. Another way to excel is by recognizing the full potential of an idea not fully developed by the innovator.

To refine an idea is more than just doing it better. Here one takes a good idea and repositions it to serve a broader or more profitable purpose. The *"Time Essay"* was a refinement both of *Newsweek*'s signed columns and its own publisher's page.

To segment an idea or technique involves lifting only part of the original innovation. This can be the best part of the model, but more often it should be the part that best fits the imitator's marketing need.

Finally, this new idea can be transplanted. This is easiest when the audience of the imitator is 100% different from the model's audience. But it can also mean using the idea in an entirely different context or for an entirely different purpose, as when a circulation manager adapts an editorial idea for a promotion piece. Elliott made a major creative contribution by putting the opinion poll, heretofore exclusively a marketing and political tool, to editorial use.

The secret of creation through imitation

As we have already pointed out, imitation serves creativity only when the idea imitated serves as a point of departure, i.e., the basis for an adaptation. Since the further an idea is removed from your situation the more you have to transform it, the less an idea seems to fit your publication, the greater is the chance that it will occasion a truly creative adaptation.

This is a fact of creative management that many publishers overlook. Most magazine executives watch other media, particularly newspapers, television, and radio, as competitors for the advertising dollar. But few study them for new ideas. Even when multi-media giants like CBS and ABC take over magazines, there is surprisingly little creative cross-fertilization. There seems to be an absolute mind block against adapting "foreign" ideas to "native" situations.

The primary reason for this mind block may be pride in specialization. Most executives like to think what they do is unique. If they are even slightly insecure, they tend to view parallels, even analogies, as a threat to the distinction of being different.

This could be the major reason why so few publishers hire talent from other media, and why groups of similar magazines become so inbred. Even among publishers, we find many who cannot see how what is written about consumer magazines applies to business publications, and vice versa—or how what is said about large magazines applies to small publications.

Truly creative executives look hardest for similarities where they are least evident. It is there that most is to be learned, and the best ideas generated.

MANAGEMENT REVIEW

Check List for Creative Imitation

I. **To determine the advisability of imitating specific innovations.**

   A. The innovation must be worthy of imitation for one or more of the following:

      _____ It worked for the innovator, and can work the same way for you.

      _____ It is widely acclaimed, and also will be admired in your publication.

      _____ You know your readers (or advertisers, or employees, etc., depending on the nature of the innovation) will like it.

      _____ It can solve a specific problem for your publication.

   B. The requirements for the form of imitation you will use must be within your resources.

      1. Copying requires:

         _____ Sales and promotion resources superior to the publication you are imitating.

         _____ A reputation that cannot be hurt by copying.

      2. Excelling requires:

         _____ Evidence that the originator did not realize the full potential of the innovation.

         _____ A clearcut plan on how to realize that potential.

      3. Refining requires:

         _____ Discovering a better purpose to which this innovation can be adapted.

         _____ Determining precisely how the innovation is to be repositioned to serve that purpose.

      4. Segmenting requires:

         _____ Isolating an element or part of the innovation as the basis of a similar innovation.

         _____ Determining precisely how the part is to be developed into an independent innovation.

      5. Transplanting requires:

         _____ Selecting the different context in which to introduce the innovation.

         _____ Adapting the innovation to the context.

C. Your imitation strategy must be in place before you start.
_____ You know precisely what changes you are making in the original idea or its execution.
_____ The changes are based on your marketing needs.
_____ The imitation will not make you look dated or inferior vs. the publication you are imitating.

II. **To evaluate your staff's use of imitation as a creative tool.**
A. Imitation is being used as a substitute for genuine creativity, if
_____ Copying is the favored form of imitation, particularly if there is little planning for supportive firepower.
_____ Excelling is more lip service than precise plans on how to excel.
_____ Price cutting is proposed to support the imitation.
_____ Changes from the original are not based on specific marketing needs.
_____ Almost all imitation is of competitors and very little of unrelated publications.
B. Imitation is being effectively used to stimulate creativity, if
_____ The imitator is interested more in the departures from the original than in the similarities.
_____ Changes in the imitated ideas clearly reflect the unique character of your publication.
_____ Imitated ideas really help in solving marketing problems peculiar to your publication.
_____ The ideas imitated are more likely to come from outside your field than from your competitors.

PART THREE

The Practice of Successful Editing

Now that we have a better understanding of the primary function of editorial material, we are ready to consider the practical side of editing—the actual techniques editors use in editing successful magazines.

Of course, a whole book could be written on techniques. Here we consider only four. But we have selected four that illustrate broad, fundamental aspects of the practical side of editing. To continue the analogy of the editor as restaurateur, these four techniques can be compared to buying food, preparing it, composing the menu, and making an event out of the meal. With the first two, the chef concentrates on essentials: nourishment and taste. With the second two, he considers incidentals: interest and excitement.

Not accidentally, the first two ask the editor to keep both eyes on the reader, while, for the second two, the editor is asked to keep one eye on the advertiser.

Chapter 10, with Fred Danzig, studies the fundamental questions in the gathering of editorial material. Where do you get it? And how do you get it? The focus is on human sources. Not only are they primary, but they also can create the most problems for editors. "The Cultivation and Handling of Editorial Sources" attends to those problems.

In Chapter 11, Jim Michaels tells us how important opinion is to the editing of *Forbes*, and we go on to show "The Value of Editorial Opinion" for every kind of magazine—how it generates excitement, enhances information, and facilitates the marketing of your magazines.

Chapter 12, with Cathie Black, considers the problem of helping others to understand what you, as editor, are doing. "Positioning Editorial So Advertisers Will See Its Value" may not seem like an editor's problem, but if the editor cannot get the point across, who can?

Finally, in Chapter 13, we examine "The Place of Special Issues in Periodical Editing." Don Gussow discusses how he has used special issues to create editorial and advertising excitement at Magazines for Industry, and we analyze just how and why this technique works.

CHAPTER TEN

The Cultivation
and Handling
of Editorial Sources

*Featuring an Interview with
Fred Danzig*

Executive Editor of Advertising Age

Every time a staffer gets editorial information from an outsider, the reputation and prosperity of your publication is at risk. Yet most, if not all, of the
material that goes into each issue has to come from outside. Hence the importance of an editor's knowing how to handle such editorial sources.

Just what do editors do to get the most out of such sources, while protecting the publication from being manipulated—or sued?

It made sense that the best person to give us some answers would be
one with extensive reporting experience, a person who had not only supervised
and guided others, but who knew first hand how to work with sources.

Fred Danzig considers himself primarily a newspaper reporter. After
graduating from New York University, he worked briefly at the Herkimer, N.Y.,
Evening Telegram and the Port Chester, N.Y., *Daily Item* before joining United
Press International in 1951.

In 1962, he left UPI to join the editorial staff of *Advertising Age*. At the
time of the interviews he was executive editor in charge of the New York editorial
staff, and had written, since 1977, the biweekly "Sidebars" column, as well as
many features and news stories. Since then, he has been appointed editor.

Fred has studied the reporter/source relationship from both sides. After years of cultivating sources and instructing reporters, he co-authored, with Ed Klein, *How to be Heard: Making the Media Work for You* (Macmillan, 1974). He has lectured and conducted workshops on the same subject.

INTERVIEW

Q: Is there much difference between people who offer you a story and those out of whom you have to dig a story?

A: The first often catches our attention with a press release. He or she is then prepared for our phone call or interview and is anxious to help. The second is usually approached without warning. We suddenly phone him or her, intrude on the working day, seek information that wasn't volunteered. Of the two, the latter is more likely to resist, but is usually the more productive in terms of important or exclusive news.

Q: The first is self-selected. But you have to select the second. How do you decide whom to contact when looking for story material, i.e., when you have no specific story in mind, but are setting up the interview with the hope of uncovering a story or finding a story idea?

A: You have to have a general subject area in mind. Then you pick the people most likely to be knowledgeable. You develop lists.

Q: In developing lists, do you follow certain norms?

A: We aim as high as we can realistically go on the level of our interests. With advertisers, for example, we frequently will not go to the president, or as high as we could go in the absolute sense, but we zero in on the marketing department. In media and agencies, it's simpler: we proceed from the top down. Ultimately you go after the person who makes the decisions, who adds substance to the kind of stories your publication needs.

Q: When you're working in a field with no established contacts, how do you get names of sources?

A: You look into the literature and reference works in your publication's library and outside libraries. News clips, annual reports, trade magazines will tell you who is important and informed. You also talk to people on Wall Street, at the advertising agencies—anyone who has to study or do business with the company or industry you are writing about. It doesn't take long to develop a thin but serviceable knowledge of whom to call and what to ask. After that there's a snow-ball effect. The more people you talk to, the more you learn and the more new names are added to your list of possible sources.

Setting up the source

Q: Once you've decided whom to see, how do you persuade that person to see you, particularly if you've never met?
A: We explain who we are: always reporters from *Advertising Age*—and why we want to see him: we're writing a story about his company.

Q: When the source wants to delegate the interview, push you off onto someone else, how do you sidestep the ploy?
A: Sometimes we don't want to sidestep. For instance, we go to the president knowing he's going to buck us down to the vice president in charge of market-ing. He's the man we really want to see. Now the v.p. marketing has to see us, since his boss told him to.

Q: Does it make much difference whether the interview is held in the source's office or outside over lunch?
A: It depends on the nature of the story. If we're talking about a specific event or project, it's preferable to conduct the interview in the source's office, where he has easy access to records and people for checking facts. Lunch is better when the interview is exploratory.

Q: How about trade shows, conferences, other events?
A: Not too productive. Speakers' presentations tend to be bland, with very little that's new. At social sessions and exhibits, when there are other people in the room, sources tend to clam up. They don't know who is watching and what they may be accused of having said if a story appears after they were seen talking to a reporter. We inhibit conversation at times.

Q: Are phone interviews as effective as face to face?
A: The phone is used more often than the face-to-face interview because it's faster and more economical. But it is second best. Eye contact, facial expres-sion and body language can say a lot, enhance the mood of the story, provide valuable clues to what to ask, what to explore elsewhere, what is really going on.

Handling the interview

Q: How do you get someone you're meeting for the first time to open up?
A: You do your homework, try to get as much information as you can about the person before the interview. You find out his interests, his extracurricular associations, his charitable works, his hobbies. Then, over lunch, you make relaxed conversation about what interests him. You cast around for "button" words—words that will trigger comfortable feelings. Get him to recognize you as sympathetic to his work and interests and he'll open up, even tell you things he shouldn't. This approach is best done face to face. On the phone it is very hard to hit these buttons.

Q: At times you can get a much better story if it's not for attribution. At other times the source may tell you things "off the record." How do you control this?
A: Many people take pride in feeling they know how to deal with the press. P.r. people have briefed them on how to handle us. In the middle of an interview a source will say suddenly: "Now this is off the record." Our response is to continue taking notes and, as soon as the source pauses, we ask whether he really means off the record. We may point out that the information is readily obtained elsewhere or is already out on the street in garbled form. What he usually means is: "Don't quote me" or "not for attribution" or "as backgrounder." The thing to do is to negotiate after the fact, to talk about the terms of the interview. You work it out.

Q: Did you ever have an interview which ended with: "Now everything I told you is off the record"?
A: Yes, retroactive O-T-Rs are the worst. They're not cricket. You have to retrace the entire interview and negotiate exactly what is meant. You have to return to each part of the conversation and work out what can be quoted, what can be used without attribution, and what can't be used at all.

Q: How do you handle a source who demands to see the written piece before it is published?
A: At *Ad Age* we can truthfully tell him there isn't time. Even the reporter usually doesn't get to see the galleys of his story. If the source insists, and time permits, we will call him when the story is written, and read back exact quotes only.

Q: Is it legitimate to offer a favorable story in exchange for information, or to persuade someone to open up?
A: It's not advisable to promise any kind of story—least of all a favorable story.

For one thing, there's no guarantee we can deliver. We do say: "If you give us this, we'll owe you one"—which means when he has another request, we'll try to oblige.

Gossip: Opportunity and danger

Q: Do you have a problem with gossips, people who want your ear but really waste your time?
A: We get many calls we can live without. A capable secretary who screens calls helps. But it's dangerous to be inaccessible. Gossip and rumor touch the life blood of our business. Today's wild rumor is often tomorrow's news story. We want to know what the street talk is. It's a vital source of leads.

Q: There are people who enjoy volunteering stories. Do you encourage them, and, if so, how?
A: We do— by listening to them. There's an incredible amount of gossip in our field, and the more we hear, the more news we can uncover.

Q: Aren't volunteer stories often biased, offered for ulterior motives? How do you keep sources from using you?
A: We try to analyze the source's ultimate motive for the story. In many cases the motive is fairly obvious. The source is pushing a private interest, using us. Such information is always tainted to some extent, and we check very carefully before we use it, consulting with other sources to correct the inherent bias. There are many instances, however, in which the self-serving motive does no harm, and gives us a real story. The story helps the source, but it is still an accurate and valid news story. We both get what we want. It's a wash.

Oil on troubled waters

Q: How do you mollify a source who is unhappy with your story after it is published?
A: By keeping the discussion alive. As long as he'll talk to you, you are on the way to patching things up. When it is really our mistake, the verbal "mea culpa" can't be overdone. If it's the interpretation or tone of the story to which he objects, no apology is necessary, but it helps to keep chewing it over sympathetically until the source admits either that there was a misunderstanding or that you had a right to express you opinion. The angrier they are at first, the more time you need for the soothing process to take hold.

Q: If, due to error or your being misled, you face a possible lawsuit, is it possible to prevent it?

A: Yes. Honesty is always the best policy. We won't reveal our sources, of course, and frequently all that the complainers want is to learn who gave us the information. But we're very polite, very understanding. We explain our position, listen to their position. We try to work out a correction or follow-up story that reflects the facts more accurately. It is very important to be respectful. There's nothing to gain by being a wise guy. If it's our mistake, we have to eat humble pie and hope it's not going to reach the courtroom. *Ad Age* has managed to avoid lawsuits.

Q: How do you handle p.r. people who threaten to boycott your publication, if you don't clear stories with them?

A: That doesn't bother us very much. If we decide in a particular case that we're not going to contact the p.r. person, that's it. It's best to ignore threats and take your chances.

Q: Are there times when a reporter can justifiably refuse to share sources with a reporter on the same publication?

A: There are times when a reporter who has spent great time and effort to gain the confidence of someone in a very high position, resents another reporter's wanting to gain access to that source. What we do at *Ad Age* is encourage the reporter who has the source to offer to get the information himself, or—if the subject is too complicated—urge him to allow the person working on the story to use his name. There can be objections, but most of the time teamwork prevails.

Q: Do you find that with many top stories, you piece them together from clues, like a detective unraveling a mystery?

A: That's the joy of business—divining what is in the mind of corporate managers, deducing what decisions they will make and why, putting facts together so that you come to the same conclusion as the decision makers at the precise moment they do. It's very satisfying to be able to piece everything together, then to make a call and find out that exactly what you thought was going to happen is happening.

Q: Are there times when you are in a position to make news by proposing solutions or ideas worth trying?

A: Yes. We get drawn into offering suggestions for marketing improvements, adjustments to turn products into more competitive brands. We talk to chief executives about companies they should be looking to acquire. We suggest potential accounts to ad agencies. There are many different areas where our knowledge and expertise can help people arrive at decisions. It gets to a point where you almost feel you're a partner, an unpaid consultant, in what is going on.

ANALYSIS

Handling Sources—A Matter of Psychology

Since they cannot be omnipresent, journalists rely more on derivation than observation. What we cannot view ourselves we see through others—our sources. Very few publications have been successful without cultivating sources, whether directly through staffers, or indirectly through freelancers. Even magazines like *Reader's Digest, Time* and *Boardroom Reports*, originally conceived as 100% derivative, end up using direct sources.

Before the interview: Be choosy

The primary step to source cultivation is source selection. Since we cannot see everyone, there is constant and dangerous temptation to select sources because they are easy to reach. It is easier to see the public relations director than the president, but he is seldom the better source. It is essential for editors to be particular in selecting sources.

The three basic criteria by which to judge a source's caliber are knowledge, power and communicativeness.

Knowledge, of course, is fundamental. What is the source's job? Is he close to the action? Do others consider him knowledgeable? Is there evidence of knowledge?

Power is important, first because it presumes knowledge, but also because it makes things happen. Position on the power scale is especially important when probing for future developments. There is no better way to get an inkling of what tomorrow's decision may be than to speak to the person who will make that decision. Power is also important to communicativeness. The more power the source has, the fewer people he has to answer to, the easier it is to make the decision to communicate.

Communicativeness is important because without it, the other criteria are irrelevant. As we shall see below, there are ways to persuade uncoopertive sources to communicate. But every source's value is limited by the extent to which he communicates. There are people whose ability to communicate is minimal, even when willing. On the other hand, there are sources who are not only knowledgeable, but have a natural journalistic sense. They not only provide facts, but interpret them, explain the significance, point out where to dig.

At the interview: Remain in control

Once the source is selected, it is important to get him to do what you want. The better the source, the more difficult this can be. People with knowledge and power are accustomed to being in command. They automatically try to get you to do their will, to serve their purpose.

There are four possible reasons why a source agrees to communicate: fear, self-interest, friendliness and pleasure. Two or more of these motives may work together, but one is usually dominant.

Fear is a far more common motive than reporters realize or sources admit—particularly in initial interviews. A publication, by the very fact that it has an audience, can help or hurt the people it writes about. That creates fear, fear which can persuade a source to refuse an interview, but can also persuade the source to cooperate. "We're running the story, whether you see us or not." "We've already talked to your competitors; now we want your side." People cooperate in self-defense.

Self-interest is a step beyond fear. Sources willingly cooperate if they think it helps them, their companies or their work. Favorable publicity is the number-one self-interest, but trading information also works. Mike Johnson, editorial director of McGraw-Hill's world news service, tells editors to drop at least one nugget of industry information into every interview.

Friendliness makes work easy and life pleasant for the reporter. Most people are willing to help, particularly if it costs relatively little. Fred Danzig's "button words" turn on friendliness. Good reporters start with friendliness, falling back on the self-interest and fear motivations only when necessary. It pays for a reporter to be likable. It is the Barbara Walters approach vs. the old Mike Wallace technique (which even Mike doesn't use very much anymore).

Pleasure includes and transcends both self-interest and friendliness. Most people enjoy talking about what interests them. To enjoy being a source, one need not be a frustrated journalist who gets a feeling of exhilaration when participating in the development of a story. Almost everyone enjoys the attention of a good listener. Reporters in the business press often find themselves in the role of surrogate psychiatrists. Many top executives have a compelling need to talk openly with someone. Neither wives nor friends understand. Their co-workers and competitors are too involved. Only the business editor qualifies.

If the interviewer is aware of the motives behind the source's cooperation, he can use them to control the interview. Almost always, it is best to start by appealing to the motive that got the source to agree to the interview and gradually lead toward the more positive and productive motives: friendliness and pleasure.

If the source is in trouble or the information is disagreeable, the interviewer may have to rely on fear. Even here, a sympathetic attitude or willingness to help may transform fear into self-interest, even friendliness.

Although a source's motivation frequently shifts in the course of the interview, there are general norms on how to query a source based on his motivation. If the source is fearful, keep him on the defensive, constantly working him toward being grateful that you want to help and are on his side. If the motive is self-interest, start with what the source is anxious to promote; then lead him in the direction you want to go by showing it will help his case. When friendliness predominates, put your need for information as a personal problem that he can help you with. When pleasure takes over, give the source his head, interrupting just enough to steer him in the direction most useful to you. The source's vanity, pride and need for understanding are your allies. Use them.

To remain in control it is essential that the interviewer keep his eyes on filling an editorial need without distracting the interviewee from satisfying his psychic need. Even sources motivated by friendliness or pleasure should not be distracted by the reporter's editorial problems. The more the source tries to visualize how the story will look in print, the less open and informative he will be. This is true even of the source who enjoys helping you write a story. Nothing spoils his fun quicker than a reporter who edits the information during the interview.

After the interview: Be responsible

Modes of attribution are better defined as ways to determine responsibility to the reader than the usual definition, which is in terms of responsibility to the source.

There are four different modes of exercising such responsibility:

1. Full responsibility. The publication presents a fact as having been checked out first-hand, an opinion as its own.

2. Limited responsibility. The publication attributes the fact or opinion to a specified source. The only responsibility assumed is for correct attribution and accurate quotation.

3. Negative responsibility. The publication or reporter assumes responsibility for withholding a fact that is editorially relevant.

4. No responsibility. The publication attributes the reliability of the information to a source, but refuses to identify the source. "Industry

sources report...'' ''A government official said...'' ''Insiders think...'' (Admittedly a modicum of responsibility is involved, for it would be irresponsible to invent the quote.)

From these definitions we draw six conclusions:

1. It is important not to allow the source to dictate the manner of attribution.

2. A not-for-attribution story demands more work than a for-attribution story, since it requires checking the reliability of the source's information.

3. It is not only legitimate but necessary to edit most quotes, since limited responsibility requires that the source say what he means—unless the inability to express himself or the peculiarities of expression are part of the story.

4. Off-the-record interviews are extremely dangerous in so far as they give a source the power to force the reporter or publication to withhold information. The easiest way to avoid off-the-record situations is to say: ''I am unable to promise that anything won't be used because I cannot keep other reporters from digging up the same facts.''

5. There are occasions when withholding information is justified, but in each case the good achieved by withholding information must be weighed against the readers' loss. When *The New York Times* published the Pentagon Papers, it faced such a decision and decided in favor of the readers.

6. Since sources of information are usually editorially relevant, concealing the source involves negative responsibility. When a publication takes full responsibility for the facts, the names of sources are not very important to the readers. Hence protecting the source, particularly if it serves the readers by assuring a continued flow of information, usually justifies withholding the source's identity.

Skilled editors and reporters know when to withhold the name of a source and how to do it so that readers cannot deduce the very information the editors want to hide. The most frequently used technique to throw curious readers off the scent is to include many non-source names, or facts and comments unfavorable to the source, or information the source could not know. The best technique, of course, is to use multiple sources for every important fact.

How much control the source should have over the final copy depends on the nature of the story and the needs of the publication. No source has a right to see a story before publication unless the reporter or magazine gives him that right. Sometimes it is to the publication's (and readers') advantage to do this. This book's interviewees were given the right to edit the semi-final draft of the chapter in which they are featured. Such an approach is advisable only when the readers recognize the source as a collaborator.

Check-backs for accuracy are often necessary and usually appreciated by the source. Reading back quotes for accuracy is especially useful if the quote has been edited. Quotes made before witnesses cannot be edited or revised, even by the source. There are times when an entire article or several paragraphs should be reviewed by the source, as when the writer describes the source's thoughts, particularly if the article gives the impression that it is a collaborative effort.

More important than checking with the source is protection from the source. No source, no matter how well-intentioned, is without bias. In every interview there are bias indicators:

1. Character. Some people are more trustworthy, more accurate than others.

2. Motive. The reason for granting an interview will color what is said, how it is presented, and what is left unsaid.

3. Attitude. Little signs betray how the speaker feels, i.e., Danzig's eye contact, facial expression, body language.

4. Involvement. The more involved, the less objective.

If bias is recognized or suspected, the interviewer should challenge or question the source more thoroughly and subtly. Afterwards he must make adjustments to compensate for the bias and query other sources who are either more objective or have compensating biases.

Legal counsel should be called in when there is any possibility of legal problems. But such counsel must be used properly. It is the attorney's job to describe the legal consequences of publishing the piece. It is not his job to edit or censor it. He estimates the risk. The editor decides whether the risk is worth taking or whether changes to lessen risk are acceptable.

Lawsuits are best prevented by care and accuracy, but, when a lawsuit is threatened, the threat should be considered an opportunity. Fred Danzig's technique of sympathetic talk can not only mollify, but it can also open the door to another story, one that advances the earlier story. A new story, correcting the old, is almost always better for the magazine, the reader and the complainant. Publishing a correction, as a correction, usually helps no one. It is ineffective; it seldom gets the same prominence as the original article. It can be damaging to both magazine and complainant, since readers who did not read the original will have it brought to their attention. Finally, it is unfair to readers because they must fit the correction into a vaguely remembered story.

MANAGEMENT REVIEW

Check List for Handling a Source

I. **Before the interview:**
   A. Be certain the prospect
   - Has the knowledge required.
   - Is powerful enough.
   - Is communicative enough.
   B. Select the motive you will use to persuade the source to give you the interview:
   ____ Fear. How? _____
   ____ Self-interest. How? _____
   ____ Friendliness. How? _____
   ____ Pleasure. How? _____
   C. Decide on the interview milieu:
   ____ Mail.
   ____ Phone.
   ____ In person, at:
      ____ His office.
      ____ Restaurant or bar.
      ____ Your office.
      ____ Elsewhere: _____

II. **At the interview:**
   A. Determine his motive in accepting an interview:
   ____ Fear.
   ____ Self-interest.

_____ Friendliness.

_____ Pleasure.

B. Decide which motive you will use to begin the interview:

_____ Fear. How? _____

_____ Self-interest. How? _____

_____ Friendliness. How? _____

_____ Pleasure. How? _____

C. Decide which motives you will work toward during the interview:

_____ Fear. How? _____

_____ Self-interest. How? _____

_____ Friendliness. How? _____

_____ Pleasure. How? _____

III. After the interview:

A. Determine the mode of attribution required:

_____ Full responsibility.

_____ Limited responsibility.

_____ Negative responsibility.

_____ No responsibility.

B. Accept the implications of this responsibility:

_____ Information has to be checked

_____ Quotes have to be edited.

_____ Off-the-record confidence has to be kept.

_____ Withholding relevant information is justified.

_____ Source's identity may and should be withheld.

_____ Source's identity is effectively hidden.

C. Decide the need for check-backs:

_____ For the entire article.

_____ For parts of the article.

_____ For certain facts.

_____ For additional information.

_____ No check-back required.

D. Protect yourself against bias by examining the indicators:

_____ Character.

_____ Motive.

_____ Attitude.

_____ Involvement.

E. Compensate for the bias by:

_____ Challenging the source.

____ Questioning the source more thoroughly and/or more subtly.
____ Adjusting the material for bias.
____ Querying other sources:
____ Who are more objective.
____ Who have compensating biases.

F. Determine whether legal counsel is needed.

G. If a lawsuit is threatened,
____ Talk with complainant sympathetically.
____ Look for a new story.

CHAPTER ELEVEN

The Value of Editorial Opinion

Featuring an Interview with
James W. Michaels
Editor of Forbes

Nothing touches the individual editor so personally as the continuing debate about how opinionated a magazine can afford to be. American journalists, far beyond their fellows in other areas of the world, have been trained in a tradition of "objective" reporting and editing. Yet every honest editor realizes that complete objectivity is impossible, and today even the newsmagazines put bylines on their stories.

Editors also know that readers want opinion—otherwise there would be no excuse for the editorial page. But just where does opinion belong in a magazine? How far should it extend? How should it be managed? And does it help or hurt a publication's success—with readers, and with advertisers?

There are few, if any, successful magazines in the United States today that have as great a reputation for being opinionated as *Forbes*. Hence the choice of Jim Michaels, its editor, for this interview.

James Walker Michaels joined *Forbes* in 1954, when the magazine had 130,000 circulation. Jim had graduated from Harvard College, cum laude, 12 years earlier. He had gone to war (Burma theater, World War II), and served as a foreign correspondent in India and Southeast Asia. You can read Jim's coverage of Mahatma Gandhi's assassination in *A Treasury of Great Reporting*.

Today *Forbes* has 700,000 circulation, and Jim has been its editor for over two decades.

As editor, Jim has had much to do with bringing *Forbes* into the age of group journalism. He now has a staff of 140 people. When he arrived, the magazine was 37 years old, with a long, solid editorial tradition. It is to his credit that he was able to graft the best of the old judgmental journalism onto the new group editing.

INTERVIEW

Q: Malcolm Forbes's contributions to Forbes *have always been very personal, very judgmental. Has this set the tone for the magazine?*
A: I'd rather say that he and we are following and updating tradition. *Forbes* was founded 65 years ago, in the era of personal journalism, by Malcolm's father, a Hearst business columnist. Today personal journalism is out, group journalism is in. But the founder's mark remains. *Forbes* is one of the last magazines owned by the man whose name is on the cover. It is steeped in the tradition of never telling a story without an opinion.

Q: Why did personal journalism go out of style?
A: Tastes changed. Americans are fact-obsessed. Compare England's *The Economist* with *Time* or *Newsweek*. The typical *Economist* article is 60% editorial, 40% fact. The typical *Time* or *Newsweek* article is 80% fact or description, 20% editorial. The American journalistic trend was toward eliminating opinion. It reached its apex in the news services, with the alleged total objectivity of the AP's style: the reporter as tape recorder.

Q: But aren't we moving away from that now?
A: Yes. Now we're moving partially back. But our magazine never left the earlier tradition entirely.

Q: Henry Luce had much to do with making group journalism dominant. Yet, though Time *was group-edited from its beginning, it was considered very subjective in its early years.*
A: *Time* and *Newsweek* still are quite judgmental and interpretive. Group journalism doesn't imply AP style. There are trends and countertrends at work here. We at *Forbes* stand partly in each tradition.

The extra ingredient

Q: Do you feel that judgmental journalism is one reason for the success of Forbes?
A: I think so. Business people are inundated by dry facts and welcome a judgmental voice. It helps us stand out from the field.

Q: I used to tell young editors that good business publications function like management assistants: they don't succeed by offering the boss questions or problems—the boss needs opinions, possible solutions.
A: That's an excellent analogy. The judgmental approach establishes you as a strong personality in the mind of the executive you're helping.

Q: Your opinion helps him or her make decisions, even if it's by disagreeing with you.
A: That is provided you're working for somebody who can take opposition. Our readers aren't "yes men." Hence our letters column is open to anyone who wants to disagree. Intelligent readers know we can't be judgmental without being wrong a certain amount of the time.

Possible negatives effects

Q: Do strong opinions ever turn readers off?
A: We get cancel-my-subscription letters.

Q: Do you think most of them stay cancelled?
A: There aren't enough to make much difference. But I would be alarmed if we didn't get any. You have to keep readers stirred up. If opinion costs you subscribers, you eventually develop a list of readers to whom you really appeal.

Q: Does having definite opinions make readers consider you less objective or less reliable?
A: I don't think readers regard us as objective. I hope they regard us as reliable. If all your judgments are based on facts and sound reasoning, being wrong occasionally does not make you unreliable. Readers rely on us to make judgments.

Q: Can you go too far—be too opinionated?
A: If you have an opinion on everything, you probably aren't reliable. I think it was Edmund Wilson who said that a good editor has a corner of his or her mind in touch with a corner of the minds of a lot of readers. We don't talk to the whole mind—just a specific corner. Our readers may be interested in pho-

tography, horses, religion. We don't touch those corners. We talk to the reader as a business person, and we come through as clearly as we can as a well-informed "persona" with opinions on business.

Should every magazine have opinions?

Q: Regardless of which corner you cover, isn't it more effective to have opinions in that area? When Family Circle *presents three recipes, doesn't it help to say, "I like this one best"? Can't every magazine use opinion to make it more important to readers?*
A: Personally, I would approach any subject that way. But other editors may have reasons for not doing it. A strong point of view might make a how-to magazine successful. It might also make it lose a lot of ads.

Q: Unless it made everybody read the magazine, and advertisers couldn't afford not to use it?
A: True, but readers of service magazines want something different from what *Forbes* provides. We are not writing on how to buy a stock, or how to get your first job. There may be less need for judgmental journalism on the level of how-to editing.

Q: Maybe the simpler you get, the greater the need for opinions, since "how to" readers feel less secure in making their own judgments.
A: You're right.

Q: The National Enquirer *seems to have a lot of opinion, and I'm sure that everyone would agree that it's edited for the unsophisticated.*
A: I suppose they're also editing life for readers.

Social climate and thirst for opinion

Q: Do you think the multiplication of media has resulted in so many conflicting opinions that the public is no longer interested in any of them?
A: I don't think that at all. I can only speak for our field, but it's very clear that we have been successful, and I think it's safe to say we're the most opinionated publication in the field.

Q: Are business executives more interested in opinion than the general public?
A: Maybe. Business happens to be a field with a relative abundance of factual information and a dearth of strongly judgmental publications.

Q: One form of opinion journalism we don't seem to see very much of anymore is the extended campaign, such as Ladies' Home Journal's *famous drive to get women to stop buying ostrich feathers back in the days when Edward Bok was editor. Today we have movements to save whales and baby seals, but they're not instigated by national magazines. Why the change?*

A: People's attention shifts more rapidly today. A couple of years back, the balance of payments was on the front page of every newspaper. Now we're running a horrendous trade deficit and nobody is paying any attention. Modern attention spans are very short—not only the attention spans of readers but also those of writers and editors. *Ladies' Home Journal* was the first true mass magazine in the United States. Bok came along when America's middle class had just expanded from a few people living in brownstones to a much larger group who could suddenly afford to buy curtains for their windows. He helped raise the tastes of people who, for the first time, had a little leisure and a little discretionary income. And life moved more slowly then.

Managing editorial opinion

Q: In managing editorial opinion, do you distinguish the opinion of the individual writer or editor from the opinion of the magazine?

A: The magazine has no detailed opinions. It favors free enterprise, believes that individual executives are the most important ingredient in management, that some companies are run well and some are run badly. That's the platform. It's up to the individual writer to make the specific judgment that John Doe is doing a great job, or Joe Smith is doing a lousy job.

Q: But, when a writer says, "Joe Smith is doing a lousy job," you don't issue a disclaimer: "This is the opinion of the author, not of Forbes.*"*

A: We adopt the opinion, but the writer has to prove it to me, the editor. If I don't think his judgment stands up, I'll ask him to change it or kill the story.

Q: Do you, as editor, encourage your staffers to have strong opinions?

A: I insist. It's not enough to tell me about a man, the company he runs, and whether it's making money. I want the man's philosophy and judgments and how it affects the success or failure of the company.

Q: Do editors sometimes tell you, "If I run this story as I see it, this company will never cooperate with us again"?

A: A lot of companies won't talk to us. Some won't talk to anybody. Some won't talk to us specifically. I take that as a compliment.

Q: Does opinion affect advertising sales? Does it ever cost you advertising?
A: We lose some advertising each year. But if readers trust a magazine and personally react to it, I think it becomes a better advertising medium.

Q: Do you believe Forbes *would lose some of its readers if the magazine suddenly changed its policy and became less judgmental?*
A: I suspect it would. Many people might figure they would not need *Forbes*, since they would have already read *The Wall Street Journal*.

Q: Are you ever afraid to take a stand because it will heighten the possibility of libel?
A: No. We have a very good attorney who looks at the copy from that point of view and tells us, ''If you want to say this, you had better report it this way.''

Q: Don't you find that if lawyers had their way, there would be no opinion in magazines?
A: Not in this case. Our attorney is very good, and has had our account for a very long time. He doesn't tell us, ''Don't say this.'' He tells us, ''Say it this way.''

Q: Doesn't having an opinion increase the likelihood of libel by making it more difficult to prove absence of malice when you make a mistake?
A: We have a very elaborate fact-checking system. Even when I write something, the researchers demand that I document it.

Q: What's the best way for an editor to change his opinion?
A: To say right out, ''I've changed my opinion.'' When you are expressing opinion all the time, honesty and frankness are appreciated. I would add that there should be a consistency in opinion. It shouldn't seem arbitrary. Everybody knows what *Forbes* stands for, and our judgments, both favorable and unfavorable, are consistent with this.

Q: You're pointing at something very important beyond individual opinion. The fact that you make these judgments, and are consistent in them, gives you a strong, clear image with readers. You stand for something.
A: The magazine acquires a personality. I think that's very important.

ANALYSIS

Opinion—An Editorial and Marketing Asset

No matter how lofty an editor's intentions, it is impossible to be 100% objective. Editing means selection, and selection requires judgment. The difference between judgmental journalism and so-called objective journalism is a difference of emphasis. What interests us are the advantages and disadvantages of emphasizing opinion in magazine editing vs. supressing it.

The first school is represented by Hamilton Fish, publisher of *The Nation*, who boasts: "We don't tailor articles so they are inoffensive. We say what we feel should be said and if someone doesn't like it, they cancel." The second is represented by *Better Homes & Gardens* editor Gordon Greer, who explains that his publication "is not overly opinionated. We're not selling anything except magazines."

Like any other publishing judgment, the decision as to whether a specific magazine should stress or repress opinion in its general editorial pages should be based on the needs of its audience. Some publications require more judgmental journalism than others.

The two most common causes of poor judgment in managing opinion are fear and vanity. Opinions that would improve a publication are frequently suppressed because some writer or editor fears a reaction. Writers and editors who lack self-confidence very often live by the principle that it is safer to bore everyone than offend anyone.

Vanity, on the other hand, can make editors and writers so enamored of their opinions that they introduce them whenever possible, forgetting the needs of their readers. There are times when opinion impedes the flow of information either by eliminating facts the reader wants or by introducing a distraction. The editor's judgment on the aesthetic value of a new car may be entirely irrelevant in a how-to publication such as *Muffler Digest*.

Opinion generates excitement

There is no doubt that strong opinions create editorial excitement. Taking definite stands on controversial matters is a sure-fire technique for involving readers. On the rational level, when the author's opinion challenges the reader's judgment, the reader becomes involved, whether he or she accepts or questions the author's line of reasoning. Involvement can also be on the emotional level, as readers respond with enthusiasm or anger. Not every garment exporter may have agreed with Mark Hosenball's story in *Women Wear Daily* on the outrage of exporting $5-million worth of cancer-causing Tris sleepwear, but very few read it with indifference.

Judgmental journalism is also more apt to generate external excitement. For better or worse, editorial opinions create publicity, whether in the form of battles with Carol Burnett and Johnny Carson for the *National Enquirer*, campus furor over "right-wing iconoclasm" for the *Yale Literary Magazine*, or newsstories for *Human Events* on being read by President Reagan and his advisers.

Opinion enhances information

The value of opinion to editorial goes far beyond added excitement. Opinion makes information easier to understand, to remember, and to use.

A basic function of all editing is to organize information so that the reader can digest it more easily. There is no technique more effective in organizing information than to develop an argument. There are, of course, other ways to organize material, but none works as well. One reason is that an argument not only creates a working order for presenting facts, but it also requires the writer and the reader to evaluate the facts and their relative importance.

For the same reason, opinion helps to make information more memorable. There are few memory assists as effective as a persuasive argument. Although most readers have difficulty remembering even a small proportion of the facts presented in the material they read, they will retain the fundamental opinion around which the writer marshalled the facts. Furthermore, in remembering the opinion, it becomes far easier to recall the facts that advanced that opinion.

Finally, opinion helps readers use information. A good business publication, for instance, performs a service very similar to that provided by a good consultant. Neither the consultant nor the magazine can make business judgments for their "clients." Yet both help their clients most when they offer judgments. A consultant, or magazine, merely providing information or restating a problem is not nearly as helpful as one offering a solution. And this is so whether the client accepts or rejects the solution.

Advertising Age's editor in chief, Rance Crain, expressed it in this way: ". . . our columnists wander all over the lot and present (hopefully) opinions in all shapes and sizes . . . the idea is to give our readers enough information on all sides to let them make up their own minds."

Opinion facilitates marketing

A magazine that emphasizes opinion has certain marketing advantages. One of these is that it heightens reader expectation, which builds reader continuity. The *New England Journal of Medicine*'s growth in circulation from 106,000 in 1967 to 205,000 today is attributed to the "love of new challenges and controversy" of the late Dr. Franz Ingelfinger, its editor from 1967 to 1977. He broadened its coverage to include opinion on medicine's social and ethical implications, and encouraged reader participation by developing an extensive correspondence department. The result: more and more doctors look for the *Journal* each week to find out what it has to say.

Significantly, the more information a reader has on a given subject, the more important opinion becomes. Sports writers have recognized this for years. The fan who saw the game is the first to turn to the sports page. His need is not to learn what he saw, but to find out what someone else thinks about it. That is why sports writers without opinions do not last very long.

Opinions also help marketing by giving the editorial product focus. A magazine with strong opinions stands for something. Opinions can give a publication a clear image, a definite position in readers' minds. FOLIO: executive editor Karlene Lukovitch quotes an anonymous publisher as saying, "The women's books have reduced themselves to commodities—they have no position at all. They are sold by the pound and they're completely interchangeable." They also have few strong opinions, unlike *Ms., Cosmopolitan* or even *Savvy* and *New Woman*.

In the business field, opinion can be a key to industry leadership. When Congress was debating the business-lunch tax several years ago, *Restaurant Business* did an eight-page insert marshalling arguments against it, and distributed 250,000 reprints. As editor Joan Bakos commented, looking back at the stand *Restaurant Business* took, "It was extremely instrumental in making us the spokesperson for the industry."

Of course, opinion can also create an image detrimental to specific marketing goals, as *Mother Jones* is finding out in its pursuit of national advertising. But even here, the strong image is advantageous in overall marketing. Advertising is something *Mother Jones* would like to get, but it is subordinate to its principal marketing goal: readership.

Finally, opinion is the easiest way to establish a monopoly position in a reader market. It provides the one reader value that is impossible for competitors to duplicate. *Time* and *Newsweek* may occasionally beat each other out in breaking or gathering news, but the only thing that really distinguishes them consistently week after week is opinion.

Opinion on this level, however, must be more than tolerance for judgmental journalism on an article by article level. A magazine with a mishmash of opinions no more stands for something than a magazine with no opinions. *Atlantic* and *Harper's* both publish a lot of opinions, yet neither stands for anything. Both lack an overall editorial point of view. In Jim Michaels's words, "there should be a consistency in opinion. It shouldn't seem arbitrary."

It is easy to see how magazines such as *Washington Monthly, The National Review* and *U.S. News & World Report* have a consistent point of view. But the need is just as important for magazines with non-political subject matter. *Reader's Digest, National Geographic, The New Yorker, Prevention* and *Yankee* owe their success to definite and consistent points of view.

Managing opinion

One of the most difficult problems in magazine publishing is how to preserve the balance of pursuing marketing goals through judgmental journalism. There are very few magazines in which opinion is encouraged as marketing strategy. Usually, editors are interested first in expressing opinion, and only afterwards in the marketing consequences.

The marketing consequences are nonetheless real, and important. It is extremely important for the editor to control the ebb and flow of opinion both to secure consistency in point of view and to make sure that opinion is always a benefit to the reader.

To be consistent in its opinions, a magazine must have a recognizable tradition or philosophy in its approach to its subject matter. It also needs an editor in tune with that tradition, but having the strength to guide it into new directions without violating it's recognized approach. Such an editor will have an overall purpose in choosing subjects and treatments.

The following principles are common to top editors making sure that opinion benefits the reader:

1. Opinion must never be allowed to become a substitute for fact. There is always a danger that the lazy author will fall back on opinion to camouflage a lack of knowledge. Unlike information, opinions can be created off the top of one's head. Yet the best examples of judgmental journalism are well-organized facts with not a single sentence devoted solely to expressing opinion. The facts say it all.

2. The greatest inconsistency in opinion is the opinion that never changes. This seeming paradox is self-evident to good editors. Opinion is the result of human judgment. It cannot be human without being imperfect, nor judgment without being responsive to new information. Writers who end up with their initial conclusions, no matter how much research they do, are either stubborn or stupid, and cannot be trusted. As Jim Michaels observes, ''When you are expressing opinion all the time, honesty and frankness are appreciated.'' The ability to recognize one's errors is a sign of wisdom.

3. Beware of sensationalism; it breeds excitement but kills respect. Sensationalism results when writers or editors become more interested in exciting readers than in helping them. Drawing conclusions for their excitement value is what got the *National Enquirer* into its lawsuit with Carol Burnett, and led publisher Herb Lipson to fire the editor and writer responsible for *Boston*'s August 1978 article on Cardinal Medeiros.

4. Respect your readers—and your advertisers. The higher one's opinion of readers and advertisers, the less fear and the more balance there is in expressing opinion. This manifests itself in several ways: a) The writer or editor thinks of the readers as intelligent, and never tries to fool them with half-baked opinion, or sensationalism. b) The writer or editor thinks of the readers as decent and kind, and will presume that they do not want titillation or gossip that hurts others. As *People*'s managing editor Dick Stolley has said, ''Part of our responsibility is to our story subjects themselves: not just to be truthful, but to be careful and tasteful and even kind.'' c) The writer or editor will state opinions without fear, since respect for readers and advertisers implies expecting them to support freedom of expression. When individual readers or advertisers cause trouble, the writer or editor will presume they are atypical and ignore them out of respect for the majority.

MANAGEMENT REVIEW

Check List for Evaluating the Use of Opinion

I. Assess your magazine's current position.
 A. Is your magazine currently
   ____ Emphasizing opinion?
   ____ Supressing opinion?
   ____ Unsure of its position in this area?
 B. Is the principal reason for the current policy
   ____ The needs of the magazine's audience?
   ____ Editorial caution or fear?
   ____ Editorial vanity or self-gratification?

II. Decide whether your magazine's position could be improved.
 A. Could the introduction of more or stronger opinions
   ____ Make the magazine more exciting to readers?
   ____ Help to generate more publicity for the magazine?
   ____ Be introduced without reducing the magazine's value to its readers?
 B. Could opinion be used to make the information in articles or features
   ____ Easier to understand (better organized)?
   ____ Easier to remember (more interrelated for association)?
   ____ Easier to use (more helpful in making decisions)?
 C. Could opinion be used to
   ____ Heighten reader expectation for each issue?
   ____ Attract readers who already have most of the facts?
   ____ Give the magazine more focus, a clearer image?
 D. Would more or stronger opinions
   ____ Improve your magazine's position as a leader in its field or industry?
   ____ Make your magazine stand out from its competitors (establish a monopoly position)?

III. Evaluate possible negative effects.
 Would the positive effects mentioned above compensate for any
   ____ Loss of readers?
   ____ Loss of advertising?

IV. Make sure that the policy you adopt is properly managed.

A. To assure consistency of opinion, does your magazine have

_____ A recognizable tradition or philosophy in its approach to its subject matter?

_____ An editor in tune with that philosophy?

_____ An editor strong enough to lead that philosophy into new directions without violating that philosophy?

_____ An overall purpose in its choice of subjects and treatment?

B. In managing opinion does your magazine's editor

_____ Never allow opinion to substitute for fact?

_____ Change opinions when the facts so warrant, and expect the same of the writers?

_____ Protect readers by avoiding sensationalism?

_____ Respect both readers and advertisers, and have a high opinion of the majority's basic decency and good judgment?

_____ Show no fear of the minority who may occasionally try to limit freedom of expression?

_____ Instill these attitudes in the staff and contributors?

CHAPTER TWELVE

Positioning Editorial
So Advertisers
Will See Its Value

Featuring an Interview with
Cathleen Black
Publisher of New York

No matter how wonderful the editorial product, if no one knows or understands it, your magazine will fail. The readers have to recognize it for what it is. And, in most cases, advertisers also have to recognize what it does, and what it can do for them. Any editor successful in positioning his or her magazine with advertisers is unlikely to have a problem positioning it with readers.

This chapter looks primarily at the task of getting advertisers to appreciate the editorial package. For the same reason, we interviewed a publisher and experienced salesperson rather than an editor. We wanted someone who had been successful in selling unique editorial products to a large number of different kinds of advertisers, someone who understands advertisers, who knows how and why they respond to a magazine's editorial focus.

We selected Cathie Black, publisher of *New York*, as the right executive for this interview. Soon after we conducted the interview, the rightness of our decision was confirmed by an outside source. A few weeks after the interview, Gannett's chief executive, Allen Neuharth, chose Cathie to be president of *USA Today*, the company's new national daily newspaper. Her job: to sell this new editorial product to advertisers.

In 1966, having graduated from Trinity College in Washington, D.C., Cathie Black got her first job in publishing, as a sales representative for *Holiday*. About two years later, in 1968, she moved to the sales staff of *Travel & Leisure* and, in 1970, to a similar job at the 18-month-old *New York Magazine*.

At that same time, *Ms. Magazine* got its start by being presented as a bind-in in *New York*. Pat Carbine, the new publisher and editor in chief of *Ms.*, asked Cathie to become the fledgling magazine's advertising manager. Four years later, Pat made Cathie associate publisher.

In late 1977, Joe Armstrong, *New York*'s then president and publisher, offered Cathie the same title if she would come back to his magazine. Cathie accepted, with the understanding that she would be appointed publisher in 12 to 18 months. And so, at the age of 35, she became the first woman ever to be publisher of a large-circulation weekly consumer magazine.

When Cathie left *New York* to take her new job at *USA Today*, the magazine, which had been in trouble a few years earlier, was in better shape than ever: it expected to finish the year with 2,650 pages of advertising, 425,000 circulation, and $27 million gross revenue.

INTERVIEW

Q: When you became New York*'s publisher, did you feel advertisers knew what the magazine was all about?*
A: One of the unique things about the magazine is that it's about the world's most media-intensive city. All the young people in the ad business, particularly on the media side, read the magazine—not as space buyers, but as people living in New York.

Q: Have you research to prove that?
A: Lots. Remember, media is a very important advertising category for us. The magazine is over 15 years old, and the tradition of high readership in the advertising community has been established for a long time.

A magazine's image

Q: Are there no misconceptions in the ad community as to the nature of your editorial, about what you are trying to do, or your success in doing it?
A: Every magazine is subject to personal interpretations and misconceptions. We did have a serious perception problem about six years ago. We hadn't changed enough with the times; we had done the same things for too long. On top of that there was all the negative publicity on ownership and management changes. Although the magazine did not lose its strength in this market or its reason for being, it lost some of its edge—the immediacy that makes its readers read it the day it arrives.

Q: I've heard complaints that New York *has become too "in," that it's written for a clique that excludes most New Yorkers.*
A: You can't be all things to all people. People who have lived in the suburbs for 15 years may find less to identify with in the magazine. *New York*'s first editor, Clay Felker, established a formula that has been imitated by some 200 city and regional magazines, and by newspaper special sections. Clearly the formula works. It attracts the bright, young readers advertisers want, the kind of people Manhattan's business and culture attracts from all over the country.

Q: But do advertisers really want the "in" crowd?
A: Definitely. They are the people who start styles, trends. I think it is a great compliment to be thought of as an "in" magazine, to be considered a leader in a market of leaders. Six or seven movies have been inspired by *New York*'s cover features, including *Saturday Night Fever*. The magazine has been the launching pad for two other magazines: *Ms.* and *Savvy*. It attracts and is a showcase for the best new writers and photographers in the country.

Q: You're talking about the magazine's editorial image. That should be primary, of course. But what do advertisers think of it as an ad medium?
A: The fact that *New York* is one of the few weeklies with 1983* ad pages 10% ahead of 1982 should answer your question. If there's a problem, it's that media buyers try to put us in a category, and we're unique. On one side we are not an ordinary city magazine. None of the other city or regional magazines are weekly. On the other, there were two other weeklies with New York in their titles: *The New Yorker* and *The New York Times Magazine*. So we have to clearly illustrate our special strength, our difference from those two publications.

---

*This interview was conducted in the third quarter of 1983.

Making the image unique

Q: You joined the sales force in 1970, a year and a half after launch. Did it take a long time to establish New York *as unique and effective?*
A: No. But let me tell you a recent anecdote. For our fifteenth anniversary, I received a letter from Philip Morris chairman George Weismann. He mentioned a sales presentation he attended in 1968 and how he immediately recognized the need for this magazine in this market. He was not alone. Besides Philip Morris, we have a number of charter advertisers still with us, including R.J. Reynolds, Revlon and several liquor companies. Although *New York* grew out of a Sunday supplement in the old *Herald Tribune & World Journal*, it started with a small circulation and a high cost per thousand. It would never have succeeded if it hadn't been considered unique and effective from the start.

Q: Are you saying it always had a homogeneous image?
A: No. If you lined up six people, each would describe the magazine differently. Some read it for its entertainment directory, others to learn what's new, others for its political or social comment. If there is a homogeneous advertising image, it is a consensus that the typical reader of our magazine is between 25 and 40, living or working in Manhattan, a trend setter, wanting to be among the first to buy or try.

Q: Yet 25% of your circulation is outside the Greater New York area.
A: That proportion has never changed. They are ex-New Yorkers, frequent visitors to the City, or people fascinated by the Big Apple. They read *New York* precisely because it is not a national magazine, but a magazine about this very important city. That's one of the principal ways we differ from *The New Yorker*. Our reason for being is to serve this city. Advertisers understand that.

Establishing an image internally

Q: Is it a problem to get your sales staff to see the magazine that way? Do you define it for them?
A: I believe each salesperson should adhere to a clear party line, as the foundation for their individual approach. Someone who's been selling the magazine as long as I have doesn't need a formal presentation, whereas someone selling for less than three months requires greater guidelines. But I don't believe there should be a written three-line statement that everyone hands out.

Q: But how do you make sure that everyone toes the party line? Is there a formal "image" program?

A: No. But we're a pretty hands-on group. Our two experienced ad managers spend most of their time on sales calls with the salespeople. Every Monday afternoon our ad director holds a sales meeting. I attend about 85% of them, and frequently invite one of the editors to attend and talk about what the magazine is doing and plans to do.

Q: One of the objectives of such meetings should be to keep the salespeople from wasting time on categories of advertising that don't belong in your magazine.

A: Naturally we'd prefer not to exclude any category of advertising. We are currently running 20% ahead of last year, and last year we had a gain of 200 pages. That's not only extraordinary for our 15-year-old magazine, but for the industry, which is just coming out of a recession. Traditionally, cosmetics, retail, liquor and travel have been our four principal categories, in that order. But in the last two years, the media category has exploded for us. In the past year we have gone from 50 to 125 pages of media ads, and this year it will be something between 160 to 185 pages.

Q: What happened? Why the sudden change?

A: We've always had media advertising due to our large readership in the ad community. But the impetus came when we introduced a regular advertising feature.

Q: Is that the reason for the 20% growth?

A: No, we've been developing two other major ad categories: first, financial services advertising, and second, major retailer apparel and fashion. The latter is just beginning to grow. We do a lot of fashion editorial, and every major retailer in the country is on our complimentary list.

Keeping in touch with the image

Q: Do you go on many sales calls yourself?

A: Not too many direct calls anymore, but I take part in every formal presentation, for it's a part of the business I love. And 98% of my lunches and entertaining are advertising-related. It's essential for a publisher to know firsthand how agency and advertiser people think about his or her particular magazine.

Q: Is that preferable to formal research?

A: Magazines use research like a sailboat uses the wind. You have to know which way the wind is blowing, but you use the information to go where you want to go. Before we merged *Cue* into *New York*, we conducted focus groups with *Cue* and *New York* readers to learn how they would react to the combined magazine. It was interesting, but not mindblowing. It indicated what we already knew. Remember we have more contact with our readers than most magazines. We're writing about them, and they live in our own front yard.

Handling image problems

Q: You mentioned the image problem six years ago. The ad community expected the new owner and personnel changes to hurt the magazine more than they actually did. In a situation like that, should you forget the image and concentrate on real problems, or is it also necessary to doctor the image itself?

A: You have to pull out all the stops. It's essential to concentrate on your regular business, but you must also communicate on every level: with presentations, breakfasts, luncheons, dinners. Images change slowly. You can put out eight successive great issues, but the negative perceptions hang on. You've got to be patient and persistent—accepting the fact that the results of your efforts won't affect your image until six months or, more likely, a year from now.

Q: Should you discuss your problems with the press, with advertisers?

A: People aren't really interested in your problems. They're interested in success. The smart thing is to stick to good news. If you can tell them only three good things, tell three and quit.

Q: The advertising community is made up of very cynical people. Everybody says things are great.

A: You've got to tell them what has happened or will happen shortly. Let the facts bear you out. We had a major advantage in that many of our readers considered *New York* ''their'' magazine and wanted us to succeed.

Q: How much did Rupert Murdoch's negative image hurt the magazine?

A: Mr. Murdoch has been misunderstood in this country. But time is obliterating that negative image. He's had too many real successes.

Q: Did acquiring Cue *help you with advertising?*
A: It gave us something positive and new to talk about. We've made a remarkable turnaround in less than three years, and it's partly due to the acquisition of *Cue*.

Q: Is being tops in your category a great help with advertisers?
A: We're not tops in any particular category. There's lots of places advertisers can spend their dollars. We have to rely on ideas. We don't sell just space. We go into an advertiser with a program. We approach them with a marketing reason why they should be reaching the trendsetters in the New York market, and a program to facilitate that strategy.

ANALYSIS

Making Space Buyers See Your Magazine Right

Since advertising makes the difference between profit and loss for most magazines, the image of the magazine in the minds of advertisers and those who place their ads is of tremendous importance.

Influencing the perception and attitude of customers is like courtship. To gain the beloved's love you must first get his or her attention and then win his or her respect.

Unfortunately, magazines, unlike most lovers, court harems rather than individuals. Space-buying decisions are determined by media buyers, agency creative people, advertising and marketing executives and top management. *Family Weekly* and *Parade* have a problem with media buyers because Publishers Information Bureau refuses to classify them as magazines. *True Story* has difficulty establishing a respectable image with top management. A magazine has to win attention, respect and love on every decision-making level.

Attention (being thought of) is essential, but not enough. Although it can be gained and in many ways, it is important to choose methods that lay the groundwork for respect and, eventually, love. Negative publicity, like the Felker-Murdoch struggle over *New York*, does more harm than good.

Respect (being admired) clears the way for acceptance both with the person who respects you and with those influenced by that person. It is much easier to win the hand of the beloved if you have won the respect of the parents:

National Enquirer and the *Star* would find it much easier to sell media buyers if they could prove that agency clients respected them.

Love (being wanted) is the goal. It is achieved by making prospects realize that you fill their need, that you are important to them. There is no doubt that Detroit's auto industry respects *Vogue, Glamour, Mademoiselle* and *Self*. Conde Nast's problem is getting the industry to realize it needs those magazines.

Appraising the image

Seeing your magazine as others see it is almost as difficult as it is important. The fundamental problem for many editors is not in the advertisers' minds but in their own. Ask ten editors for a statement of their magazine's purpose, and nine will give you rambling descriptions of the kind of material they've been publishing and/or the kind of people their circulation departments or research tell them they are reaching. They hardly ever even hint at why their magazines deserve attention, respect or love, i.e., the precise need their magazine fills.

What are the elements that go into the advertising community's image of a magazine? All the things that are important to advertiser and their agents. A magazine—in fact, every advertising medium—is evaluated by advertisers on four levels:

1. As an editorial product: nature and size of audience the publication attracts; importance to that audience; how readers use it; respect they have for it.

2. As an advertising medium: the cost/value equation; ability to produce results; use by other advertisers, particularly competitors; prestige with the advertiser's customers, distribution channels, employees and agents; time between closing and publication; reproduction quality; value as a showcase (*Architectural Digest* has more showcase value than *Better Homes and Gardens*, *Better Homes and Gardens* more than *Home*).

3. As a competitor with other media: relative standing in advertising pages and/or dollars, growth, profitability, and glamour (television is more glamorous than magazines, and magazines more than newspapers, *Playbill* is more glamorous than *The New York Times*, and the *Times* more than the *Daily News*).

4. As a business: likability of personnel; credit rating; reliability; efficiency; flexibility; knowledge and consideration of client needs; aura of confidence and/or success. (Neither *People Weekly* nor *Self* could

have won so much advertising support so quickly had they been launched by companies with less prestige than Time Inc. and Conde Nast).

Smart editors periodically assess how the advertising community thinks of their publication on each of these levels and on all the points enumerated.

Is it possible for a magazine to have a different image for different publics? As Cathie Black points out, very few readers, or advertisers, see *New York* exactly alike, but there exists an underlying consensus. Both readers and advertisers perceive the magazine as dedicated to satisfying the curiosity about, interest in, and concern with New York City common to the upward mobile, fairly young, reasonably affluent people attracted to the Manhattan lifestyle.

On the surface, different people's images of the same magazine may seem very different, but there has to be a consensus at the core or the publisher has a serious problem. Hence, the final test: If the magazine is on target, not only will the editor see its purpose clearly, but he or she should be able to relate the "different" images to that purpose. Whether *New York*'s readers see the magazine as an entertainment directory, a bargain-hunter's guide, or a commentary on the City's art and politics, they all satisfy interest in New York City as it pertains to the Manhattan lifestyle.

Focusing on the underlying purpose also cuts through the confusion when the image does not seem to correspond to certain facts. Bob Larimer, of *Cosmopolitan*'s agency, Nadler & Larimer, has pointed out that the magazine's famous media ads "ignore the magazine's true audience demos, showing a glamorous, classy gal, when in reality the average reader is almost blue-collar." Since editor Helen Gurley Brown's underlying purpose is to feed the aspirations of the glamorous, classy gal inside most modern women, whether blue-collar or not, there is no deception in these ads. The image they form is true to the underlying purpose of the magazine (and, incidentally, is the image most useful to the advertisers, since consumer buying is determined by aspirations, not demographics).

Although few magazines have *New York*'s advantage of being fervently read by the majority of media buyers, informal research is still the most common, and most practical, way of determining the nature and status of a magazine's image in the advertising community. As Cathie Black says, nothing substitutes for direct contact with clients and agencies. Editor William Withworth did not need formal research to learn that the advertising community thought "*The Atlantic* is an esoteric, intellectual magazine." Nor did editor Lewis Lapham need to find out that many other agency people agree with Calet, Hirsch, Kurnit & Spector's Stan Gerber that *Harper's* is an "old, dying, stodgy publication."

Second only to the editor's direct contacts with the advertising community is listening to the magazine's salespeople. Most salespeople are too prone to self-delusion to realize what is wrong with their magazine's image or what can be done about it. But a smart editor should be able to analyze complaints and alibis to get at the heart of the matter.

Determining the image

Determining what the editor wants a magazine's image to be should precede its appraisal, since the desired image is the norm against which actual images are evaluated.

Cathie Black is smart to reject "a three-line statement that everyone hands out." A written statement of purpose is a poor communications tool. Advertisers (and readers) are interested in immediate, personal use, not ultimate, general purpose. To communicate effectively, talk about their goals, not yours.

But stating a magazine's purpose in writing is a good way to clarify one's thinking. It can force an editor to face the fact that he or she is not clear on what the magazine is all about. A written statement of purpose is an essential preliminary to any formal attempt to research, appraise or improve a magazine's image.

Who writes this statement is not important. Who approves it is. The editor may do the initial work. The statement can even be drawn up by committee or jointly by department heads. But it should be approved by top management.

The statement of purpose should be the focal point for both evaluating the magazine's image and, more important, determining where improvement is needed and what changes should be given priority.

Changing or molding the image

As Cathie Black says, when you have an image problem, the best procedure is to "pull out all the stops." Only hermits can afford not to worry about what others think. Image-building is part of the editor's job.

Whether the publisher assigns the task to a public relations director, calls in a p.r. agency, or does the job unassisted, someone has to oversee and coordinate everything the organization does that will affect the magazine's image. And the editor has to have the ear—and the confidence—of that person. The objective is to develop a grand strategy of direct and indirect communication.

Indirect channels of communication include all the activities of the editorial, advertising, circulation and business departments that touch any of a magazine's many publics. This requires diplomacy, sometimes authority, especially when image building clashes with a department's proximate goals, as when *Gentlemen's Quarterly* decided to refuse ads "involving hair replacement products, mail-order grooming products, mail-order bathing suits and underwear, and mail-order vitamins."

Direct channels of communication are typically media ads, but take many forms from sophisticated presentations of original research (Knapp Communications's audio-visual presentation, "The Affluent Market and the Automobile"), to a simple change of title (*Solid Waste Management* becomes *World Wastes*). To establish their image as leaders for the markets they serve, *50-Plus* publishes a quarterly newsletter (*Maturity Market Update*), and *American Hairdresser/Salon Owner* promotes the use of beauty salons through ads in women's magazines.

Editors need not be directly involved in such activities, but they should be aware of them, and willing to cooperate when needed.

Although there is no fool-proof formula for deciding on the nature and extent of image-molding communications, there are some general principles:

1. Do not try to change everything at once; select the most important target and concentrate on it. If your magazine's editorial, graphics, and sales strategy are at peace with each other, the secondary targets will fall with the first.

2. Let the magazine determine what you spend, the audience what you say. The more relevant the image is to the imaginer, the longer it will last and the more impact it will have.

3. Don't let the medium contradict the message. A leaflet on how particular and elegant a magazine is should not be printed on the newsprint.

4. A vague image is worse than no image at all. Conde Nast's major mistake in relaunching *Vanity Fair* was to raise expectations without telling people what to expect, forcing everyone to form his or her own concept of what the magazine should be. The result: an avalanche of criticism.

5. People influence images more than numbers. Positive talk, an attitude of confidence can overcome sliding numbers, but raising numbers won't help much when management doubletalks, seems indecisive or pessimistic.

6. Bad news does not necessarily a bad image make. The worse thing one can do is to panic at the first hint of criticism, negative talk, or even unfavorable facts. As it takes a long time to build a favorable image, it takes a long time to destroy one.

MANAGEMENT REVIEW

Check List to Appraise an Ad-medium Image

I. To appraise a publication's current image:

A. Evaluate it first by general image of objectives:

Does the image win the attention, respect or love

	Attention	Respect	Love
1. Of media buyers?	___	___	___
2. Of agency creative people?	___	___	___
3. Of client executives?	___	___	___
4. Of client top management?	___	___	___

B. Analyze how they see it as an editorial product:

Is the image positive or negative	Positive	Negative
1. On kind of readers?	___	___
2. On number of readers?	___	___
3. On importance of readers?	___	___
4. On reader use?	___	___
5. On reader respect?	___	___

C. Analyze how they see it as an advertising medium:

Is the image	Positive	Negative
1. On cost vs. value?	___	___
2. On ability to produce results?	___	___
3. On use by other advertisers?	___	___
4. On prestige in client's field?	___	___
5. On closing time?	___	___
6. On reproduction quality?	___	___
7. On showcase value?	___	___

D. Analyze how they see it vs. its competitors:

Is the image positive or negative   Positive   Negative

1. On advertising sales?   _____   _____
2. On growth rate?   _____   _____
3. On profitability?   _____   _____
4. On relative glamor?   _____   _____

E. Analyze how they see it as a business:

Is the image positive or negative   Positive   Negative

1. On likability of personnel?   _____   _____
2. On credit rating?   _____   _____
3. On reliability?   _____   _____
4. On efficiency?   _____   _____
5. On flexibility?   _____   _____
6. On concern with client needs?   _____   _____
7. On aura of confidence, success?   _____   _____

F. Evaluate the cohesiveness of the image:

Does a consensus underlie all the different images of the publication?   Yes____ No____

G. Check your research methods:

1. Do you, as editor, have enough contact with the ad community?   Yes____ No____
2. Do you, as editor, listen to the salespeople?   Yes____ No____

II. To determine what a publication's image should be:

A. Prepare a written statement of purpose:

Is this statement of purpose   Yes   No

1. Focused on an underlying reader need?   _____ _____
2. Approved by management?   _____ _____
3. Truly the focal point for
   a) Assessing the current image?   _____ _____
   b) Planning to improve the image?   _____ _____

III. To improve a publication's image:

A. Encourage the appointment of a communications coordinator:

Does the candidate   Yes   No

1. Understand the statement of purpose?   _____ _____
2. Understand indirect communications?   _____ _____
3. Know direct communications?   _____ _____

4. Have the required diplomacy?   ____ ____
5. Have the necessary authority?   ____ ____

B. Evaluate the image-molding strategy:
   Do the plan and its implementation   Yes   No

   1. Concentrate on a single target?   ____ ____
   2. Address each audience's interests?   ____ ____
   3. Use means appropriate to the message?   ____ ____
   4. Make a definite, unambiguous statement?   ____ ____
   5. Highlight people rather than data?   ____ ____
   6. Ignore incidental negatives, whether rumor or fact?   ____ ____

C. Are you, as editor, doing your best   Yes   No

   1. To assist, counsel the communications coordinator?   ____ ____
   2. To correct or improve the image-molding strategy?   ____ ____

CHAPTER THIRTEEN

The Place of Special Issues in Periodical Editing

Featuring an Interview with Don Gussow

Chairman of the Magazines for Industry Inc., Harcourt Brace Jovanovich

There are hundreds of techniques editors use to generate excitement in their magazines, from illustrations and heads to breaking news and muckraking—and new techniques are being invented all the time. We have chosen only one for this chapter: the special issue. We selected it because it is a technique that has been around for a long time, because it can be used by almost any kind of magazine, and because it has enough impact on the editing process to exemplify the basic principles required for any successful excitement-generating departure from routine editing.

The man we interviewed on the subject of special issues qualifies on several counts. First, he has been an editor all his life. Second, he has final responsibility for the editorial products of a number of magazines that use the special-issue technique regularly. Third, he is an unequivocal advocate of the special issue as an excitement-generating technique. And finally, as head of a publishing operation, he understands not only the editorial relevance of special issues but their impact on advertising and the bottom line.

At this writing, Don Gussow is 75, still very active, and able to look back on 55 years in publishing. His first job was with *The Butcher's Advocate* in 1929. He considers himself first an editor, and then a publisher.

He did not become the full-fledged head of a publishing operation until 1944, when, with $6,000, he started *Candy & Snack Industry* because his boss at *Confectionery-Ice Cream World* refused to recognize that the magazine's audience was becoming two distinct markets.

Twenty-four years later, in 1966, the $6,000 investment had become the $2-million Magazines For Industry Inc., and Don sold the company to Cowles Communications for $1.9 million worth of Cowles stock. The contract specified that Don continue to operate the publication as president of Cowles Business & Professional Publications and serve on the Cowles board of directors.

By 1970, Don's group of business publications was grossing $3 million a year in a division totalling $12 million. But the parent company, Cowles Communications itself, was in deep financial trouble. Its flagship, *Look,* was to fold shortly, and it had lost millions on a short-lived daily newspaper called *The Suffolk Sun*. Foreseeing disaster, and recognizing an opportunity, Don managed to purchase back Magazines For Industry for $940,000—$750,00 in cash with the rest to be paid out of profits.

In 1982, Don sold Magazines For Industry, by then grossing over $8 million. Harcourt Brace Jovanovich bought the nine magazines, a semi-annual, six annuals, two newsletters and a book company. Don remains as head of the MFI division.

Don is the author of several books, including *Divorce Corporate Style*; *The New Merger Game*; *Chaia Sonia: A Family Odyssey, Russian Style*; and *The New Business Journalism*.

INTERVIEW

Q: Do all your magazines have special issues?
A: Not yet. I believe in special issues, but I've had a hard time selling my publishers. We operate with autonomous profit centers, and each publisher runs his own magazine, subject only to management review. It took me five years to sell the publisher of *Food & Drug Packaging* on the idea of "Package of the Year" issue. As in most trade journals, the December issues of *Food & Drug Packaging* were disasters. Who wants to advertise in a year-end issue, especially that of a bi-weekly? Then we introduced the Package of the Year Award, and made that issue a special. Now December is highly profitable. After that, the publisher started a number of other special issues on his own.

Q: Don't most specials become annual affairs?

A: That's right. *Beverage Industry* features a special on the International Market every year. Such a special attracts clients who don't advertise normally. The same magazine has a special issue on Primary Packaging and another on Secondary Packaging. It has a Vending issue and a Sanitation issue. And this is just one magazine, a bi-weekly.

Deciding on the special issue

Q: For a special to be repeated annually it must be successful. How do you measure success?

A: A special issue must be *special*; it must have a valid editorial approach, with a subject and editorial matter that are really meaningful to the reader.

Q: Do you measure success by the advertising attracted or by reader response?

A: If you have a good editorial product and it generates enough interest among readers, it will attract advertisers. Advertising is the bottom line. A special can't succeed without it.

Q: Is there an automatic cutoff point—so many pages of advertising or we won't do it again?

A: No. We'll do it several years. Then, if it doesn't prove a success, we drop it or try something else.

Q: Let's consider a single example.

A: My favorite is *Food & Drug Packaging*'s special for the Interpack Expo. The show is held every three years in Germany. On previous occasions I couldn't sell it to the publisher. This year he bought it, and did a marvelous job. The staff designed an Interpack survival kit: a special pull-out section on what to do when you get to Germany, how to travel, what to expect at the fair, and how to see it.

Q: Who made the decision to do that special?

A: The idea came from the editorial department, but the decision to go ahead had to be made by the publisher.

Q: What convinced him to go ahead?

A: The excitement raised by the idea of a pull-out survival kit. This show is huge. It attracts 75,000 from all over the world. It runs from 9 A.M. to 6 P.M. for a full week, including Saturday and Sunday. There are 12 huge buildings. And no publication was offering a real guide.

Q: How do you determine whether there is real advertiser interest before you go ahead?
A: You can't market it ahead of time. You have to decide this is it and go ahead. You depend on the excitement among the editors. They develop the product. Their success will attract advertisers.

How the special issue affects advertising

Q: Do the editors consult the advertising staff?
A: Not always. It depends on the subject and its interest to the sales staff.

Q: How much additional advertising was there in the Interpack issue compared to the corresponding issue of a year earlier?
A: About 25 additional pages, or over $50,000 more.

Q: From new advertisers?
A: Some were new, but most were regular advertisers who took additional space. We find, and I'm sure this is true of other bi-weeklies, that there are very few 26-time full-page advertisers. Six insertions is considered a very big contract. But they wanted to be in this special issue and, for most, it was an additional insertion. In fact, the increased excitement will result in many advertisers—I can't yet say how many—increasing their space next year.

Q: Are the salespeople enthusiastic, or do they consider the special an interruption of their regular selling?
A: If it's planned properly, the salespeople catch the excitement. Since compensation is based on sales, a special issue also means extra income.

Q: Won't a salesperson, who has convinced a client to advertise in an issue because it is a special, have a more difficult time getting him to buy space in ordinary issues?
A: I never thought of it that way. We find that anything that increases a client's interest in the magazine makes him easier to sell the next time.

Q: When you do a special issue, do regular advertisers ever say, ''That's not for me,'' and drop out of that issue?
A: Some advertisers won't have any part of specials. There are some who avoid advertising in any extra-large issue. But they are by far the minority.

Q: In most of your special issues, is the whole issue given over to one topic, or is the special material added to the regular features?
A: It is added to the regular features. Instead of running 48 pages, we'll run 72 or more pages.

Kinds of special issues

Q: You seem to be describing two kinds of specials: one connected with a news event, the other with a general topic or subject. Which is more common?
A: Special subjects. At times we combine the two, as when a show is on a special subject.

Q: The show specials you mentioned appeared before the event. Is there a special that reports on the event?
A: There's usually a special to cover the show. At the Interpack Expo we had a complete staff covering the several thousand exhibits. *Food & Drug Packaging* had two special issues after the fair, one on equipment and another on materials. *Candy & Snack Industry*, which covered the same show, had only one special issues after the fair—in addition to a very large issue preceding the show.

Q: These after-the-show issues are sold as specials to advertisers?
A: Yes. Most shows are occasions for two special issues—one before and one after, sometimes two after. *Dairy & Ice Cream Field* covered last November's every-other-year show with three special issues. September was the pre-show issue. October, the main-show coverage issue. And in November we did something really special. Those advertisers who took space in all three issues were given the opportunity to provide leaflets which were included free of charge in those copies of the November issue which were distributed at the show.

How the special issue affects the reader

Q: Do you ever get complaints that you are filling up the special issue with material that doesn't interest a particular reader?
A: We've never had an instance of that. I guess because all the regular features are always in the issue. The special issue is just bigger. The October special issue of *Dairy & Ice Cream Field* was in excess of 200 pages, while an average issue runs about 100.

Q: One of the strengths of periodical publishing is that it develops in its audience both a pattern of expectations and certain reading habits. Don't specials interrupt this continuity and, therefore, hurt the publication?

A: If the special issue provides excitement, it is an addition, not a substitute. The regular features remain.

Frequency and format

Q: Is there a limit to the number of special issues it is practical to have?

A: In a biweekly, if you run more than six specials, you have a problem. In a monthly, more than four is too many. We follow the thematic editorial approach in all our magazines. Every issue features a particular theme or subject. But that does not make every issue a special theme or subject. In ordinary issues the theme is not that important, it is not developed to such an extent; it is not a reason for special advertising. Early in the fall of the year we develop the themes for the following year's issues, including specials.

Q: What's the advantage of that?

A: The announcement of the schedule is for the advertiser, not the reader. We don't publicize it to the reader. It gives the advertiser a chance to see what you intend to do a year ahead so he can include it in his own promotion schedule, in planning his own advertising.

Q: Isn't this the equivalent of telling the advertiser, "All the issues aren't for you"?

A: It doesn't work that way. Every publication pulls together special material continually. The fact that it happens to be special adds interest for the reader and improves the environment for the advertiser.

Q: Should the special issue depart from the format of the regular issues, or should it fit, as much as possible, into the standard format of the magazine?

A: We don't change graphics at all, except in very rare cases. We have to stick to the basic style of the publication so that the reader will not be confused. He gets the same magazine. It is just bigger and better.

Circulation and pricing

Q: Special convention issues are frequently distributed to a larger audience than usual, aren't they?
A: We always distribute extra copies at the show.

Q: How about specials unconnected to the show? Do you ever mail copies to people outside the regular list?
A: Occasionally. But on other specials we seldom print extra copies.

Q: When do you charge the advertisers extra? Must they pay for extra circulation?
A: There's no extra charge, even for convention issues. The one exception is a special pull-out section to be distributed separately as *Food & Drug Packaging* did with the Interpack survival kit.

Q: In summary, what's the most important element that a special issue brings to a magazine?
A: In one word: excitement. Excitement for your readers, for your advertisers, and for your staff.

ANALYSIS

Special Problems of Special Issues

Special issues are very different from special publications, though the word "special" is used for both. A special issue is an integral installment in the series of publishing events that make up a periodical, whereas a special publication is not part of the series. *Food & Drug Packaging*'s Package of the Year Issue is clearly a special issue. *Better Homes & Gardens's How To Buy a Home, House & Garden's Building Guide* are special publications. Here we are interested only in special issues.

The importance of continuity

Publishing a magazine is different from running a book club. A periodical is not a disconnected series of anthologies. It has an identity that carries from issue to issue, a character or personality capable of winning the loyalty of readers by building expectation.

This does not mean that a good magazine is predictable. Herb Mayes once said that a good editor will surprise his readers in each issue of his magazine. Herb may have surprised the readers of *McCall's* each month, but it was the surprise of delight, not of disappointment. Successful editors know how to innovate within the range of expectation, i.e,. with continuity.

The importance of continuity to media has received far too little study. It is an essential tool for building audiences in television, radio and newspapers, as well as magazines. It is the reason why most successful radio stations have consistent formats, from all rock to all news. Failure to understand the importance of continuity has done more to hurt network television than any other single factor. CBS, under Jim Aubrey, was a firm believer in the importance of series to build regular viewers. In the late seventies, under Aubrey's successors, CBS emphasized specials to attract occasional viewers. All the shift achieved was to convert many regular viewers into occasional viewers.

What broke CBS's hold on the ratings was not the specials themselves, but the inability to integrate specials with the medium's continuity. Special events, in any medium, can either dilute or concentrate continuity. What is amazing is that programming geniuses like Bill Paley, Paul Klein and Fred Silverman have never found a way to make the television extravaganza serve the medium's need for continuity. When Norman Lear and Joseph Papp proposed a series of great plays for television, the project died because the networks wanted them as scattered specials, while Lear insisted that weekly showings at a regular time were necessary for continuity. Magazines can learn from television. Special issues must serve continuity, not disrupt it.

Editorial ebb and flow

It looks easier to preserve continuity in publishing than it does in broadcasting. As Don Gussow points out, a special issue can and should include all the regular features of other issues. Even graphics should remain in character.

But continuity requires more than regular features. A magazine has a personality precisely because it does not flow as a constant, unfluctuating stream. It has ups and downs, cycles of greater and lesser intensity. Within each issue every page cannot be equally interesting, all layouts cannot be identical. There are also cycles from issue to issue, a publishing rhythm readers learn to expect.

Special issues should be high points in a periodical's multiple-issue rhythm. They should flow naturally in the direction the magazine is going, so readers feel each special as a climax rather than an interruption. From this principle we draw four practical conclusions:

1. A special issue should build on the reader's expectations. The topic of the special issue must contribute to the overall objectives of the publication. A special issue on the World Series does not belong in *U.S. News & World Report*, nor would *Sport* do a special issue on the Presidential elections. Treatment should also be consistent with the magazine's editorial approach, a satirical version of *Smithsonian* may work for *National Lampoon*. It would not make a good special issue for *Smithsonian*. If *Time* and *Esquire* both did special issues on inflation, the results would not be alike.

2. A special issue should appeal to the majority of the magazine's regular readers. One of the ways to destroy continuity is to publish a special issue which is too specialized. Although *Chain Store Age Supermarkets*, *Progressive Grocer* and *Supermarketing* all include most of the important grocery wholesalers in their controlled circulations, the wholesalers are a small percentage of their total audiences. It would be a mistake for any of them to run a special issue of interest to wholesalers only.

3. A special issue should never interfere with the regular function of the publication. Not only should usual features be retained, but primary objectives cannot be ignored in favor of the special material. If an entire major-league team died in a plane crash, we cannot imagine *The Sporting News* backpaging the story just because it happened in the week of its Kentucky Derby special issue.

4. A special issue should be really special. This point, emphatically stated in the interview, cannot be overemphasized. Nothing is so pitiful as the special issue that is an anticlimax. This can happen in three ways: the subject may not be important enough; the treatment may not be extraordinary enough; or the publication may have so many special issues that the term becomes meaningless. Under "Special Feature Issue" in SRDS, Cahners lists every issue of *Electronic Business*, and Sutton lists at least two-thirds of *EE-Electrical Equipment*'s issues.

Special issue vs. theme issues

The problem may be with SRDS, which has not developed a format and terminology to distinguish between ''special issues'' and ''theme issues.'' The difference is in the degree of editorial excitement. Theme issues cause ripples in a publication's flow. Special issues make a splash.

Certain periodicals lend themselves to theme editing better than others—usually in direct proportion to their dependence on active editing vs. reactive editing. Active editing chooses its own subjects. Reactive editing has its subjects chosen by outside events. The National Association of Home Builders used to publish *NAHB Builder* as a magazine the first week of the month, as a newsletter on other weeks.* It was an efficient and effective device which provides the frequency required for reactive editing while allowing a once-a-month format for active editing.

Although theme selection can be affected by outside events (*Organic Gardening & Farming* would not select planting as its theme for November), most theme issues require advance planning and information gathering that precludes reactive editing. In fact, the purpose of theme issues is largely to facilitate long-range planning—both for editors and advertisers.

Unlike theme issues, special issues are frequently occasioned by news events. *Builder* put together a midweek special issue (newsletter format) immediately after President Carter announced his plans for fighting inflation. The special issue was smaller than regular issues. What makes a special issue special is excitment, not size.

Special issues vs. special sections

Since 1972, *Business Week* has developed a whole new source of revenue (and a dubious reader service) by running special sections devoted to regional markets, domestic or foreign. The sections are 67% advertising, 33% editorial. The text is 100% promotional, totally lacking *Business Week*'s customary editorial bite.

The chamber-of-commerce approach to special sections is not essential. When *Professional Woman* ran a special section on aviation in August, on education in September-October, both were predominantly editorial, though the first attracted a few specialized ads.

---

*N.A.H.B. Has since sold the magazine to a private firm, but retains the newsletter.

The big difference between special sections and special issues is that a special section does not dominate the issue. It is really theme editing restricted to a part of the publication. Hence the special section can be devoted to subjects of interest to a minority of the readers without disrupting the impact of the magazine.

Special issues are for readers, not advertisers

The topic of a special issue has to be important. To whom? To readers, the majority of the publication's readers. This is easy to forget, because most special issues are created to solve advertising problems. *Food & Drug Packaging*'s annual Package of the Year issue was invented to build advertiser interest in the year-end issue. *Advertising Age* schedules its top 100 Advertisers Report right before Labor Day; its 100 Leading Markets issue right before Christmas

In all three examples, however, the special editorial is for readers, not advertisers. The issue is made more valuable to advertisers by hyping reader interest.

This becomes a problem for many publications because the business department is more likely to think in terms of low-interest vs. high-interest issues than the editorial people, particularly where there are no single-copy sales to immediately reflect reader interest. Hence proposals for special issues frequently originate with management and are resisted by the editors.

The way to overcome this is to present the low advertiser interest in terms of low reader interest due to competition from holidays and other disruptions in reading habits. So the publisher's problem is solved once the editors start looking for special-issue ideas to hype the magazine's appeal when competition is greatest for reader attention.

Among the greatest competitors for attention in the trade field are conventions or trade shows that engage the participation of many of the magazine's readers. On the principle of joining forces you cannot lick, business papers use such meetings as occasions for special issues (in fact, some, like FOLIO: and *Advertising Age*, run their own shows). The problem is deciding the nature of the special editorial treatment. Should you anticipate the show, supplement the show, or report on what happened at the show? Few shows justify three special issues, particularly for a monthly. The decision should be based on audience needs. If most of your readers are interested but cannot attend, after-show coverage makes the most sense. If most of your readers will be at the show or have other sources of information about it, an issue with in-depth coverage of the show's theme is preferable. The latter approach has the added advantage of permitting distribution of the issue at the show. Anticipation of the show works only if your publication is connected with the show's sponsor or is the only complete source of information about the event. *Meetings & Expositions*, for instance, published the programs for the annual conventions of both Meeting Planners International and the National Trade Show Exhibitors Association.

Selling the special issue

As a climax in reader interest, the special issue has added value. It should be sold as such—to both reader and advertiser. Frequently a premium price is justified. *Advertising Age* doubles its single-copy price. Penton/IPC's *Heating/Piping/Air Conditioning* has higher multiple-page rate for advertisers in its annual catalog-directory issue. If premium ad rates are not more common, it is because most special issues are scheduled for periods weak in space sales. Once a special issue becomes well established, its price structure should be reviewed, particularly if it delivers bonus circulation.

Even magazines that are normally distributed free should study the opportunities for selling extra copies of special issues. If the special issue is of wide enough interest, it can result in extra circulation income plus the numbers needed to charge premium ad rates.

Two common mistakes in selling special issues to advertisers: first, to forget that advertisers need more notice on special issues (changing plans or budgets requires time); second, to reduce special issues to routine events for advertiser planning. The weekly *Flower News* schedules its special issues to correspond with its once-a-month "Grower Digest Issue" (distributed to an additional 5,000 growers).

Both consumer and business publications should give more attention to the use of special issues to attract new readers and advertisers. To create a special issue solely for new customers would be a serious mistake. The opportunity lies in using special issues already successful with regular customers.

MANAGEMENT REVIEW

Check List for Special Issues

I. Do special issues make sense for your publication?
   A. Are you sure they will not hurt regular issues?
   B. Will readers accept them as natural developments rather than a departure from your regular editorial?
   C. Will they add to the publication's overall value to the reader?
   D. Will they add to the publication's value to the advertiser?
   E. Will the extra expense involved be justified by sufficient added revenue (immediate or long-range; from circulation, advertising or both)?
   F. Can special issues be managed without interfering with primary editorial priorities, e.g., news.

II. Is your staff ready for special issues?
   A. Does the editorial staff have to be educated to the idea?
   B. Do you track reader interest by
        _____ Single-copy sales?
        _____ Research?
        _____ Fluctuation in renewal response?
        _____ Reader correspondence?
   C. Can the editorial staff handle the extra work without harm to regular issues?
   D. Does the sales staff have to be educated to the idea?
   E. Do the salespeople understand the relation between reader interest and advertisers' needs?
   F. Can the salespeople sell special issues without harm to regular sales?

III. Does the topic for your special issue qualify?
   A. Is it a topic readers expect from you publication?
   B. Is it important enough to your readers in both
        _____ Depth, i.e., it affects readers significantly?
        _____ Breadth, i.e., it affects a majority?
   C. Does it lend itself to special editorial treatment?

IV. **Are you positioning the special issue properly?**

A. Will your other special issues interfere

_____ By proximity?

_____ By sheer number?

B. Is the date selected appropriate for the topic?

C. Can this special issue boost a weak point in your publishing schedule?

D. Would it be more effective as an extra issue?

E. What effect will the date chosen have on the return on investment

_____ From readers?

_____ From advertisers?

F. How does this special issue mesh with editorial plans for:

_____ Theme issues?

_____ Special sections?

_____ Cover stories and other special features?

G. How does this special issue mesh with advertising sales plans, i.e.,

_____ Prior commitments to advertisers (position, multi-page ads, inserts, etc).?

_____ Salespeople's quota and bonus arrangements?

H. How does this special issue mesh with production's?

_____ Traffic flow?

_____ Paper supply?

_____ Printer's and binder's capability?

V. **Will the special issue be properly promoted?**

A. Will advertisers get sufficient notice to achieve expected advertising results?

B. Are there advertisers not on the regular prospect list who belong in this issue?

C. Will it help to mention it in new-subscription promotion? (Or requalification appeals?)

D. Will it help to mention the special issue in renewal notices?

E. Is it worth a special promotion in other media?

_____ Single-copy promotion?

_____ Subscription promotion?

_____ Advertising promotion?

F. Can extra copies be distributed advantageously?

_____ How many?

_____ Where?

_____ Sold or free?

_____ With promotional materials?

G. Does a premium price make sense?

_____ For the single-copy price of this issue?

_____ For special advertising positions?

_____ For all space sold in this issue?

PART FOUR

The Basics of Editorial Management

Planning and editing a magazine's copy and layout is only part of the editor's job. Editors must also be managers. They must run a department, i.e., manage people, organize a team, keep it working, pass on its performance, and make changes when necessary.

Editorial management can be divided into five broad areas: 1) managing oneself, i.e., understanding and working with your personal abilities, peculiarities and shortcomings; 2) managing others, i.e., controlling and motivating the people who work for you; 3) managing the product, i.e., evaluating and improving the publication itself; 4) managing innovation, i.e., encouraging and developing new ideas and products; and 5) managing external relations, i.e., judging, cultivating and using what outsiders think of what you are doing.

Chapter 14 is devoted to managing oneself, as we question Herb Mayes on "What It Takes to Be an Editor." It is not enough that an editor have talent and develop skills. There are, we discover, different kinds of editors. And it is crucial that every publication have the kind of editor it needs.

Managing others, or "The Care and Feeding of Creative Personnel" is the very important topic of Chapter 15. We learn from and with George Allen that selecting, directing and motivating creative people requires special rules and special skills.

In Chapter 16, "Evaluating Your Editorial Product," we study product management by discussing with Tom Kenney how to judge results: Is the magazine in focus? Are the contents and the selection of material what they should be? Is the presentation right—the writing readable, the graphics effective? And, finally, is the final result really exciting to readers?

Chapter 17 is devoted to managing innovation, or "Editorial Research and Development." We interview Gil Maurer, who supervised the creation and evolution of a new-product development department at Hearst Magazines, and find that, for encouraging and screening new ideas, management's attitude is as important as how the editorial department is structured.

Finally, Chapter 18 takes a look at "Awards, Competitions and Editorial Management," a significant example of managing external relations. To learn how editors can and should use management tools available from outside one's organization, we discuss American Business Press Jesse H. Neal Editorial Awards with Tom King, who was ABP's president at the time of this interview.

CHAPTER FOURTEEN

What it Takes to Be an Editor

Featuring an Interview with
Herbert R. Mayes
Former Editor of McCall's *and President of McCall Corp.*

There is no doubt that the job of editor or editor in chief is the highest job in magazine publishing. But is it one job? Will the skillful editor be equally comfortable at the top of the masthead of any magazine? Someone once said that for every magazine there is only one editor who really fits the job. If there is real truth in the observation, it has less to do with the demands different magazines make on editors than with the tendency of strong editors to remake their magazines into reflections of themselves.

There are, however, broad categories of editors, depending on the kind of editing their publications demand. We discuss the three most important of them in this chapter. Great editors, as the history of the magazine business amply proves, have often been successful in editing more than one magazine. T. George Harris made a name for himself as editor at *Psychology Today* and then *American Health*. John Mack Carter successively edited *McCall's, Ladies' Home Journal* and *Good Housekeeping*. And then there is Carter's mentor, whom we have chosen for this interview.

Few men or women are better equipped to tell us what makes an editor than Herb Mayes. It would be difficult to find another editor with a career that compares to Herb's—whether in length of service, variety of publications edit-ed, magnitude of success, or impact on the magazine business.

Herb became an editor at the age of 20. He was editor of *Inland Merchant* from 1920 to 1924; editor of the Business Paper Division of the Western Newspaper Union from 1924 to 1926; editor of *American Druggist* from 1926 to 1934.

In 1934, he moved into consumer publishing, becoming editor of the *Pictorial Review*. Four years later, in 1938, he was hired to edit *Good Housekeeping*.

After two decades as editor of *Good Housekeeping*, Herb was fired. At 58, when lesser men would have taken early retirement, Herb accepted a new job as editor of *McCall's*, and worked a revolution in magazine publishing. From 1958, when he joined the magazine, to 1965, when he retired from the McCall Corp. presidency, *McCall's* went from 5.3 million to 8.5 million in circulation and from $18.4 million to $51.4 million in gross advertising revenues.

Many of the observations Herb makes in the following interview have been considerably amplified in his autobiographical *The Magazine Maze*, published by Doubleday & Co. in 1980.

INTERVIEW

Q: What do you consider the main difference between your years as editor and your years as chief executive?
A: As editor, I enjoyed my work; as head of a company in charge of administra-tion, I didn't. As editor of *McCall's* I was infinitely more important than Gover-nor Langlie, who was president. When I succeeded Langlie, I considered myself less important than any editor in the shop.

Q: What was your prinicipal problem as chief executive?
A: Understanding the financial people. Balance sheets, profit & loss statements were easy, but sinking funds and offerings of convertible subordinate debentures knocked me for a loop. In addition to the magazines, there were the pattern di-vision and the printing operation. I had some degree of responsibility for 5,700 employees. I hated dealing with bankers, and even more, negotiating with labor unions. If it weren't for the accountants and lawyers on the staff, to say nothing of the constant availability of Norton Simon for advice, I'd have been a dead duck.

Q: Why did you give up editing to do what you hated?
A: I had no choice. Mr. Simon had the peculiar notion I could do anything, and insisted I'd be as good a chief executive as I had been an editor. I wasn't.

Q: Isn't it natural for an editor to want to become the top executive?
A: In my book, the truest, soundest editor never wants to be anything else. Editor is as high as anybody can go. If the editor is good enough, he or she is more than president, general manager or publisher.

Q: The editor is more important than the publisher?
A: Exactly, though traditionally the publisher is supposed to outrank the editor. It gripes me even today to see a magazine masthead that carries the name of the publisher at the top, which is where the editor's name belongs. The editor is the most significant person on a magazine, or should be. Editors, not publishers, give magazines their stature. If you were to list the great editors of the century, such names come to mind as *The Saturday Evening Post*'s George Horace Lorimer, Time-Life's Henry Luce, *McClure*'s S.S. McClure, *Vogue*'s Edna Wollman Chase, *The New Yorker*'s Harold Ross. But who could come up with even one name of a publisher of those magazines?

Q: But doesn't the publisher get the higher salary?
A: Generally. But editors regard influence and power as being as important as salary. I certainly did. And, in later years, my salary was higher than the publisher's.

The editor and management

Q: How were your relations with publishers?
A: I remember when I first created the slogan for *Good Housekeeping*, ''The Magazine America Lives By.'' After it appeared in the magazine, the publisher came to my office and said, ''That's a good slogan, but don't you think you might have discussed it with me first?'' I thought for a while, because I wanted to give him a sensible answer, and finally I said, ''No.'' But that was stupid. I should have discussed it with the publisher. He was entitled to that courtesy.

Q: Suppose the publisher had said he didn't like it?
A: Then I'd have told him to come up with a better slogan or go jump in a lake.

Q: Suppose management got into the act?
A: The answer would have been the same.

Q: How did you handle publishers who tried to involve themselves in editorial matters?
A: If you mean any who tried to suggest what to print, they're all dead. I didn't kill them, but would have been ready to. The editorial area is sacrosanct. Nobody, including management, has the right to stick a nose into editorial affairs. Management has the ultimate right: to hire and fire. That's enough.

Q: Is there such a thing as an ideal relationship between editor and publisher?
A: When they're able to talk to each other as nothing less than equals. The editor should participate in decisions affecting circulation goals, promotion, choice of an agency. The publisher should participate, not in what editorial content should be, but in decisions concerning changes in editorial goals.

Q: How about one person as both editor and publisher?
A: I think it's unwise. As publisher, you want to bring in as much advertising as possible, but you may be confronted with a request for editorial favors; then, as editor, you're on the horns of dilemma. I've never known an editor-publisher who was really comfortable.

The editor and advertising

Q: How does the editor relate to the ad department?
A: Very few magazines, if any, have total separation. It's impractical. The ad director and the space salesmen have every right to know what the editor is doing and planning. The more they know, the better they sell.

Q: You've been quoted as saying any space salesman on the magazines you edited could come into your office any time of day or night, provided only that he come in on his knees. Is that true?
A: It makes a good story that way, but it's only partly true. What's omitted is that I always said it with a grin, with obvious humorous intent. Actually every salesperson was more than welcome, and I thought it part of my job to answer questions, explain why we did or did not do something editorially. The toughest job on a magazine is the salesman's. He deserves all the help the editor can give him, short of providing so-called editoral support for an advertiser.

Q: Should an editor ever do any space selling?
A: If he does, I think he's demeaning himself.

Q: Should an editor ever make calls on advertisers?

A: I always did. Once a year I popped in on every major agency in the country, and on many not so major. I wanted them to have some behind-the-scenes information: gossip about authors, for example, or why we had discontinued an established department, or which features had been well or poorly received. Agency people were pleased to see me. There was no direct selling effort, but those calls made life a little easier for our salesmen. And I found most of the agency people stimulating. I can't recall editorial contemporaries more challenging to be with than, for example, Leo Burnett, George Gribbin, Bill Bernbach, Tom Dillon or David Ogilvy.

The editor and circulation

Q: Most advertising departments have more to say about circulation than editors. Is that as it should be?

A: For me, the ideal ad director is one who assembles a formidable sales staff, brings in ample ad revenue, and stays, as much as possible, out of the way where promotion and circulation are concerned. I always considered those two functions as fully in the editorial domain as in the business domain, which may suggest to you, not unreasonably, that I never suffered from delusions of humility. The editors I respected had no less authority than the publisher in the circulation and promotion areas.

Q: Did management resist you on this?

A: Let me be honest. As an editor I trespassed on territory that according to an organization chart was not mine. But if, as frequently was the case, the editors could write better promotion copy than our agencies, we wrote it. If we could write better circulation copy than anybody in the circulation department, I saw no reason why we shouldn't. When there was a first-rate writer in our promotion department, we lovingly deferred to him—as in the case of Joe Heller, on *McCall's*. But for some of his hours Joe Heller sat in the office churning out reams of copy that had nothing to do with promotion. He was writing a book: *Catch 22*. We thought he might have dedicated the book to the company.

The editor and his staff

Q: Were the reins tighter for the people you hired?

A: Of the men and women who worked for me, 90% were inherited; had been hired by shrewd predecessors. We had no hours, day or night, Saturdays or Sundays, Good Friday or Yom Kippur. We laughed a lot, loved somewhat, fought, made up, conceived some far-out ambitions. We worked like mad—had to, because of the intense competition around us. In five decades of publishing, I disposed of few associates, and about a couple of them I am sure I was wrong.

Q: How did you rank the members of your staff?
A: In no particular order. The titles on a magazine's masthead (managing editor, executive editor, senior editor, etc.) signify neither duty nor stature. The one meaningful, unambiguous title is editor, or editor in chief.

Q: Did you insist on regular hours for your staff?
A: Only for secretaries and clerical help. Creative people could come and go as they pleased. I remember that Sig Larmon, when he was head of Young & Rubicam, insisted that everybody report on arrival to the reception desk—a self-defeating regulation because executives who knew they were going to be late simply phoned in, reported sick, and didn't show up at all.

Fundamentals of editing

Q: Were there any basic rules by which you operated?
A: Every editor has his own style and makes his own rules. I'll mention a few of mine, which doesn't mean that I recommend them. 1) If we had any remote doubt about the value of a submitted manuscript, we didn't buy it; editorial inventory has a way of piling up, and it limits future choice. 2) When we did buy a manuscript, we had to know in exactly which issue it would appear. 3) We never saved good ideas. We used them immediately.

Q: Any secrets of good magazine editing?
A: If there's one editorial element I believe in, it's surprise. Every issue must have it. The editor must have a passion for surprising his readers, his staff, and once in a while himself. Before any issue is considered final, an editor should ask: Does it have balance? Is there sufficient variety? Is there something to compel the reader's attention—a knockout feature the reader is bound to remember? Is there a report, chart, piece of fiction to make the reader feel the magazine was worth buying?

Q: What's the editor's biggest problem?
A: Good times. When everything is going smoothly, with circulation and advertising high, with everybody happy—that's when complacency sets in. That's when

the tough thinking and planning must begin. Complacency is the great editorial curse. Nothing recedes like success.

Q: How has the magazine business changed since you were chief executive at McCall Corporation?
A: Editors today are too friendly. I believe editors should be not merely competitors but enemies. When Bruce Gould was editing *Ladies' Home Journal*, Otis Wiese, *McCall's* and I, *Good Housekeeping*, we were never on speaking terms. Our attitude was part showmanship, but it made for a kind of excitement. Another change: the business side of magazine publishing is now more deeply involved with editorial, holding tighter rein on the purse strings, editorial/advertising page ratios. I'm not sure editors are as significant today as the likes of Luce and Lorimer once were.

ANALYSIS

Editors—Their Genius and Species

Borrowing a definition from psychology, we can describe the editor as a publication's ego, the conscious element in a magazine's personality which mediates the demands of the publication's id (its creative resources), superego (its business management), and external reality (the reader marketplace). It is an enlightening analogy and explains why good editors frequently need strong egos.

No job in publication management relies more on intuitive judgment than that of editor. This is because editors, in addition to being artists, can never repeat what they do. Each issue of a magazine must be both a continuation of what went before and an entirely new creation, another movement in a symphony that started with the first issue and will not end until the magazine goes out of business. Good editors employ theme and formats, but never formulae. The best editors rely as much on well-honed instincts as they do on educated intelligence.

Our purpose here is to consider the editor from the point of view of publication management. Whether the editor is an employee, a partner or the owner, management must decide:

1. Whether this creative egoist is the right person for the job.

2. How management can help to encourage and develop the editor's well-honed instincts.

3. When the editor's relations with the rest of the publishing orchestra are right for making beautiful music.

The editor as creator

A publication should be the editor's baby, whether the editor is *Omni*'s Bob Guccione, *Ms. Magazine*'s Pat Carbine, *Machine Design*'s William Miller, or *Sierra*'s Frances Gendlin. Even at Time Inc., where there is a company-wide editorial office, corporate editor in chief Henry Grunwald wants the managing editors of *Time, Sports Illustrated, People, Life* and *Money* to run their own magazines with full responsibility for the editorial product.

This does not mean that every editor has the same relationship to his or her publication. There are three basic relationships, each requiring a different type of editor, and a distinct manner of handling the editor.

First, the editor may be related to the publication as its natural parent. Editors like *Rolling Stone*'s Jann Wenner, *New Woman*'s Margaret Harold, *Creative Computer*'s David Ahl not only conceived their magazines, but raised them from infancy to their current status. To be a natural parent, an editor need not have founded the magazine. It is possible for an editor to take over an established publication and to recreate it in his or her own image. There is no doubt that Helen Gurley Brown is the natural parent of today's *Cosmopolitan*, or that Norman Cousins had a similar relationship to the *Saturday Review*. *Esquire* was born and successfully reborn under Arnold Gingrich.

The essential element in this type of editor-magazine relationship is that the editor is working with his or her own conception.

Second, the editor may be related to the publication as step-parent. Someone else has the idea, and the editor is brought in to adopt the baby and guide it to maturity. The very short-lived *Vital* was the idea of publisher Bert Schuster (with the help of a $30,000 study by Market Facts Inc.). But Bert immediately turned his idea over to editor Anthony Monahan. Time Inc. chose the managing editor for *People* after management had decided what the magazine was going to be.

Third, the editor may be related to the publication as spouse. Anyone who accepts the editorship of an established publication with the assignment of continuing, advancing and improving what already exists is entering into a partner relationship with the magazine's mature ''personality.'' Such an editor can shelter, nourish and improve the magazine's concept, but only if he or she recognizes its "rights," so to speak. *The New Yorker*'s William Shawn, *Good Housekeeping*'s John Mack Carter, *New England Journal of Medicine*'s Dr. Arnold Relman, and *Photomethods*'s Fred Schmidt are such editors.

It is important to distinguish between the natural-parent editor, the step-parent editor, and the spouse, both in hiring the person for the job, and in establishing parameters for the editor-management relationship.

It is essential that the editor fit the job. Although the same person may be able to function in all three relationships (natural-parent, step-parent, spouse), it is highly unlikely that he or she will be equally at home in each. In fact, the natural-parent editor is usually temperamentally unsuited to protect and nourish another person's creation. Despite his high respect for his predecessors, Norman Cousins had to change the *Saturday Review of Literature* into the *Saturday Review*, and when he was called upon to help with *McCall's* without the ability to alter its concept, his contribution was negligible. When Clay Felker took over *Esquire*, it was presumed from the start that he would recreate the magazine. In fact, his biggest problem was that it was impossible to achieve a genuine rebirth without first killing the old *Esquire*.

There is more likelihood that the same person who was successful as a spouse editor can also function as step-parent, although even there, the balance between the editor's creative and development skills is different. One reason so many new magazines look and read like so many old magazines is that the publishers hire spouse editors rather than step-parent editors. Good step-parent editors are hard to find. Highly creative editors prefer to develop their own ideas, while editors who are not so highly creative are more comfortable with a fully-developed concept.

The leadership thrust in the management of each publication will differ with the type of editor. The natural-parent editor must be allowed to influence the rest of the endeavor far beyond editorial. He or she points the direction in which the magazine must go—even to the point of defining the limits of circulation and advertising. As a business, a publication starts with the magazine idea. Although the natural-parent editor may be a minority stockholder or just an employee, he or she conceived the idea that makes the business, and has unavoidable consequences in authority and influence.

Attempts by the business side to share leadership with a natural-parent editor almost always lead to trouble as they did between the John Veronis-Nick Charney team and Norman Cousins, when the former tried to recast *The Saturday Review* into four specialized publications.

Step-parent editors, on the other hand, accept their jobs with the understanding that someone else in the company is the final arbiter on what the company wants to do and what the magazine should ultimately be. In most cases, if they are successful, they share the leadership (in influence and inspiration, if not in title) with the founder or business head, since it is the editor, not the boss, who has taken the magazine concept from idea to reality.

Spouse editors are more likely to play a subordinate role in the overall progress of the magazine as a business. This does not mean that they have to be weaker or more malleable than parent editors. As is evident from the interview, there was nothing weak about Herb Mayes, who was a spouse editor most of his life, though some may argue that at *McCall's,* he was a natural-parent editor.

The editor as manager

Once the basic creative function of the editor is defined, we must consider the tools required for the job. From a management point of view, the editorship is a line job. The editor heads a department, the management unit responsible for the development, production and quality-control of the editorial product. As such, every editor must be able to manage people (staff or free-lance), time (deadlines), money (budgets), and ideas.

The first three requirements are common to all department heads, although the correct handling of creative personnel requires a degree of specialization. Idea management, however, deserves special attention. Since the editor should be the final judge of whatever goes into the magazine (including advertising), an important part of the editorial function is the generation and evaluation of ideas. In fact, if the staff is large enough, the editor can frequently produce an excellent product without writing or rewriting a single phrase. The editor's entire function becomes a two-phase activity of 1) stimulating the staff to provide ideas, and 2) deciding which of the ideas to use.

Because of this, editors trained on large publications frequently fail in editing small ones. The fewer staffers an editor has, the more he or she must be the originator as well as the judge of ideas. This inner-directed process can be quite different than the outer-directed process of the large-staff editor.

One of the many problems John Mack Carter had when he took over the failing *American Home* several years ago was that he had become accustomed to a large staff at *McCall's* and *Ladies' Home Journal* and was suddenly forced to work with a much smaller staff.

The editor as a politician

A good editor's influence on the other departments of a publication (advertising, circulation, production, finance) is much like that of a brand manager in a large package-goods company. The brand manager's sole concern in dealing with other departments is to protect and further the success of the brand. The editor's concern is to protect and further the success of the editorial product. Both have to achieve their goal by persuasion rather than authority.

The editor, of course, has a tremendous advantage over the average brand manager in that the editor creates and controls the quality of the product. An editor who produces a very successful magazine seldom has problems with other executives in the company. Herb Mayes may have been kidding about salesmen approaching him on their knees. But most of the salesmen at *McCall's* were already on their knees—in gratitude more than submission.

Although editors are communicators by profession, the one area where many of them fail is in communicating the editorial concept to the promotion, circulation and advertising departments. Sometimes this is due to the artist's justifiable reluctance to provide rational justification for instinctive judgments. But most of the time it is due to the fact that the editor lacks a clearly-thought-out editorial concept.

Herb Mayes's ability to communicate explains his penchant for "interfering" in the writing of circulation and advertising promotion. In Dick Deems's years as head of magazine publishing at Hearst Publications, he had each prospective editor write a detailed description of what he or she would do with the magazine. Marketing-oriented companies like Lever Brothers and Norelco prepare detailed manuals outlining the marketing/advertising strategy for each brand. Magazines should do the same, and in most cases the editor should be the one to write the manual.

The editor as employee

Whether the editor is employee, partner or owner, it is important to foresee the stress and strain on the working arrangement. No publication can be as profitable as it should be if the editor is continually at odds with management. The right chemistry is essential. This is true even when the editor, publisher and owner are one person (an arrangement some publishing experts consider a short-cut to schizophrenia). Editorial and business needs frequently pull in opposite directions and sometimes the conflict can be reconciled more easily by two minds than by one.

Finally, what motivates an editor? We believe editors should be well paid and treated with respect. Editors' remuneration should include an incentive bonus—based on profits or on circulation (the latter only if editorial is the major factor in building circulation).

But, as Mayes states, money is not the most important consideration for an editor. Most editors want power, the power to create a publication with real impact. Any magazine owner who resents giving that kind of power to the editor is a fool.

MANAGEMENT REVIEW

Check List for an Editor's Self-Evaluation

I. **Decide what type of editor the publication has or needs.**
    ____ Natural parent: when the editor is the originator of the editorial concept.
    ____ Step-parent: when someone other than the editor originated the concept, but the editor is charged with taking it from concept to reality.
    ____ Spouse: when the editor is charged with continuing an established publication with no change in basic concept.
    NOTE: A natural-parent or step-parent editor is required when an essentially new editorial concept is to be imposed on an established magazine.

II. **Judge whether you have the qualities required to be this type of editor.**
    A. If a natural-parent editor is needed, you need:
       ____ Exceptional creativity.
       ____ Genuine leadership qualities.
       ____ Pride of authorship outweighing humility.
       ____ A work history of originating and executing new ideas.
       ____ Interest in influencing the non-editorial side of publishing.
       ____ Impatience with readership research.
       ____ A tendency to dominate idea sessions.
    B. If a step-parent editor is needed, you need:
       ____ Exceptional ability to understand other people's ideas and to foresee both their potential and the problems inherent to them.

____A general willingness to share the spotlight.

____More humility than pride of authorship.

____A work history of taking charge of new projects.

____Preference for sharing responsibility.

____Interest in readership research for testing.

____An inclination to seek consensus in idea sessions.

C. If a spouse editor is needed, you need:

____A high respect for the publication's past record and achievements.

____The ability to recognize and sell the best assets of a going operation.

____Pride in the institution overshadowing pride of authorship.

____A history of working successfully for others.

____A tendency to leave non-editorial decisions for others.

____Interest in readership research as a source for editorial ideas.

____The inclination to require others to justify new ideas in the light of past experience.

III. Rate your editorial-department management skills.

	Tops	Good	Fair	Poor
A. Management of people:				
•Staff	___	___	___	___
•Free-lance and suppliers	___	___	___	___
B. Management of time:				
•Editor's use of time	___	___	___	___
•Staff's use of time	___	___	___	___
•Ability to meet deadlines	___	___	___	___
C. Management of money:				
•Preparing budgets	___	___	___	___
•Keeping to budgets	___	___	___	___
D. Management of ideas:				
•Idea origination	___	___	___	___
•Idea stimulation	___	___	___	___
•Idea evaluation	___	___	___	___
•Idea adaptation and use	___	___	___	___

IV. Evaluate your ability to work with other departments.

	Tops	Good	Fair	Poor
A. Powers of persuasion	___	___	___	___
B. Ability to avoid conflict	___	___	___	___
C. Esteem of non-editorial staffs	___	___	___	___
D. Success in communicating the editorial concept	___	___	___	___

V. Assess your relationship to management.

	Tops	Good	Fair	Poor
A. Right chemistry, lack of strain	___	___	___	___
B. Satisfaction with your salary	___	___	___	___
C. Effectiveness of incentives	___	___	___	___
D. Freedom to exercise editorial control	___	___	___	___

CHAPTER FIFTEEN

The Care and Feeding of Creative Personnel

Featuring an Interview with George H. Allen

Senior Vice President for Magazines, CBS Publishing

The tongue-in-cheek observation that the hardest job of an editor in chief is cracking the nuts that make up an editorial staff has a good deal of truth in it. In more conservative language: the most difficult—and important—job for any editor is the management of creative personnel.

To do this successfully, an editor must understand what is special about creative people and how it affects the way they are managed. How much freedom do they need? What kinds of encouragement? What forms of discipline? Can creative people work effectively as a team and, if so, how do you get them to do it?

To avoid confusing the central management problem with specific editorial needs, we interviewed an executive with extensive experience in overall magazine management rather than an editor.

George Allen trained for his career by earning a Master of Business Administration degree from Harvard University. His first job, in 1938, was assistant to the president of a theatrical company. In 1941, he moved into research and promotion, first in radio (six years, half at WOR New York), then on a newspaper (four years with the *New York Tribune*), and finally in magazines (ten years at McCall Corp.).

In 1960, George moved to Meredith Publishing, as assistant to the president. Not long after, he became the first executive to have the title of publisher of *Better Homes & Gardens*. He was also elected to the Meredith board of directors, and appointed general manager of the company's publishing division.

In 1966, he was hired away from Meredith by Fawcett Publications, as executive vice president and publisher of all Fawcett magazines, including *Woman's Day*. He was also elected to the Fawcett board of directors.

When CBS Inc. purchased Fawcett in 1977, the new management signed George on as publisher of *Woman's Day* with the title of senior vice president for all magazines, i.e., for ten monthlies and 60 specialty titles.

INTERVIEW

Q: In hiring, do you distinguish between creative and non-creative jobs?
A: There aren't too many jobs in publishing where you do not look for creative talent. People tend to think of editorial as the creative job, but creativity is needed just as much in circulation and advertising sales.

Q: Can you judge creativity from past performance?
A: Certainly not from resumes. You can deduce something from past positions, though that seldom helps with salespeople. Mostly you depend on intuition.

Q: Have you run into people with relatively little creative ability who are good at handling creative people?
A: The problem is that creative people must respect their supervisor. There is a need to respect the boss's experience. It would be most difficult for someone with no creativity to handle creative people. This doesn't mean that the supervisor is in competition with subordinates. Such an attitude leaves subordinates with no place to go. They can't hit a home run because the boss should have hit it first. You can't compete with your employees, but you can't be a complete novice either.

Motivating creative people

Q: Is it true that salary is less important than other considerations in motivating creative people?

A: It's not always true, but creative people tend to be accomplishment oriented. Pride in their ideas is often more important than salary.

Q: When you've lost creative people to other companies, what was the principal motive for leaving?
A: Usually it was desire for more recognition, that is, more responsibility. I've always encouraged people to move to better jobs inside the company. Creative people become frustrated when unable to develop their abilities. You must keep creative people on a loose rein. You have to let them grow.

Q: How do you open the door to continuous growth, when you can't continually promote your creative people?
A: In any job, there is plenty of room for growth without being promoted. Good personal-evaluation systems usually allow four or five performance levels in each job. In publishing, even secretaries move up faster than in any other business I know. There are more opportunities to move up today, fewer iron curtains between departments.

Q: How do you keep creative employees from reaching beyond their level of competence?
A: You have to let people fail on their own. You can't prevent them from trying. This doesn't mean you destroy your operation by permitting things which would endanger it. But you have to let your people try new jobs: some to make it, some to fail. In a creative operation, turnover is health—if it means people are moving, improving, testing themselves.

Q: Do you find a lot of jealousy or envy among creative people?
A: No more than among other people, though it may be accentuated by the egoism natural to anyone who has pride in his ideas—enough to fight for them. Competence requires a certain degree of ego, pride in one's product.

Q: How do you get creative personnel to share glory?
A: There are a thousand ways, but you don't know until you know the person and the situation. People learn to live with one another sooner or later. Those who can't fall by the wayside.

Q: Do most really need recognition from within?
A: They've been trained to want it since kindergarten. In school it was grades. Maybe it's different in China or Russia, but our social structure is based on rewards, not necessarily money or prizes, but recognition.

Rewarding creativity

Q: Is there a systematic way to recognize achievement?
A: Two. One is to acknowledge it, not by contests, but by listening to ideas, using suggestions and cooperatively making them work. Praise is often artificial, no substitute for a consistent philosophy of recognizing value. It's not what you say but how you act. The other is compensation. A compensation system in any company is based on merit. Payday is recognition day.

Q: How important are by-lines?
A: Usually more important when you're young. But it's always nice to be identified with what you do. It goes back to the medieval guilds, where each craftsman marked his work with his initials.

Q: Sending editors and other executives to speak at conventions or teach classes is primarily a publicity device. Does it have any motivational value for creative people?
A: Half think it's great and love it. Half think it's a burden and are unhappy about it.

Q: Do you feel their attitude has any relation to their overall creative ability or usefulness?
A: The most important thing is to produce a good product. The publicity you get from the product is more important than that from speakers.

The use and abuse of criticism

Q: You said you have to let creative people make mistakes. After they've made the mistake, how do you tell them they are wrong?
A: Very often you don't have to tell them. They know it. Of course, if a person doesn't realize a mistake, you may have to tell him. But usually it's unnecessary. His contemporaries will tell him. His conscience will tell him.

Q: Do you encourage criticism by one's peers?
A: Criticism by one's peers is not in itself helpful, especially after the fact. Before the fact it may contribute to improving an idea.

Q: When a department head comes up with a really innovative idea, should the editor bring other members of the staff in for evaluation and criticism?
A: That's the editor's prerogative, and depends on his or her style. Some editors operate on one to one, others through group discussion. No two styles are alike.

Q: How practical is it to bring in an outsider to tear apart a couple of issues with the editors, just to get them thinking of things from a different angle?

A: Unless it is done regularly, it will do more damage than good. It is too far from the reality of producing the next issue. The best relationship of a consultant is a continuously advisory one. That doesn't mean you can't have someone from management or a reputable expert decide that the magazine is bad and sit down with the editor or staff to insist on the need for improvement. But you can't handle any staff, editorial or sales, principally by criticism. Many times it's better to change a staff than to try to whip it into shape.

Goal-setting and discipline

Q: When a creative person goofs off, how do you discipline him or her without damaging creativity?

A: Creativity is not a product of laziness. The ability to produce something better is no accident. It results from a great deal of concentration and hard work. As in sports, there are no champs without discipline.

Q: In sports, the coach can see that the team does its laps around the track, that it keeps to its diet, but how do you discipline creative people?

A: By watching production. The disciplined creative person produces more and better.

Q: What do you do with creative people who go stale?

A: There is little you can do with people who go stale. They have to do it themselves—change either their job or their attitude. It has nothing to do with ability. It's motivation. You can offer a new challenge, but the individual has to accept it.

Q: Is there a practical way to relate salary to creative achievement?

A: There had better be. But the problem is in evaluating each creative contribution. I don't know of any industry where value judgments are more necessary than in ours.

Q: Is it practical to require specific production levels from creative employees?

A: No, but you can set goals. That's a basic management tool. You should discuss objectives for the year ahead, review them periodically and at the end of the year. The goal need not be numerical, but you and the person reporting to you should be able to tell whether the goal was accomplished or not. The management technique known as goal setting is entirely appropriate on every level of our industry.

Q: What would be an example of an editor's goal: that he produce a predetermined number of stories that year?
A: Not necessarily numbers, but types of stories, or shorter stories. Goal setting also helps executives think ahead.

Q: Do you insist on fairly strict hours with people whose jobs are basically creative?
A: Successful creative workers resent strict hours. At the same time, they usually put in more than the normal number of hours. You can't let the organization go to pieces, with nobody knowing where anyone is, but you've got to be flexible. It's silly to make a fuss over five minutes with people who always take work home, in their minds if not if their briefcases.

Q: In engineering, one great management development has been the task force. How practical are such project-oriented teams in magazine management?
A: You might assemble a task force to start a new magazine, but in general such teams would be artificial in publishing, where most projects are for individuals.

Q: Is there a difference in the way you handle editorial people and the way you handle art people?
A: If you handle them differently, it's because they are different individuals, not because they do copy or art. Managing creative talent requires an instinctive sense of thinking creatively, recognizing creativity, identifying the contribution with the creator. Empathy is an indispensable part of the process.

Q: Don't really top executives feel personal recognition is secondary to getting the job done?
A: That's real leadership—like a hockey team that becomes greater than its players. Creativity is creating something greater than the sum of its parts. In such a group, the members learn faster, feel freer and have more fun. It is easier to achieve this creative spirit in a small organizaton—100 to 200 people, at most. Projecting that spirit to thousands is very difficult.

Q: You seem to imply that team work is vital to creativity in publishing.
A: Very few creative ideas spring whole from a single thought process. They are usually conceived rough and have to be shaped, often on the anvil of rationality. It's management's job to keep the flow of ideas along rational lines, subordinating egos to objectives. To waste time on nonsense ideas is not creative. Creativity is constructive. It works within the parameters of meaning—not always practical, but always meaningful. To encourage ideas, you must have the respect of those you are helping. Otherwise, there is no encouragement; they consider you a fool or a time-waster. Sincerity is essential for managing creativity.

ANALYSIS

Understanding Creative Personnel

Creativity is the ability to produce something new through imaginative skill. It is limited to no area of activity. The "something new" may be a way of handling people or how to raise money in a tight economy.

Creative people are risk-takers. Since the end product of creativity is always something that has never been done before, creativity is by definition unprecedented and untested. Every act of creation is a gamble.

Creative people are problem-solvers. Accidents and mistakes can result in "new" things, but we do not call accident-prone people creative. The results of creativity must be intended, even though the creator may not fully visualize the creation until it is realized.

The ability to subordinate risk-taking to problem-solving is what distinguishes truly creative people from non-constructive risk-takers, such as daredevils, dreamers and compulsive gamblers. Encouraging risk-taking for problem-solving is the key to the successful hiring and managing of creative personnel.

Fear—creativity's foremost foe

The first rule of managing creative people is to allow them to take risks without fear. In George Allen's words: "You have to let people fail on their own."

This is the primary reason why creative personnel need more freedom, fewer rules. It is not the freedom that nourishes creativity, but the sense of confidence. *Mother Earth News* former publisher John Shuttleworth once wrote an ad for editorial talent: "Name your salary, pick your own assignments, design your own office, head up your own special projects, travel when and where you choose, and oversee your own research facilities and personnel." That several of the editors who answered the ad later quit because John did not let them do their thing only confirms the need for a fear-free environment.

It is important to note that one does not remove fear by removing discipline. One removes fear by granting authority. Creative people are allowed to make mistakes because they have the authority to take chances. The biggest mistake managers can make is to think they are providing creative freedom by being tolerant of failure. Creative people have to be in charge of the entire project in which you expect them to take risks, so that both success and failure will be theirs. Even assistant editors and junior salespeople must have the authority to experiment in the areas in which you expect them to be creative. Ron Travisano, one of the Madison Avenue's top creative directors, says: "Power is not to hold on to but to give away." Nowhere is uncompromising delegation more vital than in the management of creative personnel.

In promoting creative people to manage other creative people, the editor should watch first for this ability and willingness to delegate. One complaint about Joe Armstrong's reign at *New York* was that he would not delegate full editorial authority. Ironically, the same reason was given to explain why Joe's replacement as editor, Ed Kosner, was dismissed from *Newsweek*.

Fear of criticism can inhibit creativity. Constructive criticism before an idea is used can be helpful in polishing and improving the idea. After the idea has been used, criticism serves no purpose, except to aggravate the pain of failure. Smart publishers know that risk-taking is essential to publishing. It is the publisher's responsibility to evaluate the operation's resiliency to risk, and not to authorize creativity in areas where the operation cannot survive failure.

Creative people who really have authority to take risks should not have to clear their creative ideas with the boss. A smart boss will be there to help, knowing how to draw his or her people out, and letting them prevail even when he or she disagrees with them. On the other hand, the smart boss sees a red flag when creative people bring ideas to their supervisor in order to avoid responsibility and failure.

One source of fear that can crush creativity is insecurity due to a lack of knowledge. It is vital that creative people know both their tools and their field. The imagination needs material to work with, and acquiring this material is a continuous learning process. This is one reason why a lazy creative person is a contradiction in terms (though creative people often seem lazy to those who do not understand the work of observation and contemplation).

In an excellent article titled "Getting the Best From Your Creative Staff" (*Industrial Design*, Sept./Oct. 1979, p. 52) management consultant John Graham writes of the need for creative people to have a "useful data base of information." Creative people, he observes, tend to have a generalist's approach to knowledge and a broad scope of interest. They are experience gatherers. The smart manager encourages and facilitates this.

Problem solving—creativity's sense of direction

Since creative people have no motive to get their creative juices flowing until they face a problem, the most effective way to manage creative personnel is by defining problems for them.

This is easy to overlook, which is a major cause of wasted talent. If you want to drain a creative person, urge him or her to be creative without presenting a problem. Whatever creativity is not exhausted from lack of challenge will be devoted to trying to look creative.

The technique of defining problems to spur creativity is similar to what is called "management by objectives." A good manager will be able to formulate both final and intermediate objectives in terms of problems. This is important because the creative process is basically a successful search for a new solution. The difference between creative jobs and non-creative jobs is that while non-creative workers use predetermined solutions (how typists should fill the page is known before they start typing), creative workers have to come up with new solutions (nobody knows how the writer will fill the page).

There are six basic rules for defining problems for creative workers:

1. Define the problem according to the extent of the responsibility you are giving the subordinate. If an editor is responsible for the whole issue, then that is the problem; if for a page, then a page is the problem.

2. Define the entire problem. One does not wait until after the art director has redesigned the magazine to tell him the printer cannot handle bleeds. The limitations under which a creative person must work are part of the problem.

3. Don't be afraid of limitations and restrictions. So long as they are presented as part of the problem they will stimulate the truly creative person—a sculptor uses the wood's grain, a poet, the sonnet's structure.

4. Never prescribe part of the solution when defining the problem. This obscures the real problem with a secondary problem: how to incorporate the boss's solution. It is wrong to ask your art director for a new masthead and then add you think he should do it in red. It is right to ask for a new masthead in red, if the problem is that you need a red masthead.

5. Set deadlines and stick to them. A problem that never has to be solved is not a real problem. Deadlines, like other restrictions, challenge creativity. As Graham points out in the article previously quoted, the anxiety associated with the approach of an imminent deadline increases until the creative person breaks into his or her subconscious to release an outpouring of ideas. Individual creative people have different pressure thresholds. A perceptive editor will keep the pressure on, but vary it according to the individual.

6. Remember that in most assignments people are part of the problem. McGraw-Hill sends editors to human behavior courses as part of its program to bring edi-

tors into top management. Perhaps it should not wait that long; even the lowliest reporter has to manage sources.

The last point highlights another: much of today's best creative work is the result of teamwork. George Allen observes that task forces are the exception in magazine publishing. But he makes a strong case for the publishing-team spirit which inspires a group to collectively surpass the individual creativity of its members.

Conceptualization—creativity's basic tool

We have defined creativity as the ability to use imaginative skills to produce something new. In studying how this takes place, psychologists have observed that creative people have a well-developed ability to abstract from factual contexts a pattern of relationships. They call this conceptual ability. The fall of an apple was the factual context in which Newton saw a pattern of relationships we now call gravity.

Management should look for conceptual ability when interviewing candidates for creative jobs. Since creative people tend to use a generalist's approach to knowledge, a person whose interests are narrow is a poor gamble for a creative job.

A lot of the inbreeding that stultifies creativity in publishing is due to conservative hiring practices that stress knowledge of a special field. Specialists can be creative, but they can also be pedants. Publishers who give specialization precedence over imagination will end up with the pedants.

This attitude extends to the environment in which creative people thrive. Some managers find it difficult to tolerate the freedom creative people need to exercise their minds. They resent the time spent by subordinates to gather information that does not seem to be related to the magazine. They do not understand why Pete Bonanni, when he was publisher of *Woman's Day*, encouraged editor in chief Geraldine Rhoads to take a trip to China.

It was mentioned earlier that creative people frequently do their best work under pressure. It should also be mentioned that it is up to the editor to see that these periods of pressure are followed by recuperative letups. Time Inc. gives occasional six-month sabaticals at half pay for executives. For many monthlies it would make a lot of sense to declare the day after closeout a company holiday.

The generalist approach is also vital in creative teamwork. One of the criterions for selecting the members of a creative team is their diverse interests—not so diverse, of course, that the members of the team cannot relate. Watch how your creative team interacts. If your casting was on target, the members will find each other stimulating, and will not feel threatened by the others' evaluation of their ideas.

Recognition and remuneration—creativity's rewards

The need to give creative personnel proper recognition is undoubtedly the basis for the legend that creative people are peculiarly vain. The fact is dubious and, for management, irrevelant. The purpose of recognition is to build confidence, the confidence required for risk-taking. *Guitar Player* publisher Jim Crockett devoted half an editorial column to recognition of art director Carla Carlberg. *Mining Equipment International* editor in chief Ruth Stidger goes out of her way to give credit to staffers in the presence of the publisher. But recognition is not as important as success itself for truly creative people. In fact, obsession with recognition is a symptom of insecurity, and insecurity inhibits creativity.

Remuneration should be weighed on the same scale. Money is the primary symbol of recognition in our society. People who are well paid tend to be confident—particularly if the amount that is paid is visibly determined by what they create. The commission system is the most effective form of compensation for salespeople. At McGraw-Hill, cash awards are given for ideas that produce revenue. *Parents* president John Beni has suggested that editors receive bonuses based on circulation.

How to recognize creativity

To sum up, we can outline five recognizable qualities that indicate creative promise:

1. Possession of basic skills. A writer must know the language; an artist, the medium; an executive, management techniques. Gralla Publications gives editorial candidates a basic editing test.

2. Ability to recognize problems. Editors define problems for writers; salespeople, for prospects.

3. Zest for tackling problems. People who duck problems, or panic when they face one, are not creative.

4. Willingness to work. Zeal for problem solving and laziness do not mix.

5. Broad interests and ability to conceptualize. Creative people have a way of finding extremely relevant ideas in seemingly irrelevant places.

MANAGEMENT REVIEW

Check List for Managing Creative Personnel

*All answers should be YES. The fewer NO answers,
the closer your operation comes to being ideal.*

I. Are creative jobs properly identified by

	Yes	No
A. Including every job in which the position's objectives require non-routine solutions?	___	___
B. Giving the people in these jobs complete authority in their areas of problem solving?	___	___

II. Are creative personnel properly screened by determining that they have

	Yes	No
A. The basic skills needed in the job?	___	___
B. The ability to identify and define problems?	___	___
C. Zest for tackling problems?	___	___
D. Willingness to work?	___	___
E. Broad interest and the ability to conceptualize?	___	___

III. Are creative assignments defined as problems

	Yes	No
A. According to the extent of a job's responsibility?	___	___
B. Always in their entirety?	___	___
C. Without fear of limitations or restrictions?	___	___
D. Without prescribing part of the solution?	___	___
E. With definite deadlines?	___	___
F. Remembering that people are frequently part of the problem?	___	___

IV. Is a creative environment fostered by

	Yes	No
A. Moderating the assignment load according to the individual's pressure threshold?	___	___

B. Making certain that criticism never becomes a source of fear, and is limited to constructive assistance? ___ ___

C. Providing sufficient recuperative time after periods of pressure? ___ ___

D. Affording ample opportunities to observe, experience and otherwise build a generalist's data base? ___ ___

V. Is creativity properly rewarded with

	Yes	No
A. Adequate recognition in the eyes of:		
1. One's supervisor?	___	___
2. One's peers?	___	___
3. People outside the company?	___	___
B. An adequate salary structure?	___	___

C. A merit system that visibly determines at least part of one's compensation on the basis of specific creative achievements? ___ ___

VI. Is creative teamwork being developed by

	Yes	No

A. Defining larger problems so as to establish team objectives and build a spirit of team achievement? ___ ___

B. Selecting members of the team diverse enough in their interests to stimulate each other? ___ ___

C. Putting no one on the team whose criticism would inhibit the others? ___ ___

CHAPTER SIXTEEN

Evaluating Your
Editorial Product

Featuring an Interview with
Thomas M. Kenney
Former President of Charter Publishing, now Head of CBS Magazines

No matter what the profession, there is no task more difficult than judging one's own performance. Whether you work for another or own the magazine you edit, it is important to periodically stop and evaluate the success of what you are doing.

A very practical way to do this is to look at the magazine you are editing from the point of view of management. If you were they, how would you judge your work; would you examine this editorial product and judge that you had the best possible editor?

Because we wanted the overall management view, we interviewed a publisher rather than an editor. He had to be someone who had been in charge of one or more significant publications, and who had actually changed editors on one or more of them. Our choice was Tom Kenney since, as president of Charter Publishing, he had appointed new editors for both *Ladies' Home Journal* and *Redbook*.

Tom is a Dartmouth University graduate with an A.B. in Economics. He also took business courses at New York University. At Dartmouth he was chairman of the university's daily student paper. In the Marines (1969-1972) he served both as editor of a base newspaper and liaison officer to the New York press. (He also became a captain and junior aide of the commanding general in Vietnam.)

Back in civilian life, Tom landed a job in advertising-sales marketing at Time Inc. Six months later he was assigned to the new-magazine development group, which resulted in his becoming assistant circulation director of *People Weekly* when it was launched. In 1974, he was moved to assistant circulation director at *Time*, and was promoted, in 1976, to circulation director of *Sports Illustrated*.

Three months later, Charter Publishing's chairman, Ray Mason, hired Tom to be circulation director of *Redbook* and a member of the board of Select Magazines, the single-copy national distribution unit. A year later, Tom was made circulation boss for all of Charter's magazines, and, eight months later, publisher of *Redbook*.

In 1980, Tom became president of Charter Publishing. Two years later, after making the changes discussed in the interview, Mason decided to dissolve Charter Publishing, and Tom had to supervise the sales of *Redbook* to Hearst and *Ladies' Home Journal* to Family Media.

His job done at Charter, Tom was hired by CBS Publishing. In 1983, CBS promoted the publisher of *Woman's Day*, Peter Diamandis, to president of the magazine division. One of Pete's first decisions was to make Tom publisher of *Woman's Day*. Later, when CBS purchased Ziff-Davis's consumer magazines, Pete promoted Tom to executive vice president for all the magazines.

INTERVIEW

Q: At Charter, you hired new editors for both Ladies' Home Journal *and* Redbook. *How was that done?*
A: We began by setting overall long-term goals for each magazine. Only then could we set criteria for the new editors. Then followed many personal interviews, to get a feel for who was out there. I used a headhunter for the *Journal*. I found that less helpful than I expected. I did not use one for *Redbook*.

Q: Did the headhunter specialize in finding editors?
A: I found there weren't many well-known headhunters for senior editors, although many worked with editors on the secondary level. Perhaps I did not look far enough. Anyway, we combed through as many names as we could find and selected those who, at least superficially, looked right against the criteria. There followed a lot of lunches, breakfasts and dinners—to select the few finalists. These were

asked, first, to prepare a general statement of purpose and approach for the magazine with a list of what they would change and retain. Finally, and this turned out to be the most revealing, they were asked to state what they thought the readers thought about specific articles in two issues, which we had researched article by article.

Q: To evaluate their insight into the audience?
A: Yes, and it showed how differently some New York editors think compared with the average U.S. reader. Some substantial editorial talents did great on the general prospectus, pretty well on specific changes, but were far off in understanding readers' tastes.

Editing and readership studies

Q: Didn't you find that those who did best had edited for similar audiences and had seen similar studies?
A: Definitely. And it shows that much that applies to one kind of magazine, doesn't apply to other kinds. The test led me to zero in on candidates with experience on mass-circulation books. Their skills were more related to our needs than those of wonderful editors on small magazines.

Q: I'm suspicious of readership studies. Even the best ones are thwarted by three facts: 1) respondents are never 100% honest; 2) research examines yesterday's audience, while editors edit for tomorrow's; and 3) the secret of great editing is to know what readers want before the readers do. All research can do is help evaluate past achievement.
A: I don't think research can be used to predict specifics. It is a comfort, however, to know that when the editor edits for tomorrow, it's done with knowledge of the basic proclivities of the reader. That's vital, and research can help you get it, even if not totally. One of the surprising things I learned was how extensively major circulation magazines use readership research.

Q: I can think of an exception: Cosmopolitan.
A: And I don't mean to suggest that research is essential, or can edit a magazine, but it's an awfully good tie-breaker to separate editors who talk a good game from those who know your readers.

Q: Research can be very valuable, but I feel the large amount of research is a symptom of something that is hurting the magazines—a play-safe attitude. Costs have driven management to use every possible test to avoid mistakes. That dampens a lot of spontaneity.

A: That depends on how it's used. It would be extremely foolish for management to use research on an article-by-article basis—to tell the editor, "You wasted that page; only 20% of your readers saw it." At Charter, readership research was managed by the editors, used or ignored by editors. Management shouldn't use it as a club. But we're talking about screening, and as a screening technique, it was extremely helpful.

Editing and management goals

Q: Take a step back. How did you formulate those long-range goals—before looking for the editor?
A: Over the last couple of years we've been trying to identify the leverage points for the magazines, what will make them successful in the years to come.

Q: What do you mean by leverage points?
A: A leverage point could be a more favorable image in the advertising marketplace, which might mean more advertising revenue; or getting audience up so cost per thousand would go down; or changing the proportion of revenue from circulation and advertising; or adjusting manufacturing costs in proportion to total revenue.

Q: The fulcrum that makes the magazine cost effective?
A: The moves that make the whole magazine come together so that all the various pieces of the operation reinforce one another.

Q: And what did you come up with?
A: In general, we decided that we wanted *Redbook* to be supported proportionately more by the reader, less by the advertiser. For the *Journal*, we decided the emphasis had to be on more revenue from advertising, although we should also increase income from readers.

Q: The changes were basically on the business side?
A: What's been happening to the women's service field is more a function of the business side than a lot of the stuff we've been reading about how the ways women are changing are alienating them from the traditional women's magazines. That's simply not the case. What has changed is the extremely low advertising cost per thousand circulation and the costs of paper, printing, ink and postage.

Competitive pressure has kept the women's service magazines from raising their cpms to meet costs.

Q: Did your strategy include any plan to make the magazines different from their competitors editorially?
A: Media buyers usually put *LHJ* and *McCall's* together. One of our criteria was that the editor should not be from *McCall's*. We had nothing against that great magazine, but over the years there's been this almost incestuous personnel relationship between the books, and I think it helped make them similar. One of our goals was a magazine different from the competition.

Q: Did you specify how it would be different?
A: That's the editor's job. Management can say make it different, but that's as far as management should go. The editor has to decide how to make it happen.

Q: Weren't you afraid that an editor from Family Circle *might make* Ladies' Home Journal *another "store book"?*
A: One of our criteria was open-mindedness; no need to do what was done before. Though *LHJ*'s new editor Myrna Blyth came from *Family Circle*, she could edit any kind of magazine. She's blessed with that kind of open mind.

Editorial changes and continuity

Q: How about continuity? How important was knowing the Journal*'s history, what it has been doing and why?*
A: Also extremely important. Among the worst mistakes that can also be made in altering editorial direction is to have sudden, jarring changes. That has brought more magazines to the graveyard than anything else.

Q: Like the Saturday Evening Post.
A: And *American Home*, and many others. We definitely wanted to avoid that. That's why changing editors has to be viewed long-term. The changes have to be evolutionary, even for an eventual revolutionary effect. The larger the magazine, the more necessary a consistent, long-term approach. I wanted people who could conceptualize, implement and adjust over a multi-year period. An editor had to be in place to take this from beginning to end. We were also changing printers and the printing process, which was an opportunity to redesign the magazines. We also needed a designer who would be around for at least five years to see it through.

Supervising the editor

Q: Once the editor is in place, how do you monitor performance to make sure you've made the right choice?
A: On a big magazine you can watch share of market in newsstand sales. If most issues over a long period do poorly, you have a problem. There are other signs like research, street talk, and the number of returns from insert subscription cards, but they're secondary.

Q: Do renewals mean much?
A: Renewals tell you even less than insert returns, especially in the short term. Subscribers originally bought the magazine because of what it used to be. Some of them will resist the changes. Long term, of course, the objective is to get renewal rates up.

Q: I suppose the way for management to warn an editor, when sales go badly, is to keep him or her posted on the figures. You can't tell the editor what to do.
A: Management's role is to set objectives, and to specify in advance how it will determine whether the goals are met. The editor, like every executive, should be included not only in that process but in overall business planning. Our editors sat in on our long-range planning sessions, listened to and commented on what business, circulation and advertising were doing. So there's no need for management to tell the editor what to do. It's self-evident. One of my criteria for the editor was the ability to participate in management. At Charter, the editor in chief was also an officer of the company.

Q: How important is it for the editor to have a very clear picture of the magazine's core readers?
A: Very. I've done studies at two separate publishing companies showing that in the course of a year, approximately 30% of a magazine's newsstand customers account for 70% of the copies sold. I suspect the same proportion applies to small magazines. Editors had better be sure they know everything they can about the source of 70% of their sales. On the other hand, if the editor edits exclusively for the loyal core, where are new readers to come from? So it's a balancing act: to keep the core happy while attracting replacements and additions. The fringe can make the difference between having something to take to the bank or not.

Q: Isn't sloppiness in writing and layout a symptom that management should watch?
A: You can't have real editorial excitement unless you first provide the basics

of good journalism: tight, clear, accurate writing; neat, appropriate, professional graphics. Without that, all the pizzazz and excitement in the world comes to nothing. One of my criteria for the editor was that she be a hands-on, operational editor. Consumers pick up on that stuff. They may not be able to tell you how well a book is edited, but they know when a product isn't done well.

Q: How do you recognize editorial excitement? Or do you have to wait for sales figures?
A: Again, it differs greatly in terms of the kind of magazine. I define excitement as any combination of editorial ingredients that compels a reader to pick up the magazine, to read it. It can be graphics, it can be subject matter. More typically it's a combination. It operates personally with each reader. One way to spot it is to find members of your target audience and watch how they react—when they are reading the issue, or when they see it on a supermarket rack.

ANALYSIS

Five Norms for Editorial Excellence

Anyone who wants to run a business intelligently should stop periodically to ask, "What are we doing, and how well are we doing it?" For magazine publishers, this is called editorial evaluation and, unfortunately, it is not done often enough.

Yet without editorial evaluation one cannot supervise the editor. It is not a publisher's job to tell the editor how to edit, but it is his or her job to judge whether the editor is right for the magazine.

The publisher, of course, can wait to see what the effects of the editor's work will be on sales—particularly, as Tom Kenney points out, by watching how the magazine does on the newsstands vs. its competitors. But Tom's technique, as he also points out, is not equally applicable to all magazines, and there are so many other factors that can affect results, that sales alone are not always a fair test of the editor's performance.

The publisher who refuses to evaluate the editorial package that is the soul of his magazine is ignoring a necessary management tool. Prior editorial experience is not necessary to do this job adequately. You do not have to be a hen to smell a bad egg—or enjoy a fresh one.

A practical way to evaluate editorial from the publisher's position (i.e., from outside the editorial department) is to select a representative number of issues of the magazine and examine them closely in five areas:

1) The overall editorial focus.

2) The selection and arrangement of material.

3) The writing used to present the material.

4) The graphics used to present the material.

5) The excitement generated by the interaction of each of these elements.

Note that steps 2 to 5 cannot be taken until step 1 is completed, since it is impossible to judge how well someone is doing something until you understand what he or she is doing.

Does the editorial package have a clear focus?

Magazines are (or should be) started because somebody recognizes a need and knows how to fill it. You do not discover that need by asking the market to tell you what it is. As *Good Housekeeping* editor John Mack Carter put it, "Never ask your readers what they want—they won't know until they see it." Advertisers are just as helpless in defining the medium they want until they see it.

Though a real need must exist, and the market must have a general awareness that it exists, it is up to the editor to see the need with the clarity required to fill it. This is why Tom Kenney asked his prospects for a statement of purpose, and why great editors, like Helen Gurley Brown, have such confidence in their editorial judgment. They have no doubts, for they see too clearly what is needed and how to fill that need.

When *New York* editor Ed Kosner admitted ambivalence as to whether his is a city or national magazine (see his interview in *Advertising Age*, April 5, 1982), he was courting trouble. An editor cannot look in two directions at once and maintain editorial focus.

If there is a single explanation why the women's service books published by Conde Nast are doing so much better than *Ladies' Home Journal* and *McCall's*, it is because the Conde Nast books are more clearly focused. It does not matter whether this is due to management genius, or due to a need to keep *Mademoiselle*,

Glamour and *Vogue* from stepping all over each other. The result is that each fills a distinct need: *Mademoiselle*, to show young females how to become sophisticated women; *Glamour*, to teach young women how to both look and be successful in the working world; and *Vogue* to show mature women what is fashionable.

The most common cause of blurred focus is concentration on audience instead of need. Although the audiences of *Seventeen, Mademoiselle* and *Glamour* overlap, *Seventeen* is less sharply focused than the other two because, unlike them, it tries to serve all the needs of young women in its audience (13- to 19-year-olds).

In brief, a magazine's focus should be determined not by the nature of its readers, but by their reasons for reading it (see Chapter 6). Thus two magazines can have heavily overlapping core audiences but absolutely distinct foci. Although many women read both *Time* and *Vogue*, they do so for very different reasons.

How does one judge whether a magazine is clearly focused? Read several issues carefully, then describe in four sentences or less the typical reader and why that reader reads the magazine. The quicker and more specific your answer, the clearer the focus.

If you feel it is necessary to reinforce judgment with research, have reader traffic studies done on the issues you are considering, and study the results. If concentration of reader attention shows a definite pattern from issue to issue as to the type of articles and subject matter read, the publication is probably well focused. If concentration is erratic and seems to jump all over the place from issue to issue without logic or discernible pattern, the magazine lacks focus.

How well does the content serve the readers?

Evaluating content is largely deciding how it fits the focus, i.e., how effectively it fills the need that brings the readers to the magazine.

The first measure of content is how accurate and complete the material is—relative to the publication's focus. *American Health* need not treat a subject with the thoroughness required by the *Journal of the American Medical Association*. And both have to be more accurate than the *National Enquirer*.

The second measure of content is what is published vs. what is left out. Selection is a primary function of editing, and determines how well the magazine serves its readers. Again, success, is measured in terms of the magazine's focus. Some subjects a magazine cannot ignore without betraying its readers. With other subjects, readers allow the editor wide discretion—in fact, they depend on that discretion. Editorial selection is a basic element of the reader's need.

A third measure of content is how the material is arranged, the editorial approach: long vs. short, features vs. departments, multiple-view vs. single-view, comment vs. news, human-interest vs. technical analysis, and so forth. Readers expect a magazine, in accordance with its purpose, to consider the subject's relevance to the reader and the reader's need for perspective, background, opinion, examples, etc.

A fourth measure is variety. A well-focused publication requires variety, as well as singleness of purpose, both to hold core readers and to attract fringe readers. Tom Kenney calls it a balancing act. Like a great composer, the editor finds simplicity in diversity by orchestrating a multitude of instruments into one great, purposeful sound.

Finally, content should be evaluated as to how well it fits the various ways a magazine is read. *The New Yorker* has cartoons and fillers for readers who are not ready for its relentless parade of uninterrupted text, and *National Geographic*'s content serves both those who read and those who look at pictures.

How readable is the text?

Although most publishers agree with Tom Kenney on the importance of professionalism in writing, stylistic fine-tuning gets relatively little of their attention. Yet it remains basic, and careless writing is often the first sign that an editor is neglecting his or her job.

Good writing is first of all clear. It has an inner logic controlling order and selection within sentences, paragraphs and stories. Good writing is a guide line for the reader's mind, neither so loose as to encourage the mind to wander, nor so tight as to make it stumble. Good writing gets to its point, as pleasantly as possible, but never sacrificing purposeful progress to irrelevant entertainment. Good writing observes the rules of grammar, but knows when to break them.

The purpose of writing is to facilitate communication. Hence a writer must consider the reader, his command of the language and how he thinks, as well as what is said. You cannot write the same way for *Physics Today*, *Poetry* and *Popular Mechanics*.

Besides clarity and ease, language can be decorative. This is the area in which it is easiest to separate the professional writer from the amateur. Professionals use cleverness, imagination and emotion to improve clarity and reading ease. Amateurs let their cleverness interrupt the flow of thought.

How effective are the graphics?

As with writing, the first requirement for design and layout is clarity. They should advance the objectives of the magazine by helping the communications process.

Graphics should also make the magazine easier to use. Back in 1979 (*Marketing & Media Decisions*, October), Warwick, Welsh & Miller media director John Meskil wrote that magazines had "revised their format to avoid story jumping." Would that were universally true. Magazine layouts too often consider advertisers rather than readers, thereby serving neither.

Consistency and appropriateness are very important in graphics. Art directors who do not understand how a magazine works often reduce a publication to a series of unrelated spreads, graphically independent of each other. It takes a good deal of taste, and artistic self-control, to achieve the elegant graphic simplicity of magazines like *Scientific American, Smithsonian* and *Gourmet*.

Major graphic elements (vs. decorations, rules, white space) should be evaluated as content as well as graphics, whether they are used to catch attention and lead readers into the text, or supplement the text. Graphics can add to the text by clarifying (e.g., diagrams), illustrating (e.g., photos), or serving as independent features (e.g., cartoons, picture stories).

How much excitement does all this create?

Tom Kenney defines excitement as that "combination of editorial ingredients that compels a reader to pick up the magazine, to read it." Readers look to their favorite magazines for leadership, and excitement is to editorial what charisma is to leadership.

Although surprise frequently creates anticipation by arousing curiosity, surprise is not essential. Readers do not have to be surprised by the puzzles in *Games* to find every issue exciting. What is fundamental to editorial excitement is the anticipation of being delightfully stimulated, whether it be by the *Star*'s juicy gossip, *Architectural Digest*'s thrills in taste, *The Atlantic*'s political insights, or the incredible fantasies of *Heavy Metal*.

For anticipation to be strong enough to be exciting, what is coming in the magazine must be important enough to generate strong desire and, once read, fulfilling enough to nourish future anticipation.

How do editors know what is important enough to really involve the reader? Principally by being involved themselves. Show me an exciting magazine and

I will show you an editor with strong convictions, whether it be *Chemical Engineering*'s Calvin Cronan, *Cosmopolitan*'s Helen Gurley Brown or *Playboy*'s Hugh Hefner.

There are six basic rules for making editorial material more exciting. Looking for them in observance or the breach may help a little when a publication's excitement is not self-evident.

1. Be concrete rather than abstract.

2. Don't write about things when you can write about people.

3. Do write about individuals rather than groups.

4. Put the reader's personal concerns before the concerns of others.

5. Pay more attention to tomorrow than to yesterday.

6. Remember that one convincing conclusion is more exciting than a million irrelevant facts.

MANAGEMENT REVIEW

Check List for Editorial Evaluation

I. To evaluate editorial focus:

	Tops	Good	Fair	Poor
A. It is easy to figure out the precise reader need the publication is trying to fill.	——	——	——	——
B. Editing decisions are governed by this need rather than by all the interests of the audience.	——	——	——	——
C. The reader-traffic pattern is consistent and clear from issue to issue.	——	——	——	——

II. To evaluate content and selection:

	Tops	Good	Fair	Poor
A. The material is accurate.	——	——	——	——
B. The material is as complete as the type of publication demands.	——	——	——	——
C. Selection of the material makes it as useful as possible.	——	——	——	——
D. Arrangement of the material makes it as useful as possible.	——	——	——	——
E. Intriguing variety is achieved without undermining singleness of purpose.	——	——	——	——
F. The content is expertly adapted to the various ways the publication can be read.	——	——	——	——

III. To evaluate readability:

	Tops	Good	Fair	Poor
A. The writing is clear and easy to understand.	——	——	——	——
B. The writing is purposeful and direct.	——	——	——	——
C. The writing is appropriate for the audience's reading level.	——	——	——	——
D. The writing is pleasant to read, graced with cleverness, imagination and color.	——	——	——	——

IV. To evaluate the graphics:

	Tops	Good	Fair	Poor
A. The graphics add to the clarity of the content.	——	——	——	——
B. The graphics make the publication much easier to use.	——	——	——	——
C. The graphics are appropriate to purpose and audience.	——	——	——	——
D. The graphics are consistent from page to page and from issue to issue.	——	——	——	——

E. Major graphic elements make a
worthwhile contribution to the publication's content.
    —   —   —   —

V. To evaluate the excitement:

	Tops	Good	Fair	Poor
A. Readers look foward to the publication with very evident anticipation.	—	—	—	—
B. Reading the publication increases anticipation for the next issue.	—	—	—	—
C. The strength of the editor's convictions shows through in the publication's editorial.	—	—	—	—
D. Within the limits allowed by the publication's purpose, the six rules for exciting writing are expertly observed:				
1. Be concrete rather than abstract	—	—	—	—
2. Don't write about things when you can write about people.	—	—	—	—
3. Do write about individuals rather than groups.	—	—	—	—
4. Put the reader's personal concerns before the concerns of others.	—	—	—	—
5. Pay more attention to tomorrow than to yesterday.	—	—	—	—
6. Remember: one convincing conclusion is more exciting than a million irrelevant facts.	—	—	—	—

CHAPTER SEVENTEEN

Editorial Research and Development

Featuring an Interview with Gilbert C. Maurer

President of the Hearst Magazine Division

In today's publishing business, very few successful magazines stand alone. *National Geographic* now publishes *National Geographic World* for children and *National Geographic Traveler*. *Penthouse* has *Omni* and *Forum*. Even *The New Yorker*, forever carefully isolated, put its money into other publications: *Horticulture* and *The Cook's Magazine*.

When a magazine's management considers diversification into other publications, the editor, as a key member of the management team, has to be involved. In fact, he or she frequently will be asked to pass on or supervise new magazine ideas. He or she may be the source of the new idea, or be responsible for encouraging, assisting at birth, and nourishing new ideas that originate with members of the staff.

Hence, this chapter is on how new-magazine ideas are discovered and managed. Since Hearst Magazines has developed one of the most successful magazine-development groups in the industry, we interview the man who not only set it up, but has the ultimate responsibility to see it operates properly.

Gil Maurer is president of Hearst Magazines. He began his career in publishing (after graduating from St. Lawrence University in Canton, N.Y.) as an editorial researcher at the old *Look* magazine. Cowles Communications promoted him, first to the sales staff, then to assistant to the advertising director.

Gil spent 19 years with Cowles Communications, and held several important management positions: general manager of the Cowles Book Division, publisher of *Venture*, and president of *Family Circle*. He was also on the board of directors, and a member of the executive committee.

In 1973, Gil left Cowles to become vice president in charge of Hearst's Motor Division. Sixteen months later he was promoted to executive vice president of Hearst Magazines. In December, 1976, he was made president, and a year later, became chief executive as well.

Gil has an M.B.A. from the Harvard Business School, and is a past chairman of the Magazine Publishers Association.

INTERVIEW

Q: Does Hearst have a system to encourage ideas for starting new magazines or repositioning old ones?
A: It's less a system than a management principle that keeps lines of communication as short as possible between creative people, who are most likely to generate ideas, and top management, which has the power to act on them. At Hearst, both to encourage ideas and to maintain editorial quality, every editor reports directly to the president of the magazine division, unlike many other companies where editors are insulated from management by having to report to publishers, who report to a group manager, who reports to the president.

Source for new ideas

Q: Have most of the new-magazine ideas at Hearst come from your editors?
A: Usually. *Colonial Homes*, for instance, was the idea of Dick Beatty when he was editor of the *House Beautiful* special publications. Dick spotted an interesting trend in *House Beautiful*'s mail: people who had conservative tastes in home decoration were hostile to the contemporary, while people who liked the contemporary were not hostile to the traditional. This led to the conclusion that the potential audience for a home magazine devoted to traditional values was much larger than supposed. So Dick and his publisher, Arnold Wasserman, proposed a one-shot newsstand test.

Q: Since Helen Gurley Brown's transformed Cosmopolitan, *has a new-magazine idea come from outside the company?*

A: No, though we get a tremendous number of ideas from outside. I refer all of them to our Magazine Development Group, but most are impractical. Ideas generated by enthusiasts are frequently not well thought out.

Q: How great a problem is fear that an outsider may sue if later you try something similar?

A: The danger exists, but we don't run into it often. There are almost no really new ideas. Most are variants of ideas examined again and again. Ultimately it's not the idea that's important. It's the execution.

Q: Do you always use the person who came up with the idea to develop the idea?

A: No. The person with the idea is not always the best person to execute it. There's enormous difference between having an idea and executing it. We now enter a very important area of judgment. It has to be management's judgment. And it's pure judgment. You can't codify it.

The magazine development group

Q: You mentioned a magazine development group. Does that exist to initiate new ideas?

A: The idea for *Country Living* came out of the group, but its primary job is to appraise new ideas, and explore them if they have merit. It's a relatively small group. John Mack Carter heads it, with Curt Anderson as editor.

Q: Is its staff full-time, or borrowed?

A: Full-time, except for John, who is editor of *Good Housekeeping*. The unit is small, so it won't get involved in more than two projects at a time, or depend on staff talent to develop ideas. We have a strong conviction that each title needs a distinct identity, its own personality. Each established title is operated independently. Each new idea is developed with different freelancers to get varied input. If the same people created everything, there would be serious danger that everything would look alike.

Q: How long has Hearst had this group?

A: Almost four years. *Colonial Homes* was launched before the group was formed. The group's first product was *Country Living*, but it also had a lot of input in redeveloping *Science Digest*.

Q: The group gets involved in repositioning?

A: Radical repositioning is very much like a launch. You are acquiring a franchise. The best opportunities are frequently found in underperforming properties in your own stable. It is easier to reacquire an existing franchise than to create a new one.

Q: Is that the same as repositioning?

A: Repositioning can take many forms—from a subtle change in an advertising approach to a total revamping of a magazine. The reacquisition of an underperforming franchise is a very fundamental form of repositioning. What we did with *Sports Afield* is a good example. The magazine had a 1.6 million circulation, a low cost-per-thousand, with very modest demographics in a field where all the magazines looked alike. We drastically repositioned the magazine, changing it physically, editorially and graphically. We dramatically repriced it, reduced circulation to half a million. Today that former underperformer is one of our most profitable properties.

Q: Do you find that a magazine needs a different kind of management during its launching stage?

A: Absolutely. The whole purpose of our Development Group is to have launch specialists. *Country Living*, for example, was run by the development group for about three years, while it was a one-shot, then a biannual, then a quarterly. It was bimonthly when we took it away from the development group and turned it over to its present management.

Evaluating new ideas

Q: Are there any established norms, such as size, for judging a good magazine idea?
A: Size is vital. A company's most valuable resource is talent, both managerial and creative. This talent has a finite amount of time in which to operate. You can spend the same amount of attention and intelligence on a magazine with a potential of 100,000 circulation and one with a potential of a million. It's a matter of maximizing leverage with the same talent.

Q: But how do you know? When Helen Gurley Brown took over Cosmopolitan, *I'm sure neither she nor Hearst management dreamed it would become what it is today.*
A: At the Henry Johnson Award dinner, recipient Andy Heiskell said something

similar about *Time*. Once created, magazines have a life of their own. We're never sure what they'll become.

Q: That's because magazines are not products. They're services. You're selling expectation.
A: Which means the relationship with your customers is continually evolving. The problem is that magazine franchises evolve at different rates, and the rate depends on both the market and the management.

Fielding new ideas

Q: Do you have a routine procedure for people who come to you with new-magazine ideas?
A: There's no precise procedure. It depends on the nature of the idea, its source, and how it fits Hearst.

Q: Who makes the decision to develop or test the idea?
A: We all work together. It's under John Mack Carter's guidance, but he keeps me intimately informed on what comes in and how the staff reacts. It's consensus management. Obviously I must give the ultimate yes. But before the final decision, a complex sifting process takes place consisting of many mutual conclusions (everybody agrees on the idea's workability or unworkability).

Q: How is new-magazine development budgeted?
A: We have an on-going operating budget for salaries, overhead, spot research and occasional use of freelancers. When we decide to proceed more deeply into a project—put a dummy together or do formal research—a special budget is established.

Testing a new magazine

Q: There are two primary ways to test a new magazine. One is to make a direct-mail offer and count returns. The other is to put the magazine on the newsstands as a one-shot, and gradually increase frequency if it sells. You've used the latter so often, people call it "the Hearst method."
A: Both are appropriate, depending on the market challenge. Each has its own advantages and difficulties. One advantage of a newsstand test is that you must create the product. It tests execution as well as idea.

Q: We made the point earlier that a magazine is a service and not a product. It's not a book. But a one-shot is a book. It can't sell expectation.
A: I don't agree. You're selling an interest area. In fact, an important part of this technique is that your one-shot should not look like a one-shot, not even like an annual. It should look like the first of many to come. For the same reason, I've become convinced that a one-shot is not a real test. You need at least two or three issues. One reason is that, if you publish a recognized one-shot, dealers don't know where to put it on the newsstand, which can vitiate the whole test.

Q: That's an area where the large company has enormous advantage over the small company. You have the clout to get space on the newsstands for a test.
A: I recognize that what works for us, may not work for other publishers. But I lean heavily to the newsstand route because of the heavy expense and slow response of a subscription test. Direct mail requires a huge investment, and you can't judge results until after the billing cycle, often until after the renewal cycle. Besides, in direct mail, the person who designs the mailing piece is not the editor. Too often the copywriter's concept is a good deal different from what the editor delivers.

Q: Isn't that less likely to happen if the magazine is on a clearcut special interest? Some magazines are recognized as wanted before people read them; others have to be sampled before people know they want them.
A: If Gillette had sold his new safety razor by direct mail, he would have failed. He had created something people didn't know they wanted until they used it. On the other hand, you can't introduce a magazine on the newsstands. When a magazine appeals to a very specialized interest, direct mail may be the only way.

Q: Are your newsstand tests national or regional?
A: In between. We distribute all over the country but not to every wholesaler. The objective is to conduct a national test with minimum investment. Then you study the returns to see not just how many copies were sold, but where they were sold. Distribution patterns and placement tend to be irregular. That's another reason I'm convinced you need several issues.

Terminating new-product status

Q: When is the magazine no longer in test? When you take it away from the development group?
A: It's certainly before we take it away from the development group. It's really when we decide that we can make a long-term commitment to publishing it.

Q: But when is it moved from the development group?
A: When development is over. The product mix is set, distribution and sales patterns established.

Q: Do most of the people whom the development group hired to execute the magazine, stay with it?
A: Of course. The staff is in place and the development group is satisfied that the staff can run it. So we set it up as one of our regular magazines.

ANALYSIS

Are Management and Innovation Incompatible?

In publishing, as in every business, the bigger the organization, the more resistant it is to change. The National Science Foundation did a study over four years ago which concluded that, per dollar invested, R&D in small companies produced 24 innovations for every one produced in large companies.

Two years later, Jim Kobak's study of consumer-magazine launches (FOLIO:, February 1982) concluded that "existing publishers, rather than dominating the new-magazine scene, are often quite conservative in their approach to new ventures," while "individuals without previous experience in the field start more magazines than any other group." More than 55% of Kobak's list of 239 U.S. magazine launches were under the guidance of entrepreneurs, i.e., outside an existing company.

The significance of the above studies goes beyond new-magazine development. If corporate management tends to stifle innovation in creating new products, chances are it is also smothering innovation in other areas.

Since every innovation begins with an idea, it is vital to examine what management does, if anything, to encourage new ideas. Management's goal should be to rid itself of the three monkeys on its back: Hear No Ideas, See No Ideas, and Speak No Ideas.

Listening to new ideas

Management's first responsibility is to listen. Thus Gil Maurer's dictum at Hearst: short and direct lines of communication between editors and management. Gralla Publishing uses a similar system with all editors reporting directly to executive vice president Milt Gralla or editorial director Howard Rauch.

Listening involves more than being available. In fact, the manager who listens to everyone may be hearing no one. It is difficult to pay attention to more than one thing at a time, and shorter lines of communication can result in too many lines. One solution is a screening mechanism, something like Hearst's Magazine Development Group. At Hearst, the same group screens and develops ideas. This may not be the wisest course, since a person committed to developing one new idea is least likely to recognize the potential of another.

This is especially true if the new idea from outside in any way competes with an idea from inside the company. Hearst's last "outside" new magazine idea was Helen Gurley Brown's *Cosmopolitan*, and one wonders what chance that would have had if some insider had had another idea for saving the dying magazine.

Although we know of no company with such a committee, we strongly suggest that publishers who want to encourage innovation set up the screening unit separate from the development group. Ideas should be presented to them anonymously, in writing. And committee members should be disqualified whenever their areas of responsiblity may conflict with the new idea.

Recognizing innovators

As important as listening to new ideas is the ability to see, to recognize sources of—and obstacles to—new ideas. Innovation begins long before an idea is ready to be heard, or screened. Management must recognize latent entrepreneurs, creative innovators. Hearst's *Cosmopolitan* coup resulted not from accepting Helen Gurley Brown's idea (she wanted to start a magazine), but in recognizing her potential.

There is no foolproof way to recognize an innovator, but there are basic guidelines:

1. Innovators are born, not made. You cannot create an innovator by instruction or appointment. Innovators assign themselves.

2. Innovators are more interested in creation than compensation. This is why then tend to be misfits in large companies. They prefer the detour of new-product development to steady progressions up the promotion ladder, a detour that can be a short-cut to success—or a blind alley.

3. Innovators are more concerned with making an idea work than with getting credit for it. This is the key in distinguishing the real innovator from self-promoters and creative exhibitionists.

4. Innovators will gamble with their careers, but not with their ideas. The same entrepreneur who has taken a major career risk to pursue an idea, takes only the most calculated and insured risks in implementing the idea.

5. Innovators are confident but cautious. They do not need management for support or assurance, but appreciate management for advice and assistance.

Encouraging innovation

Finally, management must put its mouth where its ears and eyes are, remembering that management's actions speak louder than its words. A major value of the magazine development groups at companies like Hearst and Time Inc. is that they tell everyone that management is serious about fostering innovation.

Establishing encouragement of innovation as part of a company's corporate culture is the most difficult task of all. On one level it can be done by talk. When the chief executive summarizes that year's progress, how much attention is given to innovation? Who are the company heroes? Compensation may not be a primary goal of the true innovator, but compensation is a primary tool in establishing a corporate culture's value system.

In American business today, corporate progress and success is measured in terms of growth. Successful chief executives have to talk growth, think growth, plan for growth. A strong determinant of corporate culture is what management indicates is the preferred route to growth. It can be sales and profits. It can be mergers and acquisitions. Or it can be innovation.

The initial go/no-go judgment

Once a new idea is found, management must decide whether to act on it. It is possible for a chief executive to delegate the decision process to others, but not the ultimate responsibility. Gil Maurer leans heavily on Hearst's Magazine Development Group. Bob Guccione at *Penthouse* and Jann Wenner at Straight Arrow Publishing rely largely on their instincts.

The decision as to whether to pursue a good idea requires positive answers to four questions:

1. Does it fit the company? Wonderful ideas die quickly in the wrong environment (e.g., *Human Behavior* at Harcourt Brace Jovanovich, *Next* at Medical Economics). A company can be wrong for a new idea due to lack of resources, opposition of key personnel, inexperience with this type of publishing, or direct competition with an in-house property. A major danger sign: total lack of synergism with anything the company is already doing.

2. Does it have real potential? This is a very difficult question to answer, one that should be made on the basis of probability. A chief executive who insists on guarantees will kill every new idea.

3. Does the required investment make sense at this time? Management must evaluate the investment from two sides: the needs of the new idea, and the cash and/or credit position of the company. The most common error is too ready acceptance of the innovator's estimate of development costs.

4. Is the potential return worth the investment risk? Innovation-oriented chief executives have a knack of recognizing when the odds are right.

5. Does the new idea come with an implementer or implementing team? A first-rate entrepreneur can turn a second-rate idea into a success (Owen Lipstein with *American Health*), while a second-rate entrepreneur will doom a first-rate idea.

Obtaining staff approval

No matter how a company is organized for developing new products, an innovation will wither and die if there are key executives, or even proximate second-echelon people, who consciously or subconsciously want it to fail. Management must transmit its enthusiasm.

Gil Maurer's "consensus management" is a way of assuring staff approval before moving ahead with a new idea. Something similar is done at Conde Nast, although Si Newhouse and Alexander Liberman take more of an authoritarian position than Maurer.

Deciding whom to put in charge

Once the corporate staff is sold on pursuing the new idea, the chief executive is ready to formally install the idea's implementer. Most experts in the development of new products suggest that responsibility for the project in its developmental stage be given to an independent full-time manager, and that the manager, as we said earlier, be the innovator/entrepreneurial type.

How safe is it to allow a group of innovation-minded executives to start a new publication while continuing with their old jobs, as Fairchild did with *Sportstyle* and *"M"*? It works only if there is extensive synergism between their old duties and their new operation. This usually means that the innovation is a repositioning of the old product. *"M"* is definitely a repositioning of *Men's Wear*, which it will replace.

How important is it to choose an idea's originator as the idea's implementer? It can be convenient, but it is not important. Walter Annenberg had the idea for *Seventeen*. His sister, Enid Haupt, was the implementer. As Gil says, "there are almost no really new ideas. Ultimately it's not the idea that's important. It's the execution." Insistence that an idea is 100% your own is sheer vanity. Most ideas are conscious or subconscious borrowings or embellishments of other ideas. The most original ideas are constructs, different but dependent on ideas of others. What is important is that the implementer be an innovator enthused with the idea.

Testing the new idea

Tests of new ideas and/or publications fall into two classes: methodology tests and feasibility tests. Most methodology tests, like the mailing-piece test Rapp & Collins did for *Vanity Fair* in December of 1981, should be studied by the implementer and ignored by top management.

The rare case of a test to determine the feasibility or market potential of a new product is different. Such a test is not only of interest to management, but the chief executive and the implementer should agree beforehand 1) how the test is to determine the viability of the innovation, and 2) the precise point at which the results of the test will prove the idea will not work.

The most common method for such a go/no-go test is a direct mail subscription solicitation to a list of prime prospects. Other ways of testing viability range from selling a one-shot on representative newsstands (Hearst's *Colonial Homes*) to publishing a prototype in another magazine (*Ms.* in *New York*).

It is a serious mistake to adopt a standard testing procedure for every new idea. There are many publication ideas that cannot be fairly tested except by publishing. *People Weekly* was the first magazine idea Time Inc. ever tested. A go/no-go test makes sense only when there is an area of serious doubt which can be settled by a test. When Chuck Tannen proposed a quarterly on running election campaigns, his backers agreed to put up money for a mailing to test the idea. When response indicated insufficient interest, everyone, including Tannen, agreed the no-go point had been reached.

Establishing a budget

Hearst has two magazine-development budgets: an annual budget for the routine operation of the magazine development group, and an ad hoc budget for individual projects. It is the ad hoc budget that concerns us.

Since there is no prior budget, ad hoc budgets must be determined by the task method, but the big difference from an annual budget is that innovation budgets should be geared not to the calendar, but to project goals. Thus if the objective is to test the market before going ahead, a single budget should be created to cover the test. If the budget is for launching the publication, it should cover whatever is needed to reach a specific goal, whether in circulation, advertising, or both.

MANAGEMENT REVIEW

Check List for Encouraging Innovation

I. To evaluate management policy on innovation:
   A. Listening to new ideas.

	Yes	No
1. Are communication lines to creative people short enough for direct access?	___	___

2. Are communication lines few enough to give adequate attention? ___ ___

3. If there is a screening mechanism, is its objectivity protected by:

   a) Anonymity in new proposals (so that outside ideas are on same footing as those of insiders)? ___ ___

   b) A system to exclude participation of executives with a conflict of interest? ___ ___

B. Recognizing innovators.

	Yes	No
1. Is this person a self-assigner?	___	___
2. Is this person more interested in creation than compensation?	___	___
3. Is this person more concerned with making the idea work than with getting credit for it?	___	___
4. Will this person gamble with his or her career, but not with the idea?	___	___
5. Is this person confident enough not to need management support, but cautious enough to listen to management advice?	___	___

C. Fostering innovation in corporate culture.

	Yes	No
1. Does innovation get prime attention in management pronouncements?	___	___
2. Does compensation for innovators establish their importance?	___	___
3. Is innovation primary in corporate plans for growth?	___	___
4. Is there anything in corporate or departmental structure to indicate management's desire for innovation?	___	___

II. To evaluate the management of specific new ideas:

A. Deciding whether to develop a new idea.

	Yes	No
1. Does it fit the company?	___	___
2. Does it have real potential?	___	___
3. Does the required investment make sense at this time?	___	___
4. Is the potential return worth the investment risk?	___	___
5. Is there an enthusiastic and truly innovative implementer available to develop the idea?	___	___

B. Obtaining staff approval.

	Yes	No
1. Is there a management mechanism to assure that the company will not try to develop ideas without staff acceptance?	___	___
2. Has everyone who is consciously or unconsciously opposed to the idea been converted or removed?	___	___

C. Determining whom to put in charge.

	Yes	No
1. Is he or she a true entrepreneurial type?	___	___
2. Is he or she enthusiastic about the idea?	___	___
3. Will he or she be sufficiently independent and free of other responsibilities to give the project full attention?	___	___
4. If he or she is to retain other responsibilities, is there sufficient synergism to warrant the division of attention?	___	___

D. Testing the new idea.

	Yes	No
1. Is it a genuine feasibility test?	___	___
2. Do management and implementer agree on:		
a) How the test will determine the new idea's viability?	___	___
b) The precise point at which results prove the idea is or is not viable?	___	___

E. Establishing a budget.

	Yes	No
1. Is it an ad hoc, task-method budget?	___	___
2. Is it geared to project goals rather than the calendar?	___	___

CHAPTER EIGHTEEN

Awards, Competitions and Editorial Management

Featuring an Interview with Thomas H. King

President of the American Business Press

Among the outside helps editors can use to encourage excellence are editorial awards. Smart editors do not allow editorial awards to interfere with their own judgment as to what is good and what is not. But smart editors also realize that awards can set standards in their industry, and—more important— can be used as management tools to get better performance from their staffs.

To find an expert to talk about awards, we decided to select a single competition and interview the chief executive responsible for its administration. The Jesse H. Neal Editors Awards, administered by the American Business Press, seemed to be the awards competition with typical, if not the greatest, impact on the magazine business. Hence Tom King, president of the American Business Press, was the logical choice for this interview.

Tom began his publishing career in 1956, as an advertising-sales trainee in McGraw-Hill Publications' Boston office. Two years later he was appointed district manager for the company's *American Machinist*. In 1967, he became that magazine's advertising sales manager.

In 1971, Tom moved to Morgan-Grampian, which had purchased several McGraw-Hill publications and recruited a number of McGraw-Hill people.

In 1974, McGraw-Hill hired him back as advertising sales manager for *Chemical Engineering*. Within two years he was named associate publisher of *Aviation Week*. From then on promotion was rapid: 1977, publisher of *Fleet Owner* and *National Petroleum News*; 1978, vice president for manufacturing; 1979, group vice president.

In 1981, ABP president Charlie Mill announced his retirement. Several ABP members recommended Tom as Charlie's replacement. Paul McPherson, then McGraw-Hill Publications president and Tom's boss, was head of the search committee, but Tom talked to each of the members of the search committee before he accepted their offer and signed on as ABP's new president.

Although the Neal Awards are the focus of this interview, they are not the subject of this chapter. We are interested in them merely as a typical example of magazine awards and their significance in editorial management.

INTERVIEW

Q: What's the principal benefit magazines get from winning something like a Neal Award? Publicity?
A: There is some publicity. The announcement of the winners is always covered in the trade press, and in many cases the winners get local newspaper coverage as well. But the publicity is not that significant. The principal benefit of the Neal Awards is that they give editors something to strive for, it encourages editors and publishers to raise their standards of excellence.

Q: Does winning an award sell any advertising?
A: I've sold advertising for magazines that had won Neal awards, and we promoted our winning extensively. But it's hard to say that there were any advertising sales as a direct result. It's one of the many things you use, a way of pointing out that you have an outstanding editorial product. More important than the effect on the advertiser is the effect on the staff. Winning an award is a great morale booster—for everyone, sales and circulation people as well as editors.

Q: Do other magazines study the winners, as examples of excellence?
A: People do come to the ABP office to study the winner's entries, presumably to improve their own entries. And a lot of publishers study our *Editorial Excellence* booklets. These are a relatively recent ABP embellishment on the Neal Awards. The booklet describes each winning entry and adds a brief commentary on its impact on the publication's readers.

Is the cost worth it?

Q: I've heard a lot of gripes about awards. Let's look at a few. Does anyone complain about the cost? Even ABP members have to pay $65 for each Neal Award entry, and non-members pay $150. If you have several entries it can add up.

A: I'm not aware of many complaints. A few non-member companies have grumbled about having to pay more than twice as much as ABP members, but they enter anyway. We don't make money on the awards. The entry fees don't even cover the expenses involved.

Q: But fees aren't the important cost. A publisher has to invest a good deal of time, and editorial attention, to selecting and preparing an entry. Is that a common reason for not entering?

A: It's hard to say. People seldom volunteer why they are not entering. Most of the entries, in a business accustomed to deadlines, arrive at the last minute. It's unnerving until you get used to it. About 85% of the entries don't arrive until three or four days before deadline, and then the phones are constantly ringing with editors and publishers asking for extensions we can't allow.

Q: I suppose it's the usual thing: the publishers tells the editors to enter the competition but don't give them any extra help or time for the work involved.

A: Some publishers and editors are very organized. They have planning sessions long in advance. They may even have a Neal Award in mind before the feature is assigned. But the majority seem to wait until the deadline approaches and then go back over the past year to see what they can enter.

Is it a distraction?

Q: Is there a danger that editors will start editing for awards rather than for their readers?

A: That's always a danger, but the great majority of editors think of readers first, and then only, "If I go the extra mile, make this extra special, maybe I can win an award with it."

Q: Editors aren't going to admit, even to themselves, that they are editing for awards rather than for their readers.

A: Subconsciously, it may exist in some cases.

Q: This year four of the six Neal awards in the $2 million or less classification went to advertising trade publications (three to Magazine Age, *one to* Industrial

Marketing). I don't say they weren't deserved. But doesn't it indicate that entries on topics of interest to the judges have a better chance than entries from highly specialized publications—that editing for the judges does require choices different than editing for readers?

A: Very specialized magazines have always won awards. Still the difficulty of selecting judges to compare a large number of entries from widely different fields has worried the ABP editorial committee. We've been looking for a way to modify the judging, which hasn't changed much in 30 years. And we think we've found it. Next year it will be done on two tiers. The first will be an initial screening by experienced business press editors (taking care, of course, that no editor judges his own or a competitor's entry.) The second will be selected by the screening committee. The idea is to reduce the workload of the judges, while making certain that nothing can win which has not first won peer respect.

Can it hurt morale?

Q: If winning is great for staff morale, won't losing, especially when a magazine never seems to win, hurt staff morale? Maybe some publishers shouldn't even enter.
A: In our business everyone has to get used to rejection. For the Neal Awards there are 500 to 600 entries and, except for an occasional tie, only 15 winners and some 20 or so runners-up. It's very prestigious to win, but it shouldn't be surprising or discouraging when you don't.

Q: What about internal contention? Even the by-lines on an entry can cause jealousy and discontent among staffers who were left out.
A: Each entry is allowed six names as co-authors, anyone who contributed, except the publisher. The average number of by-lines on submissions is close to five. We do get phone calls from winners asking us to drop or add names. Someone left the company, or someone was overlooked.

Q: So it does cause problems.
A: Sometimes, and each year we emphasize that chief editors make certain that by-lines are complete and accurate before they are submitted.

Q: Would you advise publishers to put down as many names as possible? Or is it safer to just list the primary author?
A: From a morale standpoint, it's usually better to put six names on every entry if you can legitimately document involvement. Then, if you win, six people get medallions and six people enjoy the publicity involved. Remember the Neal Awards

are to individuals, not to magazines. It's not correct to say *Magazine Age* got three awards. The winners were editor Wally Wood, senior editor Maureen McFadden and three contributing columnists.

Q: Then there's the decision of whose articles to submit. Do magazines enter a lot of articles by freelancers, for instance, or do editors prefer to submit their own work?
A: We've never counted them, but I don't think many winners have been freelancers. That could be because today most trade press material is staff written. My experience has been that most editors are very generous in listing contributors, often excluding themselves so they can include someone else.

Internal awards

Q: Do many magazines reward their winners?
A: We have heard of companies giving staffers a cash bonus or a special trip, if they win.

Q: Wouldn't it make more sense to reward the people whose work you submit, whether they win or not?
A: The submission itself is an award, recognition that the individual contributed the best work of the year. Further reward is nice but not always necessary for morale. People don't live on bread alone.

Q: Do you think it's a good idea for publishers to have their own intra-company or intra-publication competitions with their own internal awards? Gralla Publications, for instance, gives monthly editorial awards.
A: Quite a few publishers have such awards. They're morale builders and help to keep standards high. When I worked at McGraw-Hill's *Chemical Engineering*, they had three annual editorial awards for their staff of 28 editors. The editor in chief and managing editor were the judges.

Q: Were there any company-wide editorial awards at McGraw-Hill Publications?
A: None that I was aware of.

Q: Just how important should a publisher consider awards? How much management attention and company resources should they invest in participating in awards competitions?
A: Each publisher has to decide according to the needs of the publication. The Neal Awards are very prestigious. It's worth entering just to put the editorial

staff on notice that management wants a top quality product, that management considers editorial an extremely important part of the business.

Q: Publishers can do that even better by paying editors more.
A: Of course. That's primary. But everything that contributes to improving quality is worthwhile, a management tool that should be used. A competition like the Neal Awards can really contribute to editorial performance. When editors fail to win it becomes a reason to try harder and do better. When they do win, they're anxious to surpass their last effort and become multiple winners.

ANALYSIS

Awards as a Management Tool

It is foolhardy to pretend awards are meaningless in our business. They do exist. They help set standards of performance for the industry. Hence every significant awards competition forces each publisher to answer three questions:

1. Can this competition help our publication and, if so, how can we maximize the benefits?

2. Should we enter this competition?

3. Can we and should we get involved in defining and administering this particular award competition?

Smart publishers will not ignore these questions. The problem may seem far down on the list of management priorities, but it is still a real problem and, as such, it deserves a real answer. When the answer is "yes," smart publishers will follow through all the way. It is frequently much more damaging to embark on a course half-heartedly or with insufficient resources than not to proceed at all.

Influencing the administration of awards

A publication's management can get involved in a variety of award administration concerns ranging from voting on setting up the award, to contributing to its financing, to accepting membership on an administrative committee or serving as judge.

Unless publishers restrict their contribution to personal time and resources, they have the obligation to base involvement on how much it directly or indirectly benefits their company. Before getting involved, a publisher should ask the following questions: Will the time and effort required be worth the possible benefit? Am I volunteering my services to help my company or to feed my vanity? Will my impact on the competition make a difference, and will that difference be worth the cost—to my company, my magazine?

Although the questions are simple, the answers can be complex. And a too literal interpretation of what benefits one's company can be very shortsighted, forgetting that contributions to the overall benefit of an industry eventually benefit each member company. There is also little doubt that most award programs could be improved and do a great deal more for their industries, if half the energy devoted to negative criticism was transferred to positive thinking and constructive cooperation.

To enter or not to enter

Whether or not a magazine should enter an awards competition depends on four factors:

1. The awards should honor an achievement that means something to the publication. Even though a trade magazine may publish occasional cartoons to lighten up the text or coax through-the-book readership, it would make little sense to compete for funniest cartoon published this year, unless, of course, the editor felt there was a need for more cartoons and entering the competition would be a relatively inexpensive way to attract more cartoonists.

2. The awards are bestowed on the basis of standards similar to the publication's own. Here the point is not that entries in a contest having different standards may have less chance of winning, but that to enter would confuse the staff by introducing objectives different from those set by management. Catalog-like publications, such as *Potentials In Marketing*, have good reason not to compete for a Neal Award. In fact, it is likely that many news-oriented newspaper-type publications, e.g., *M.I.S. Week*, feel the same way.

3. The publication has a chance of winning. Publishers who are certain their entries will not even win an honorable mention are foolish to enter. This is not as self-serving as it sounds. Entering costs time and money. Losing is no help to morale. And, unlike marathons, there is no benefit in running unless there is a chance of winning.

There is a benefit in trying to produce award-quality editorial during the year, but that effect can be achieved without entering products that did not make the grade. In practice there should be two decisions on entry: one should be made early in the year for purposes of planning, and another when management decides what, if anything, should be entered.

4. The benefits of winning an award must be worth the cost of entering the competition. Since entering an award competition is a business tool, it must be cost-effective. Admittedly, it involves a gamble. No one can be certain of winning. But risk is part of any business investment. Hence cost should be equal to or less than the value of possible benefits divided by the likelihood of losing.

Although it is not ideal that awards be limited only to those who are willing to pay, entry fees have become a widely accepted practice. Few companies will consider such fees a major expense, but they are a good place to start in figuring costs, adding to them the expense of preparing and delivering the entries.

Time is a much more important cost. A simple way to figure time costs is to multiply man-hours spent in selecting and preparing entries by the per-hour salaries of the individuals concerned. A more accurate, though more difficult way, is to calculate the cost in terms of what the individuals would have done for the publication if they did not have to devote time to selecting and preparing the entries.

It is even more difficult to calculate the costs of attention. How much does participation in an awards competition distract employees from their primary work? It is impossible to give a specific dollar value to attention, especially among executives and creative personnel. In fact, one cannot even be certain when it is fully present, certainly not in others, and perhaps not even in oneself. Yet it is something that a good management person has to gauge constantly.

Attention is like water in an irrigation system. A farmer cannot create water or even control how much nature provides. Yet he must manage it. He does so by directing its flow, seeing it is not wasted, keeping it from being diverted into secondary channels when it is needed elsewhere. In brief, he concentrates more on terrain, conduits and leaks, than on the water itself.

Hence the cost of attention should be measured in how much participation in the competition interferes or diverts attention, not in dollars or time. Publishing companies, particularly editorial and sales departments, have never been amenable to time and motion studies. Periodical publishing is governed by goals and rhythms. It is the manager's job to measure the cost of entering contests by the extent to which it diverts from the goals and interrupts the rhythms.

Much depends on the personalities of the people involved. A major distraction for one person may hardly affect another. *RN* is a regular contender for the Neal awards and its editor, Dave Sifton, was a 1983 winner. Yet Dave can say, "I simply don't think about prizes while we develop articles."

The value of winning

As Tom King points out, the principal value of awards lies not in publicity but in giving editors "something to strive for," encouraging "editors and publishers to raise their standards of excellence."

Therefore it is important to ask just how much of a standard of excellence a particular competition will raise. How much will winning mean to the employees? How much will trying to win mean?

The direct publicity value is not hard to evaluate, but there is an indirect value often overlooked. Award competitions, if they are widely accepted, force everybody in the industry to raise their standards and compete on a level of worth. Since high standards are publicly recognized—and, in a sense, publicly established, it becomes more difficult for other publications to cut corners, publish garbage, and tell the advertisers and readers that is all that is necessary. In a word, award competitions force an industry's publications to fight on more equal terms.

On the other hand, the administrative and promotional skills of the group sponsoring an award can make a great deal of difference in the award's value to the winners. An award that earns poor support from its industry or attracts proportionately few entries is usually not worth the cost of entering.

Maximizing the benefits of participation

Once the decision to enter a competition is made, the smart publisher does everything possible to do it right.

1. Plan far enough ahead. Participation should be incorporated into a publication's planning at least a year ahead—not so much to avoid the confusion and carelessness of a last-minute rush, but to maximize the morale effect. If the award is worth striving for, the sooner the staff starts striving the better.

2. Put someone in charge. An executive should be assigned to prepare for and administer the publication's participation in the competition. This need not be (probably should not be) the publisher or editor in chief. The function of the awards-participation administrator is something like that of a brand manager in a package-goods company. Its purpose is to focus concern in one person, to have someone who will remind, encourage, prod, see that this concern is not slighted or overlooked.

3. Assign time (and personnel) to do the work involved. One reason for all the last-minute entries mentioned by Tom King is that too few publications provide time and talent to do the job. There are enough emergencies in publishing without creating another unnecessarily. Personnel should also be given an opportunity to study previous winners. One of the things that helped *Word Processing & Information Systems* editor Willoughby Ann Walshe win a Neal award was that her publisher allowed her to attend the awards ceremonies the previous year, where she read and was inspired by the winners.*

4. Integrate participation with internal incentives. Since the principal purpose of awards participation is morale building, participation should be coordinated with a publication's internal morale-building programs. It would be self-defeating for magazines like *Sales & Marketing Management* or companies like Billboard Publications and Gralla Publications not to choose their Neal Awards entries from the articles that win their monthly editorial awards.

5. Insulate participation against morale short circuits. Tom King points out that selecting entries and authors can cause staff friction. A primary step in preparing for a future competition is to set clearcut rules for authorship long before entries are considered, and to stick by them when the entries are chosen. It is also important to give the duty of selecting the entries to an individual or committee that is accepted by all as impartial.

The same care and objectivity should be taken in choosing entries as is taken in selecting internal awards. Billboard's in-house winners are chosen by a committee consisting of the circulation director and two editors. CBS selected an outside panel of judges for its internal awards for excellence in graphic design, innovative ideas and staff writing. At Gralla, the selection of monthly winners among second-echelon editors (top editors are not eligible) is made by Milton

---

* Someone should publish the complete text of all the Neal Awards winners in book form. Even publishers who do not compete should be interested in buying copies—for their staffs and for journalism school libraries. ABP publishes a booklet listing each winner and its authors with a brief description of the winning entry's impact, but that is small help as a guide to excellence.

Gralla and Howard Rauch, the two men with corporate responsibility for editorial quality.

6. Have a publicity strategy in place before winning. No sane public relations executive or department will spend a lot of time on a campaign about an award not yet won. But a lot of time is not necessary to be ready when the good news comes. If public relations people were consulted on the initial decision to enter the competition, they have already made the basic decisions on what can be done if the publication is a winner.

MANAGEMENT REVIEW

Check List for Entering an Awards Competition

I. **Involvement of yourself or other members of your staff in the definition and administration of an awards competition makes sense only if all of the following conditions are present:**
    _____ A. The existence of the awards and the way the competition is conducted must be significant to the welfare of your publication.
    _____ B. Your involvement must be effective enough to help your publication.
    _____ C. The benefit to your publication of your getting involved in the definition and administration of the competition must be worth the required investment:
    _____1. In time.
    _____2. In expense.
    _____3. In attention.

Be sure that the reasons for your answers consider indirect long-run, industry-wide benefits as well as more immediate direct benefits to your publication or company.

II. **Your publication should enter the competition for a particular award only if all of the following conditions are present:**
    _____ A. The award should honor an achievement that is significant to your publication.
    _____ B. The standards used to judge the awards should be similar to the standards your publication uses to judge excellence.

____ C. The benefits of participation in the awards competition must be worth the cost.
    1. Evaluate benefits of participating in terms of:
        a) Improvement in staff morale.
        b) Improvement in staff performance.
    2. Evaluate benefits of winning in terms of:
        a) Impact on staff morale.
        b) Publicity.
        c) Usefulness for circulation promotion.
        d) Usefulness for advertising promotion.
    3. Discount value of (b) by possibility of not winning.
    4. Calculate cost of participation in terms of:
        a) Time.
        b) Expense and entry fee.
        c) Attention.
____ D. Your entries must have a chance of winning.

The judgment should be made before plans are set to enter the competition, and reviewed when management has the publication's possible entries in hand.

III. If you decide to enter a specific award competition, make sure that you do all of the following:
____ A. Start planning for the competition far enough ahead.
____ B. Put someone in charge.
____ C. Assign time and personnel to do the work involved.
____ D. Integrate participation with your company's internal incentive programs.
____ E. Insulate participation against morale short circuits.
____ F. Have a publicity strategy in place before your publication or staffers win.

PART FIVE

Change: Editorial Threat or Challenge?

It has been said that magazine publishing is changing faster today than in any period since the invention of the printing press. But magazines have always changed editorially. In fact, no function of magazine editing is more fundamental than the management of change.

Change can destroy an editor, but it can also become the occasion for greatness. Hence, like most other unavoidable perils, it is viewed by the weak as a disaster, by the strong as an opportunity.

In this section we look at three basic forms of change that editors have always had to face, and one that is new and special.

We first study the changing marketplace—the reason and inspiration for all changes made by editors. In Chapter 19 we interview Bob Anderson, editor in chief of *Runner's World*, on "The Editor's Response to Changing Markets," and discover how an editor can not only survive, but thrive, when his magazine is serving a rapidly expanding market.

In Chapter 20 we face the opposite circumstance. What do you do when your market changes so radically that your magazine loses its reason for being? You decide "How to Reposition Your Publication Editorially." Our authority is Helen Gurley Brown who did just that at *Cosmopolitan*.

But all change need not be drastic. What if you want to keep the same fundamental position, but introduce changes to improve your magazine? In Chapter 21, we talk with publisher Bob Potts about "How to Introduce Editorial Changes," and learn how he and his editor went about changing *Dun's Review* into *Dun's Business Month*.

Finally, in Chapter 22, we interview the president of McGraw-Hill Publications, Paul McPherson, on the meaning and significance of the so-called wave of the future: Database Publishing. Can we determine precisely "How an Editor Should Think about Database Publishing"? We can and do.

CHAPTER NINETEEN

The Editor's Response to Changing Markets

Featuring an Interview with Bob Anderson

Publisher and Editor in Chief of Runner's World

The broadest and least controllable change that can affect a magazine is change in its market, primarily its reader market, secondarily its advertiser market (and one seldom changes without bringing about changes in the other). If they cannot recognize and keep up with the changes in the marketplace, editors—and their magazines—quickly become obsolete.

Since no market ever remains static, in theory almost any good editor would have qualified for an interview on changing markets. But we wanted one who had navigated major changes—particularly the positive change of rapid growth. We found our expert in a relatively young man who had recognized a wave when it was only a ripple and has ridden it to success.

Bob Anderson launched *Runner's World* in 1966, when he was 17 years old and still in high school. He graduated in the publication's first year and went on to Kansas State University. He not only attended classes and did his homework, but he joined the university's cross-country running team. In the time that was left (every waking moment of it) he worked at publishing his magazine.

As the magazine grew, Bob graduated from college, married, started a family, moved to California, became a skier, trained for and ran in ten marathons.

He founded National Running Week and the Corporate Cup Association (which promotes the Corporate Cup Relays), was chosen one of the U.S. Jaycees' "Ten Outstanding Young Men," and was named to the board of directors of the American Federation for Volunteerism.

While all this was going on, not necessarily in the order given, Bob was running his magazine company, watching as the market he had chosen grew and blossomed, and—most important of all—changing and developing his publishing venture to keep one step ahead of what was happening. So much was he in tune with the market that it was frequently very difficult to distinguish between the changes the market made in *Runner's World* and the changes *Runner's World* made in the market.

In its first year, *Runner's World* had two issues and a circulation of 365. Its entire revenue, including mail-order sales, was $800. When this interview was conducted, *Runner's World* was published 13 times a year and its circulation was more than a thousand times larger. It grossed over $7 million from subscriptions and single-copy sales, more than $4 million from advertising, and about $4 million from mail-order. The 13 issues included the *Runner's World Annual* published each January, and the mail-order included a book-publishing division with approximately 150 titles.

Shortly before this book went to press, Bob sold his magazine to Rodale Press, the publishers of *Prevention, Organic Gardening* and *New Shelter*.

INTERVIEW

Q: When you launched Runner's World, *in 1966, running was not a big thing. How did you see the market?*
A: I knew there were people interested in running, people out of school who participated in marathons, or ran to keep in shape. Actually, in 1966, there were some 8.5 million people interested in running, though, at that time, I did not realize there were that many.

Q: What kind of an advertising market did you see for such a magazine?
A: None at all. I was 17. I was a member of my school's cross-country team. I enjoyed running and figured a magazine on running was a good idea. I had no idea of making a lot of money, striking the big time.

Q: What kind of circulation did you start with?
A: I closed the first year with 365 paid subscribers. I got those by writing to track coaches and running clubs. It took five years to reach 10,000.

Q: When did you break even?

A: The very first year, with a profit of $15. From the very beginning, I figured that if I spent $100, I had better have $100 coming in. Since our subscription price was $1, and I sold only $25 worth of advertising that year, I had to get the money from someplace else. So I began a mail-order business with several running-related items. One was a stop watch.

Q: And you made money to pay the bills?

A: Between mail-order sales and subscriptions I managed to get $800 in revenue from the 365 subscribers. That covered my expenses. Remember, this was all done out of my home. The publication had no rent, no utility or phone bills. The only expenses were printing and postage. *Runner's World* operated in the black from its second issue.

Q: Your investment was your work.

A: I published two issues the first year and put in about 38 hours a week—and went to school full time. I graduated from high school in June of that year, and started college in September. By the second year, with four issues, I was working 60 hours a week—and still going to college full time.

Growing with the market

Q: Why and when did Runner's World *become a monthly?*

A: I felt from the beginning that I had to be in touch with my readers more often. In the third year we went to six issues and, in 1972, monthly. The greater our frequency, the easier it was to obtain and sustain circulation. The big step was going bimonthly.

Q: How much of the growth was due to the fact that the market was expanding, that more people were taking up running?

A: That's hard to say. The market was growing, but the magazine influenced that growth. *Runner's World* had a marked influence on the running scene. It was the first publication to advocate that women be allowed to compete in races over 880 yards, that men over 40 could be marathoners. We sold the concept that finishing a marathon was an end in itself, that coming in first was not the only goal.

Q: You were in the right place at the right time. Can you really say you made the wave rather than rode it?

A: We didn't make the wave, but we helped to shape it and make it as high as it became. I honestly feel that if it were not for *Runner's World* there would not now be close to 35 million joggers in this country. The magazine's impact has been recognized by objective outsiders. In 1977, the President's Council on Physical Fitness & Sports bestowed its annual service award on *Runner's World*, the only time it has ever been given to a publication.

Q: As the sport expanded, did you change your methods of circulation promotion?
A: Our 365 original subscribers were divided evenly between track coaches, athletes in training, and people who participated in marathons without being formal competitors. We recognized the importance of the last class and went after them almost from the beginning.

Q: With advertising or direct mail?
A: Neither. I've tried ads and they didn't work. We never did large-scale direct mail, for there weren't enough good lists. Initially, we depended on coaches, since they knew the people who ran. Some of them even sent us lists. Almost all our direct mail was directed at our subscribers. We hit them continually, not only for mail-order sales and our other magazines, but to get them to tell friends and fellow runners about *Runner's World*.

Q: What about single-copy?
A: I tried to get onto newsstands as early as I could. But I had to depend on arrangements with local distributors. It wasn't until 1977 that I was able to convince a national distributor to handle the magazine.

Managing growth problems

Q: In your growth period, what were some of the rough spots and how did you negotiate them?
A: The first big hurdle is realizing that you can't do everything yourself. *Runner's World* was growing and I was editor, publisher, ad salesman, circulation director, and business manager. I hired a couple of secretaries who shifted between the front desk and the mail room. In my search for new sources of revenue, I decided to start another magazine so that I could sell bicycle advertising. That forced me to hire someone to sell, not an expert, just someone to call advertisers on the phone. At that time you could hire such a person for $500 a month. Then I needed another editor. When I started my third publication, on cross-country skiing, I had hired someone to help with marketing.

Q: What was the frequency of Runner's World *at the time you launched* Bike World*?*
A: Bimonthly. We published on the alternate months.

Q: You thought it was better to start another magazine than to go monthly with Runner's World*?*
A: There was more potential for advertising. One year we actually sold more advertising in *Bike World* than we were selling in *Runner's World*. Eventually, of course, *Runner's World* outdistanced all the other publications and we sold them off. Now we've just launched a new one called *Fit*—on physical fitness for women.

Q: Why did you get rid of the other magazines? Didn't cross-country skiing and biking grow fast enough?
A: The decisions differed, but each was made on the basis of the property's impact on cash flow at a given time. I'm a great believer in watching break-even and profit points, and on having alternative plans. When plan A isn't attaining your objective, move immediately to plan B, and then, if necessary, to plan C.

Q: Are these plans made up as you go along? Or are they in place when you start?
A: Alternative plans were always in mind, even if not completely worked out. Now, of course, we are better organized. When we launched *Fit*, plans A, B and C were in place before the first issue.

Positioning shifts

Q: As the market for Runner's World *grew and developed, did you have to change your editorial approach, reposition the magazine with the changing reader market?*
A: To a degree, yes. We've always been responsive to our readers. We get a lot of mail from readers and watch their needs carefully. Our basic format has not changed since 1966. The editorial emphasis is on articles rather than news. But we have more professional input than we had in 1966, and we provide more service material, such as special diets for runners, special exercises, etc.

Q: What did you do to change your position with advertisers?
A: We helped to bring it about indirectly. By increasing the number of consumers who considered running important, we helped open up a whole new market for running clothing and equipment.

Q: Did you get this idea across with media ads?
A: I doubt if we've spent $15,000 on media ads since we began. Media advertising is near the bottom on my list of priorities. You always have such a list for things like adding a New York office, another salesperson, a direct-mail campaign. It covers not just advertising sales, but subscription and single-copy promotion. You allocate expenses against what will produce income, using available money according to need. You forgo what is not crucially needed until you cover the more urgent needs.

Q: But spending that looks like a loss can pay off in the long run. Discounting subscription prices, for instance, can pay off in renewals.
A: We do some of that. We've cut our $14.95 subscription price to $11.76 for special offers. Our five-year price reduces the cost per year to $10.68. But remember, circulation still has to make money for us.

Changes in cash flow

Q: What are your sources of revenue today?
A: It breaks evenly into four sources: 25% from advertising, 25% from subscriptions, 25% from single-copy sales, and 25% from mail-order sales.

Q: Over the past years you merged some publications and sold others. You've indicated it always had something to do with cash flow.
A: In almost every case it came down to the fact that our operation could no longer make money with a publication that had less than 100,000 circulation.

Q: That wasn't always the case. You once made money with 365. When did the situation change?
A: The moment we reached 100 employes and agreed to pay the rent for our present quarters. If I wanted to start a publication in a different field, and had none of my present executives work on it, and I housed it in a different location, got a publisher who would work for 50% ownership, and dissociated it from our present company so that the audience would not expect our high standards, then I might be able to make money on a magazine with 20,000 or 30,000 circulation.

Q: How about your time?
A: That's just it. Even if I were able to restrict my involvement with the publication to two hours a month, I would know that I could take the same two hours now and make a lot more dollars with them in my present company. I also know

that it would be a delusion to think I could make a meaningful contribution with two hours a month. I should either give much more time or get out of it altogether.

Q: So it's not just a matter of your market growing, or your magazine growing, but also of you growing personally. Your time is worth much more now than when you first launched Runner's World.

A: Exactly. Magazines are like people. They succeed and fail on their personalities. They may be born with certain innate characteristics, but these characteristics are molded, developed by the individuals who nurture them and the environment in which they grow. *Runner's World* was first an idea, but it became what it is partly because of all of us who wrote, edited, produced and marketed it, and partly because of the market that both nourished it and was nourished by it.

ANALYSIS

Changing to Cope with Abundance

Bob Anderson is one of the fortunate few who launched a publication when both he and the field it served were young, with both he and field having potential beyond his wildest dreams. He, of course, is not unique. Walter Annenberg did it with *TV Guide*. Hugh Hefner did it with *Playboy*. J. I. Rodale did it with *Organic Gardening* and *Prevention*. And, in the business field, there have been magazines like *Billboard, Broadcasting* and *Modern Plastics*.

Some markets appear out of nowhere and boom all at once, like the personal computer field. Others exist for years but suddenly take off, like interest in fitness or interest in science. Publishers can, and have, entered such markets at all stages—at the very start (*Runner's World*), when it begins to take off (*Byte*), or after it is in full flight (*Discover*). Then there are established magazines whose markets change, bringing about rapid expansion in new directions. Fortunate publications catch the new current and make tremendous progress (*Cosmopolitan*); unfortunate ones are capsized by it (*Charm*).

Our interest is in what publishers must do to take advantage of the rush of opportunity without losing control. Every surfboarder dreams of the big wave. Yet, unless you are ready and expert, that wave, when it comes, can wipe you out.

In magazines, sudden expansion happens either in reader market or the advertiser market, frequently in both. And it can change the way a magazine runs its business, the way it does its marketing, and the way it develops its editorial package.

The business response

Both the size of a market and its rate of growth affect the way a magazine does business. If the market is relatively small, has not yet been discovered by other publishers, and is growing slowly, it is possible to start a publication with relatively small resources, as Bob Anderson did. When the wind is still a gentle breeze, a single man can launch the boat and take his time setting the sails. As the wind grows, so must the crew, and so must the speed with which they furl the sails. It took a lot more money for George Hirsch to start *The Runner* 12 years after *Runner's World*.

As the market expands, the numbers get bigger—both the number of potential readers, and the number of potential advertisers. This requires more money—more to reach the audience, more to call on the advertisers, more to pay the printer. If you are starting, you need a bigger staff and more capital. And you are taking greater risks. If you are already in business, you must keep up with the market, which is more difficult and expensive in direct proportion to the market's growth.

Market expansion also means more competition. And competition means higher costs. Direct competition offers your market an alternative, causing greater resistance to subscription and cover prices, and to advertising rates. Competition forces you to raise production standards, to pay higher salaries to the staff and higher fees to free-lancers. One reason why Time Inc. needed $100 million to launch *Cable-TV Week* was that magazines like *On Cable, Cable Today* and *TV Guide* were already in the market.

Can a big company run a little magazine for an emerging market—and operate on a small scale? It can be done, but it requires a very disciplined (and disciplining) chief executive, and they seldom find it worth the bother. Bob Edgell did it with *Gourmet Today* and with *Roofing, Siding, Insulation* at Harcourt Brace Jovanovich Publications, as did Joel Harnett, with *Biomedical Communications* at United Business Publications. But most big companies find it very difficult to operate small scale once a big-scale corporate culture has taken hold. Bob Anderson now requires at least 100,000 circulation.

The marketing response

Expansion of the reader market forces a magazine to change promotion strategy. Young markets are made up of innovators—leaders and enthusiasts. They are usually easy to locate and easy to convince. As the market grows, more conservative people start to enter—followers rather than leaders. They tend to be hesitant, and need a lot of convincing. Subscription promotion must change accordingly, and renewal percentages decline. Newsstand sales depend more on cover lines and less on the logo, and single-copy sales fluctuate more, making it more difficult to keep print run close to rate base.

When the advertiser market expands, you need a larger sales force to reach all the prospects. The field diversifies and the salespeople have to be acquainted with more businesses.

More important, sales strategy must be much more sophisticated. In young advertiser markets, companies tend to be small, advertising decisions are made by principals, relatively few companies use advertising agencies, and hardly anyone requires research. As the market grows, advertising budgets become bigger, ad directors more expert, and ad agencies get involved. There are usually a few market leaders who dominate the share of voice and require special handling.

Magazines that serve emerging markets have small audiences and must rely on narrowly targeted advertising closely related to their editorial content. But as soon as the market, and the magazine's circulation, become large enough, secondary advertisers become interested. To them the editorial content is less important than the general characteristics of the audience it attracts. The salesforce has to think in terms of demographics, and the publisher has to consider selling efforts like Petersen Publishing's Action Group and Ziff-Davis's Magazine Network.

The editorial response

Mark Edmiston, the president of Newsweek Inc., once remarked that it is necessary "to recreate your magazine every once in a while"—to redefine what it is. No market can expand without undergoing some changes. And the biggest problem for the publisher who serves an expanding market is how to track those changes and reposition the magazine to catch the shifting winds without being buffeted by them.

Repositioning can be done gradually, abruptly, or somewhere in between. It is the editor's responsibility to plot and implement gradual repositioning. It is the publisher's job to approve—and often to plan—abrupt repositioning. The market itself can make abrupt repositioning necessary. Sudden gusts of change do happen. But most market changes, even when very rapid, are gradual, and abrupt repositioning is necessary only when gradual repositioning was neglected due to lack of editorial foresight.

The earlier a magazine sets the direction of its repositioning, the more successful it will be—provided the direction chosen was the right one. And that is not easy. Growing markets tend to expand and then fragment. Short-lived trends start up and die, often obscuring the important long-term trend.

As more and more people become interested in a field, for instance, the editor must decide whether the magazine's coverage of the subject should be broad and shallow or deep and narrow. Scholastic Inc.'s *Electronic Learning* chose the broad and shallow route to assist educators facing classroom computers. United Business Publication's *Home Video* took the deep and narrow route for owners of VCRs and video hybrids—too narrow, as it turned out, and it is now merged into *Video Review*.

Usually the decision is made on the basis of the magazine's competitive position. The publication that leads its market does best by trying to hold its lead, by doing the best possible job of filling the broadest needs of that market. *Computerworld* continues to serve the general information needs of the entire computer industry.

A magazine that has the resources to challenge the leader is wise to position itself against the leader's principal weakness. Although it was not enough, *Cable-TV Week* offered listings more complete than those provided by *On Cable* (which was a monthly) or *TV Guide* (which had to appeal to readers who did not have cable).

Magazines with neither leadership nor comparable or superior resources do best to position themselves in an uncontested special area. *Apple Orchard* was launched to serve only users of the Apple computer; *Rainbow* to serve Radio Shack's color computer units; *PC*, IBM's personal computers.

Static or declining markets more often require a radical shift in editorial focus than do growing markets. (The problems that led to the sale of *Psychology Today* to the American Psychological Association are due largely to a dying market, for popular interest in psychology, so strong in the '60s, has been absorbed into the growing general interest in science.) In expanding markets, a radical editorial shift is usually necessary when a publication has missed the main stream of the expansion and wandered into a backwater. The business-news-and-information market is not new, but it has expanded in recent years. Changes in *Fortune* and *Dun's Business Month* are apt examples of what it takes, and how difficult it is to get out of such a backwater.

Preparing for response

The real problem for publishing management is how to prepare for the changes an expanding market may demand. This requires constant alertness—preceded by understanding of the market, the publication, its resources, and the effect of its marketing practices.

First, the publisher must understand the market. Markets are defined not by subjects, demographics, titles, or industries, but in terms of needs that a magazine can fill. It would be a serious mistake to define *Psychology Today*'s market by psychology, education, the profession of psychologist, or by the membership of the American Psychological Association. Its market is everyone who feels the need to know more about psychology. The publisher must continually ask and answer, "How fast is the need my magazine serves spreading?" and, "How is the need changing?"

Second, the publisher must understand the magazine—the editorial product. What is the editorial focus? How precisely does it fill the need? What bearing does format, frequency, size, price, distribution and the way the magazine is promoted have on filling the need? When Time Inc. decided that *Fortune* had to be repositioned, article length and publishing frequency were among the changes made.

Third, the publisher must understand company resources. How much money is available to make changes? What are the capabilities of the staff—editors, salespeople, circulation personnel, production department? Can the company afford to supplement or replace them? And, if so, how quickly? Like every business plan, strategy for change must be built on the real world of what can be done. Sometimes the market gets so big and rough that a small ship has to be abandoned.

Fourth, the publisher must understand the consequences of the publication's current and past marketing practices. Understanding how they affect readers involves studying both the sources and type of new subscriptions, and the nature of newsstand appeal. A magazine, such as *The New Yorker*, which does little circulation promotion and depends heavily on renewals, will find more reader resistance to change than publications with big reader turnover, like *Modern Bride* or *Seventeen*.

Similarly, the way space has been sold in the past can make a big difference in repositioning a magazine with the advertising community. The difficulty magazines like *Prevention* and *Yankee* have in selling general advertisers—despite widely recognized success and enormous circulation growth—is largely due to their having been sold as specialty publications for so many years.

MANAGEMENT REVIEW

Check List to Prepare for Market Growth

I. Forecast the state of your magazine's market in the:

	1st yr.	2nd yr.	5th yr.	10th yr.
A. Number of reader prospects:	____	____	____	____
B. Total money spent on this interest ($):	____	____	____	____
C. Number of advertiser prospects:	____	____	____	____
D. Total of their ad budgets ($):	____	____	____	____
E. Number of direct competitors:	____	____	____	____

II. Forecast the share of the market you expect in the:

	1st yr.	2nd yr.	5th yr.	10th yr.
A. Circulation:	____	____	____	____
B. Reader revenue ($):	____	____	____	____
C. Ad pages:	____	____	____	____
D. Ad revenue ($):	____	____	____	____

III. How will this growth affect your operation in the:

	1st yr.	2nd yr.	5th yr.	10th yr.
A. Printing:				
Annual copies:	____	____	____	____
Annual pages:	____	____	____	____
Annual cost ($):	____	____	____	____
B. Distribution:				
Annual cost ($):	____	____	____	____
C. Fulfillment:				
Annual cost ($):	____	____	____	____
D. Promotion:				
Annual cost ($):	____	____	____	____

E. Advertising sales:
   No. of people: _____ _____ _____ _____
   Annual cost ($): _____ _____ _____ _____
F. Editorial:
   No. of people: _____ _____ _____ _____
   Annual cost ($): _____ _____ _____ _____
G. Administration:
   No. of people: _____ _____ _____ _____
   Annual cost ($): _____ _____ _____ _____

IV. How will growth affect circulation marketing in the:

	1st yr.	2nd yr.	5th yr.	10th yr.

A. Renewals:
   Renewal price ($): _____ _____ _____ _____
   Avg. renewal (%): _____ _____ _____ _____
   Avg. profit (loss) per
     renewal: _____ _____ _____ _____
   Total renewals: _____ _____ _____ _____
B. New Subscriptions:
   Avg. offer price ($): _____ _____ _____ _____
   Avg. promo return (%): _____ _____ _____ _____
   Avg. profit (loss) per
     new sub ($): _____ _____ _____ _____
   Total new subs: _____ _____ _____ _____
C. Single-copies:
   Cover price ($): _____ _____ _____ _____
   Avg. size of draw: _____ _____ _____ _____
   Avg. % of returns: _____ _____ _____ _____
   Avg. profit (loss)
     per copy drawn ($): _____ _____ _____ _____

V. How will growth affect marketing of ad space in the:

	1st yr.	2nd yr.	5th yr.	10th yr.

A. Total ad sales ($): _____ _____ _____ _____
   Primary adv. ($): _____ _____ _____ _____
   Secondary adv. ($): _____ _____ _____ _____
B. Rate per page ($): _____ _____ _____ _____
C. Rate as cpm ($): _____ _____ _____ _____

D. T&E budget ($): ____ ____ ____ ____

E. Adv. & Promotion ($): ____ ____ ____ ____

F. Research budget ($): ____ ____ ____ ____

VI. How will growth affect editorial positioning?

A. Does your competitive situation tell you to

_____ Defend your leadership position?

_____ Position yourself vs. the leader's weakness?

_____ Position yourself in an uncontested area?

B. To achieve this does your editorial indicate

_____ Sufficient gradual repositioning?

_____ A need for abrupt repositioning?

C. Does the repositioning plan fit all the following:

_____ The nature of the market?

_____ The nature of your publication?

_____ The resources of your company?

_____ Your current and past marketing practices?

CHAPTER TWENTY

How to Completely Reposition a Publication Editorially

Featuring an Interview with Helen Gurley Brown

Editor of Cosmopolitan

The deepest and most controllable change that can affect a magazine is to change its editorial focus or reposition it editorially. In its extreme form, such a repositioning turns a magazine into a publication so different that it can almost be described as entirely new.

The history of magazine publishing includes a number of outstanding examples of how a strong editor took an existing publication and made it over into a huge success: Norman Cousins with *The Saturday Review*, Arnold Gingrich with *Esquire*, Herb Mayes with *McCall's*, Paige Rense with *Architectural Digest*. And, most famous of all is Helen Gurley Brown with *Cosmopolitan*.

In 1965 the great Hearst Corp. was on the verge of closing down its venerable, and once highly successful, *Cosmopolitan* magazine. Then the author of a best seller (*Sex and the Single Girl*) made a proposal to start a new magazine as a follow-up on her book.

Mrs. Helen Gurley Brown was then 43 years old. Besides writing, her work experience was in an ad agency. She had never worked on a magazine or run an editorial staff. Her husband, a successful copywriter (today a movie producer), had helped her with the new-magazine presentation. Several publishers had listened to it, and turned it down.

Hearst had no interest in launching a new magazine. But it offered Mrs. Brown the opportunity to apply her ideas to the dying *Cosmopolitan*. Thus began one of the greatest repositioning feats in the history of magazines.

Helen Gurley had begun her career, literally, as a poor working girl, glad to get a job as a secretary. But she was bright, personable, full of ideas and willing to work. She got a job at an advertising agency, Foote, Cone & Belding. One of the agency's founders, Don Belding, was her boss. He recognized her talent and promoted her. And it was not long before she was making very good money as a copywriter.

Helen learned a lot as a working girl—a successful working girl. And she decided to put it all in a book. The result was the 1962 best seller, *Sex and the Single Girl*, which led to another book, *Sex and the Office*.

Sex and the Single Girl has been published in 28 countries, in 17 different languages, including Hebrew, Finnish and Afrikaans. Helen re-edited it in 1970 as *Sex and the New Single Girl*. She is also the author of the *The Outrageous Opinions of Helen Gurley Brown* (1966), *Helen Gurley Brown's Single Girl's Cookbook* (1969) and *Having It All* (1983).

But her greatest achievement is today's *Cosmopolitan*. In 1964, the year before she became editor, *Cosmopolitan* had 776,000 circulation and carried 250 pages of advertising. Today circulation is approaching 3 million and ad pages run about 2,300 a year.

INTERVIEW

Q: Did the idea of repositioning a magazine scare you?
A: I didn't know enough to be scared. Had I known then what I know now, I probably would have been.

Q: Why did Hearst decide to change Cosmopolitan *rather than start a new magazine?*
A: It is much easier to start with something that already exists and improve it than to start from scratch.

Editorial staff reaction

Q: Weren't you worried about the staff's reaction?
A: Of course. I had no experience at magazine editing or at being a boss. I relied on advice especially from my husband, David, who was wonderfully supportive

and had executive experience. I knew enough not to rush in and make a fool of myself. I kept a very low profile and just observed for a while. I fired no one. A few people left eventually, but I never fired anyone. There's always resistance to a new editor. Staffers are always loyal to a magazine, particularly when it's failing. It's like having an idiot child. You become extra protective and determined. The staff was polite but cool. I let them go ahead with the April, May and June 1965 issues, as planned.

Q: How did you eventually sell your ideas to them?
A: I really didn't have to. The beauty of the job was that I was put in charge from the beginning. If I told the art director, for instance, "Here's what I want." He could do it or he could leave. I had worked in ad agencies for 15 years, where art directors had greater power, and copywriters had to fight for what they wanted. It came like a revelation, the first week there, that I was boss, and we were going to do what I planned to do. What made it easier was that they all knew how close they were to not having a magazine to work for.

Q: Did you introduce changes all at once or gradually?
A: I intended to do it gradually. But my very first issue was an almost complete departure from what they had before. There was an article, assigned before I arrived, about women and the Pill. Oral contraceptives were just coming on the market then. I grabbed that article and it set the tone for the issue. The one helpful thing in all this was that I always knew exactly what I wanted. I was never confused. It might not work. It might be lousy. But there was never any doubt.

Reader Reaction

Q: Was circulation 100% newsstand at that time?
A: Management had the courage about 18 years ago to get rid of most of *Cosmopolitan*'s subscriptions and rely on newsstand sales. We still do.

Q: Perhaps that made it possible to suddenly seek a new audience without disastrous consequences.
A: That's true. I was lucky to come into a magazine that was all newsstand and has remained that way. To subscribe to *Cosmo* you have to pay a premium: $21 vs. 12 newsstand copies for $18.

Q: Didn't the fans of the old Cosmopolitan *complain?*
A: Who knows? All I could do was go by newsstand sales. When the first report

came in, over 80% of the copies had been sold, almost a million copies. Really terrific. I neither knew nor cared if old readers were outraged.

Q: Didn't any readers write in to complain?
A: I never read the mail. I don't to this day. My toughest chore is to get good writers, and reading letters from readers doesn't help me do that.

Q: Do you feel the same about reader research?
A: Yes. My problem is not learning what to write but finding people to write it. We don't do reader research.

Objectives in repositioning

Q: Which of the following best describes your objectives in making changes? 1. To make the magazine more exciting, more meaningful. 2. To change the demographics. 3. To introduce more subjects that would attract advertising. My guess is the last two meant little to you.
A: I'm not sure even the first one is right on the nose. My motivation for changing the magazine was to make it the kind of magazine I could produce. It didn't matter what readers said or what advertisers said. I only knew how to do one thing. *Cosmo* is an extension of *Sex and the Single Girl.* It is a magazine for women who don't want to work through their husbands or children, who want to do it themselves. I was helping that woman solve her problems. Maybe that's thinking about readers. But I don't have to search for what they need. I already know what they need. I was there. I started working when I was 18. I had a rough time with lots of problems.

Q: But are you sure you are typical?
A: So many women go to college now and are better educated than I am, it's getting to where I'm not typical. But I've always thought of myself as the Evita Peron of the secretarial pool. My only extraordinary quality, I believe, is drive. Otherwise I consider myself pretty average. I've no education. I come from a very poor family. I started in an ad agency's lowest job.

Q: Did you make any attempt to find out what sort of women were the core audience for the old Cosmopolitan?
A: No. I put out a magazine to gradually attract the people I was writing for. I never worried about the old readers. I hoped some would stick around, but most of them probably departed. I know my mother felt I ruined the magazine. She remembered it in the '20s and '30s. It was a very illustrious magazine then.

Business staff reaction

Q: How did the ad department respond to what you did?
A: The publisher, Frank DuPuy, was supportive from the beginning. He had tried to persuade my predecessor to make changes. Many of his ideas on what should be done were along the lines of what I planned to do. Coming from an ad agency, I respected advertisers totally. I always felt there should never be any conflict between publisher and editor. I've heard of editors who want nothing to do with advertising. They must be nuts. Advertising pays the bills. I immediately offered to help sell advertising. I still do. Every Thursday, we give a luncheon at the 21 Club for 20 to 30 advertising people, and I explain *Cosmo* and what we are doing.

Q: Did you make any direct contribution to the famous "Cosmopolitan Girl" advertising promotion campaign?
A: Frank DuPuy though of the line, "If you want to reach me, you'll find me reading *Cosmopolitan*." I wrote a few pieces of the early copy and I've been doing most of it ever since.

Q: What's your contribution to circulation promotion?
A: I do as much television as I can—on the Tonight Show and the Merv Griffin Show. I've been doing it for 15 years. I think it helps.

Positioning editorial

Q: How do you choose articles and article subjects?
A: Every article we publish must have wide appeal, and it must appeal to me. My one concession to other people's tastes is astrology. I think it is a bunch of baloney, but we've always had a column.

Q: Do you edit more for single women than for married?
A: Half our audience is married. And at least half of our "emotional" material is on getting along with your marriage partner. We don't write about child-raising because I can't relate to children. Occasionally we'll treat a subject like being a working mother.

Q: When you started, was there any other magazine that came close to what you had in mind?
A: No. I had the field entirely to myself. Since then others have come into the field with somewhat similar editorial. Yet no magazine does exactly what we do. *Viva* came and went. It was much sexier. *Playgirl* is also sexier, and really not

like *Cosmo* at all. *New Woman*, a very good magazine, is patterned, I think, somewhat after *Cosmo*. But it has no graphics or art, and relies too much on book excerpts to compare with us.

The repositioning time frame

Q: Did Hearst give you any time limit, when you took over as editor of Cosmopolitan?
A: I had a two-year contract. They couldn't fire me for two years, but it was understood that, if *Cosmo* failed, I would work out the contract writing for other Hearst magazines. But my first issue did so well they didn't have to wait very long to know it would work.

Q: Did your second issue do as well as the first?
A: Better. The second issue was August, traditionally a good month for *Cosmo*. The August 1965 issue sold over a million copies. Today we sell over 2.7 million. We got there inch by inch.

Q: I believe that's one reason for your success. Management let you get there inch by inch. They did not force the circulation up, then tell you to sustain it.
A: I've always felt circulation should not be forced.

Q: You remarked recently there's been little change in Cosmo *since you took over. Haven't you had to change with the audience over the years?*
A: We do reflect what's changing. I've never considered us revolutionaries or ahead of our time. I think we're with the times, not behind them, but right there with them. The articles we publish have to deal with current problems. Some problems change very little. A man who is unfaithful, a girl who needs help on her job—such concerns continue. But there are new subjects, such as a husband you support. That wasn't common in 1965.

Emotional vs. rational positions

Q: Do you think the majority of your readers actually intend to act and think as the articles say they should?
A: The house-husband may be a bit special because most husbands work. But every article, aside from profiles of stars like Barbra Streisand or Nancy Lopez, has to be something the reader can identify with.

Q: But one can identify with something in one's imagination without wanting to live it in reality.

A: You mean voyeurs, people who read *Cosmo* and feel it has nothing to do with their real lives? Occasionally, we may have an article about a call girl, someone with a life altogether different from that of the readers. But most of the articles are practical, and applicable.

Q: In its death agony, Viva *had an ad campaign: "The* Viva *woman does what the* Cosmopolitan *girl dreams about." I think there was a germ of truth in that, and I think nourishing fantasies can be good journalism. Back when John Mack Carter was editing* American Home, *I asked him, "How many of the home-book readers can afford the kind of homes you show?" And he said, "It is not what they can have, but what they'd like to have. We provide them with dreams." How many* Cosmo *readers can hope to look like your cover girls?*

A: In graphics, especially, we tend to show the ideal. The models are more beautiful than our readers can hope to be, and some of the dresses are more expensive than our readers can afford. But readers do buy the clothes we show in the magazine, or we wouldn't show them.

Q: It's a question of psychological approach. Should the magazine portray what people aspire to do or what people actually do?

A: What people actually do is look scruffy most of the time. The magazine shows an idealized version of how the reader should look.

ANALYSIS

Repositioning: How to Change a Magazine

The word "positioning" has been appropriated by Madison Avenue to describe one element in the marketing-communication process: establishing a special place for a company or product in the minds of its prospects. To use the precise words of the foster parents of positioning, Jack Trout and Al Ries, "To succeed in our overcommunicated society, a company must create a 'position' in the prospect's mind. A position that takes into consideration not only its own strengths and weaknesses, but those of its competitors as well."

Trout and Ries frequently use *Sports Illustrated*'s "Third Newsweekly" campaign as an example of successful positioning. They never mention their agency's attempt to improve the positioning of *Dun's Review*. According to an insider, they failed there because they made no recommendations on improving the editorial product, but tried to do it all with advertising.

This incident is mentioned not to belittle Trout and Ries, two topnotch pros who have made a major contribution to the advertising business. The *Dun's Review* positioning campaign ran a long time ago, and is relevant only because it highlights a vital fact about magazine positioning: It is very difficult to position a publication with advertisers and it is impossible to position it with readers unless the positioning effort begins and ends with the product. A magazine is its own greatest ad, and no external campaign, whether for circulation or advertising, can establish a lasting position while gainsaying the publication's message.

To position a magazine (whether in its reader market or advertiser market) is to focus it on filling a need so that prospects think of it as filling that need. To reposition a magazine is to shift its focus to a different need. *Cue*, for years, was positioned as a listings guide to entertainment activities in Metropolitan New York. Then, as *Cue/New York*, it was repositioned as a city magazine with entertainment as its primary service category. The first *Cue* focused on people's need for an easy tool in deciding where to go for entertainment. The second *Cue/New York* seemed to be focused on the broader need to know and evaluate what the city offered as entertainment.

When is repositioning advisable?

When a magazine is in trouble, the first question to ask is whether the problem is the focus or the need. Focus is to need as implementation is to objective. If the implementation is at fault, repositioning in itself won't help. On the other hand, no matter how much implementation is improved, it can do little if the objective is misconceived.

In practice, however, a new editor may reposition because he or she is better equipped to implement the new objective. Helen Gurley Brown's decision as to how to change *Cosmopolitan* was based on a simple fact: that was to do what she knew best. It was Hearst management that made the decision to reposition when it hired her.

So the decision to reposition may be made because:

1) The need the magazine has been filling has become less urgent (it no longer motivates required income). *Furniture Methods & Materials* is repositioned as *Furniture Manufacturing Management*.

2) Competition to fill the need has made retention of a profitable share of market impossible. Hugh Hefner once tried to reposition *Oui* as a "*Cosmopolitan* for young men."

3) The staff will be more effective if it focuses on a different need, e.g., *Argosy*'s unfulfilled scheme to become the flagship for tax-foe Howard Jarvis.

The one thing to remember is that there is far less risk in improving the implementation of the positioning you now enjoy than in repositioning. Therefore, repositioning should be the last resort.

Once the decision to reposition is made, there are four rules for success: 1) know where you are going, 2) start with what you have, 3) make as little noise as possible, and 4) reposition your staff. Let's consider each of these rules separately.

Know where you are going

As Mrs. Brown stresses, her big advantage when she joined Hearst was that she knew precisely what she wanted to do. There was never any doubt or confusion. How different from Clay Felker and Milt Glaser at *Esquire*!

A frequent mistake in repositioning is to try to test the goal as you proceed. During the repositioning process it is possible to test methods, techniques, personnel—but never the goal. You have to know where you are going before you start. In fact, approaching the goal is the standard against which you evaluate the tests. *Sports Afield* learned this the hard way when it briefly experimented with interesting its readers in mountain climbing.

It is advisable to research the need you plan to fill before you start. Mrs. Brown researched her market through more than 15 years of direct experience and by writing two books. Many attempts at repositioning fail before they start because publishers research audiences rather than needs. Result: The need itself is never brought into focus, and the "repositioned" publication tries to fill a potpourri of needs which leaves it with no position at all in the minds of its prospects (and in the minds of its editors).

Five basic questions should be answered with confidence before one is ready to reposition:

1) What is the precise need to be filled? If it is a reader need, is it predominantly practical or emotional? *Travel & Leisure, Montgomery Ward Auto Club News* and *Signature* focus on practical needs. *National Geographic, Arizo-*

na Highways and *Aloha* satisfy emotional needs. If it is an advertiser need, is it for cumulative or direct advertising? What is the value frame?

2) How will the publication fill the need? Filling the need must be the reason for the type of editorial, format, frequency, amount and nature of advertising. Felker's decision to make *Esquire* a fortnightly was based on neither a reader nor an advertiser need.

3) Who has the need? It is practically impossible to really understand the need without being able to answer this question. Yet Filipacchi tried to resurrect *Look* without an adequate answer, particularly in the advertiser market.

4) How can the publication reach them? This covers promotion, distribution and, to some extent, production. Failure to answer this question was one of many reasons that Leda Sanford failed in repositioning *American Home*.

5) How will filling this need affect the total financial structure of the publication? Particularly, how will filling a reader need affect the filling of the advertiser need and vice versa.

Start with what you have

In Mrs. Brown's first months at *Cosmopolitan* she was both supremely confident as to what she wanted to do and extremely diffident about disturbing what was there. She fired no one. She spent three months just observing. And the key article for her first repositioned issue had been accepted by her predecessor.

There is no contradiction here. On the contrary, it was the confidence of the true innovator that enabled her to use whatever she could of the old as foundation for the new. Only people who are unsure of themselves feel obliged to show their impact by violent change.

The secret of successful repositioning is to salvage as much as possible of the present publication. If nothing of the original is worth preserving, it is better to kill the magazine altogether and start 100% new.

A periodical's continuity exists only in the minds of people: the staff, the advertisers, the readers. The less you disturb all three of these groups while moving toward your goal, the better your chances for success. Mrs. Brown retained the old staff. She worked willingly with publisher DuPuy and made a singular effort to explain what she was doing to advertisers. She seemed to ignore the old readers. This might have caused serious trouble had Hearst not previously eliminated subscription circulation. It is much easier to change an audience committed issue by issue than one committed for a year at a time.

In 1977, when McGraw-Hill's *Construction Methods & Equipment* was in serious trouble, the then publications president, Gordon Jones, appointed a task force to study whether it should be dumped or repositioned. The group recommended repositioning because there was room for a magazine on construction contracting, and it was less costly to resposition *CM&E* than to start new. So *CM&E* became McGraw-Hill's *Construction Contracting*. Although a number of editors were added, a special circulation drive launched, and a new sales staff organized, the cost savings were based on holding most of the editors, circulation and advertising.

The easier it is to use the magazine's current assets as leverage for its new position, the less expensive the change will be, and the greater its chances for success. Hence, if you have the choice of two possible new positions of equal promise, choose the one that will cause less upheaval.

Make as little noise as possible

A lot of fanfare may help in launching a new magazine; it never helps in repositioning an old one. It does no good to tell the world you are going to change. The news will frighten your loyal readers and advertisers. They like the old magazine or they would not have stayed with it. As for those who have a low opinion of the publication, the announcement confirms their judgment. Besides, change means uncertainty, and for most people (especially media buyers), uncertainty means wait and see.

Since change is news and news means pickups, publishers have a difficult time keeping publicity people quiet when repositioning plans are underway. But here silence is essential. Clay Blair helped kill the old *Saturday Evening Post* with his "sophisticated muckracking" presentation.

If you want to score a repositioning knockout do not signal your punches. Let readers and advertisers discover the improvements for themselves. A single reader or advertiser, enthusiastic about his or her own discovery of your new merit, is worth a hundred releases. The time for publicity is afterward, when the evidence of success is on hand. In a word: publicize results, not promises. A kindred rule: publicize the facts, not your opinions. *Success Unlimited* was right to publicize its change in size from 8½" x 7½" to 8" x 11". It was wrong to publicize "improved" graphics.

Reposition your staff

The first shoals the repositioning navigator has to cross are almost always internal resistance to change. The ability to handle people (and you have to meet Mrs. Brown to realize how much of this she has) is essential for any leader. We cannot teach it here, but we can describe five principles to help win cooperation from the staff in a repositioning situation:

1) Stress the publication's problems rather than your solutions. This turns resentment away from yourself and makes change look more attractive.

2) Where possible, let staffers "discover" the solutions themselves. There is no better way to get people to fight for your idea than to convince them it is their idea.

3) Look for each staffer's strong points and use them. People are more productive and happier when doing what they do best.

4) Listen patiently, never acting as if you are sure your people are wrong. For the staffer it is much more important that you value the thinker than the thought. For you, it is a way to learn where each staffer is at.

5) Act firmly, always taking responsibility for the final decisions. Confidence and respect are built not on your always being right but on your willingness to take the blame when you are wrong.

Repositioning your staff is less a job of convincing them that where you are going is right, than it is of convincing them that you know where you are going.

MANAGEMENT REVIEW

Check List for Repositioning

I. Decide on the advisability of repositioning.
A. If the problem is one of need (objective):
1. Is the need you have been filling no longer urgent enough to supply the revenue your publication requires? ____ Yes ____ No
2. Has competition in filling that need made it impossible to retain the market share your publication requires for profit?

____ Yes ____ No

B. If the problem is one of focus (implementation):
   1. Is it impossible to solve the problem by improving the implementation? ____ Yes ____ No
   2. Will a new position really improve the implementation? ____ Yes ____ No

If all answers are no, repositioning is not advised.

II. Make sure you know where you are going.
   1. Can you clearly define the new need to be filled? ____ Yes ____ No
   2. Have you researched the need sufficiently before you start? ____ Yes ____ No
   3. Are you confident enough in the new position you have chosen that no tests will be necessary after you start? ____ Yes ____ No
   4. Do you know precisely how the publication will fill the new need? ____ Yes ____ No
   5. Do you know who has the need, i.e., who your prime prospects are? ____ Yes ____ No
   6. Do you know how you will reach these prospects? ____ Yes ____ No
   7. Will the changes you make really improve the total financial structure of your publication, i.e., are you certain what you gain in one area will not be lost in another? ____ Yes ____ No

Do not proceed until all answers are yes, *even if it means choosing an entirely new or redefined need.*

III. Start with what you have.
   1. Can the changes you plan be made without a major upheaval in your current staff? ____ Yes ____ No
   2. Can the changes be made so as to retain a significant proportion of current readers? ____ Yes ____ No
   3. Can the changes be made so as to retain a significant number of current advertisers? ____ Yes ____ No

Two no *answers mean your plan to reposition is in real trouble. Three* no *answers mean it is preferable to fold and start an entirely new publication.*

IV. Make as little noise as possible.

1. Before you start, are announcements restricted to those necessary for customer relations, e.g., changes in rates, size or frequency? _____ Yes _____ No
2. Once underway, do your public relations people understand that they must restrict publicity to results? _____ Yes _____ No
3. After changes are made, are all releases screened to avoid opinions and stick to facts? _____ Yes _____ No

Do not proceed until all answers are yes.

V. Reposition your staff.

In persuading current staffers to accept and work for the new position:

1. Do you stress the publication's problems rather than your solutions? _____ Yes _____ No
2. Are you making an effort to let staffers discover the solutions themselves? _____ Yes _____ No
3. Do you look for each staffer's strong points and use them? _____ Yes _____ No
4. Do you listen patiently and never act as if you are sure your people are wrong? _____ Yes _____ No
5. Do you act firmly and always take responsibility for the final decisions? _____ Yes _____ No
6. Are you willing to replace staffers incapable of working toward your goals? _____ Yes _____ No

Make sure all answers are yes, *if you really want to succeed.*

CHAPTER TWENTY-ONE

How to Introduce Editorial Changes

Featuring an Interview with Robert A. Potts

Publisher of Dun's Business Month

Editors, as we have said, are making changes in their magazines all the time. But occasionally, it becomes necessary to make a major change, one distinctive enough that readers and advertisers will take notice. When such changes are made, the editor—in coordination with the publisher—has to formulate a special strategy.

This chapter is about that strategy. The most important thing about this strategy is that it is not restricted to the editor's domain. It must involve the entire publishing operation. Hence the need to work closely with the publisher.

For that reason we chose Bob Potts, a publisher, as our expert. This interview was conducted shortly after Technical Publishing (a division of Dun & Bradstreet) had changed *Dun's Review* to *Dun's Business Month*. We are less interested in the advisability or importance of the change itself, than in the management, promotion and marketing methods used to introduce it.

When Bob Potts was a very young man, he worked at Fred Gardner Advertising as a copywriter. He was a 14-month veteran who had been earning $25 a week when Gardner lost a major account and Bob found a termination notice. He obtained a more secure position in the advertising department of *New*

York Daily News. And, determined to safeguard his future, he enrolled in evening school at Pace College.

After graduating from Pace, Bob left the *Daily News* for a better job selling advertising space for Watson Publications, a business-paper publisher. When Watson was purchased by Cahners Publishing, Bob went along. He soon became founding publisher of Cahners's new *Traffic Management* magazine. When he left Cahners, he was a vice president and group publisher. He worked for a while as the advertising director for Railway Express, and—in December of 1975, went back to magazines as publisher of *Dun's Review*.

INTERVIEW

Q: How was the decision made to change Dun's Review?
A: A publisher is always looking for ideas to make the product more valuable to readers. Although *Dun's Review* has had healthy growth in the last five years, we are a monthly up against a superb weekly, *Business Week*, and probably the best national daily in the world, *The Wall Street Journal*. While I don't think the biweekly *Forbes* and *Fortune* are earth-shaking, they have a good deal of clout. In the market we have been number four. For almost two years we looked for a unique editoral service, one that would give our monthly, if possible, the essentiality of a weekly. Then Jack Abely, our president, suggested a back-up editorial section for all other business information sources.

Q: That was the seed of the new Dun's Business Month?
A: Yes: A service that would recap every important happening in the last 30 days for executives who, in the press of travel or business, missed their regular reading or overlooked something they should know. So we've created a section to do for business what *The New York Times* "Review of the Week" does for the general news.

Pretesting

Q: Did you pretest this idea?
A: The Gene Riley Group conducted 10 focus groups around the country, each with up to 11 participants: a total of 109 executives from the top 500 companies, vice presidential level and up. They were told that a major publisher was plan-

ning a business-management publication and wanted to learn more about their information needs. Some of the sessions took three hours. The interplay was fantastic. These guys are drowning in information. They've a strong sense of guilt or fear that they're missing stuff they ought to know.

Q: What do they read regularly?
A: They all felt that the daily newspaper and *The Wall Street Journal* are absolute "must reads," even though most admitted they quite often didn't read them, or had to give them such a fast scan they missed a lot. Quite a few included *Business Week*, but most felt that, after those three, everything else was leisure reading.

Q: What did they want?
A: They all agreed that they liked a departmentalized format. They praised *The Wall Street Journal*'s front page wrap-up. They complained that *Business Week* carries more feature material than news review.

Q: Did they discuss your actual plan?
A: Yes, as a proposal, and the reactions were universally positive. One guy said, "Boy, if I could have something monthly and departmentalized, it would be a godsend. I'd insist my employees read it."

Q: One of the problems of focus groups is the danger of talking about a magazine with people unequipped to formulate realistic editorial ideas.
A: We were careful about this. Less than 15% of the two- to three-hour discussions was spent on magazine or editorial solutions. We didn't want to make the mistake of designing an Edsel based on what people think they want. The moderator skillfully focused the discussion on personal problems and needs without relating them to how a magazine might be a solution.

Q: Several studies I've done gave me similar feedback: "I've got too much to read. I wish someone would come up with a summary of what I need to know, so I could skip all the reading I do now." People think that's what they want, but don't follow through. They don't trust others to decide what they have to know, and they're afraid to wait for the summary. The strength of your idea lies in you're presuming they are going to read other publications, using you only as failsafe.
A: That's exactly it. We do not replace anything. We can only recap significant news, in some cases, 30 days after it happens. To the busy executive who missed something important to the future of his business, even 60 days is not too late. We can't help them with things they have to know weekly or daily.

Staff involvement

Q: How involved were your editors in the changes?
A: Totally. There were continuous discussions over two years between Clem Morgello, the editor, Gerry Rosen, executive editor, and myself. When we read Jack Abely's memo, asking us to "Take a look at this idea," we all accepted it so quickly we thought there must be something wrong. Morgello and Rosen watched every focus group from behind one-way mirrors and later reviewed the videotapes with their staff.

Q: How about the advertising sales staff?
A: They weren't involved. They were told what was going to happen at the June 9 sales meeting this year.

Q: And the circulation people?
A: There was no reason to involve them. The changes do not affect our circulation. We are keeping the same circulation thrust.

Q: Were there any objections internally?
A: The only objection was from the editors who doubted the job could be done with the staff they had. So we added staff.

Q: Other than the researchers who conducted the focus groups, did you use any other outside help?
A: After the decision was made, we brought in Will Hopkins, the design consultant who did *Horizons, American Photographer, Geo, Science 81* and other top jobs.

Timing

Q: Why did you decide to introduce the changes all at once, in September?
A: We considered and rejected a two-step approach. The new section couldn't be introduced gradually, and the new name describes it. Besides, when you make major changes in a publication month by month, people wonder whether you really believe in them. You're putting your toe in the water rather than jumping in.

Q: Why June 1 for the first public announcement?
A: We felt we needed 90 days prior to the issue for both readers and advertisers. If we went longer, spent six months talking about the change, it would become ho-hum. You can keep excitement going for 90 days; I don't think you can keep it going for 180 days.

Q: Yet advance publicity discourages precious word-of-mouth advertising. People don't talk about something they presume the other guy knows.
A: When I have a choice, I'll go the advertising and advanced-publicity route. Word of mouth can't be controlled; it frequently takes three to four months to really work. We needed immediate effectiveness.

Telling the readers

Q: How did you introduce the changes to the readers?
A: We started with letters from the publisher in the July and August issues telling readers what was going to happen. In September, when the revamped magazine appeared, there was a lead editorial page by Clem Morgello, and we ran full-page ads in *The New York Times* and *Crain's Business Review* in Chicago, with smaller ads in other papers in major and secondary markets.

Q: Why was it necesary to prepare the readers? Aren't there advantages in pleasantly surprising them?
A: Even though we are still using *Dun's* we are using a new name. Our readers are very busy. They'll take a fleeting look at a magazine and discard it if they don't recognize it at once. We had to prepare them.

Q: Why did you change the name?
A: We first named the section "Dun's Business Month," but we soon realized that was a pretty good name for the magazine. It truly described what we were doing, and we had always been a little unhappy about "Review" in our title.

Q: Yet what you planned to do was "review" the month.
A: True, but that word has been associated too long with historical and scholarly publications.

Q: There's no magazine in the world that hasn't got some enthusiasts who resent any change. How are you handling those readers?
A: There's sure to be some nostalgia. *Dun's Review* has been around since 1893. But we have no indications of any real problems. The fact that the magazine will continue the trend-oriented articles on which we've built our reputation, that the new feature is an addition, takes the sting out of it. Even the difference in the name is not radical. We've kept *Dun's* and most people call it *Dun's*. Very few call it *Dun's Review*.

Telling the advertisers

Q: How did you prepare advertisers for the change?
A: Advertisers react to changes in one of three ways—either: "It's a good idea, fine"; or: "It's such a good idea that I'll move my August insertion to September"; or: "You're offering me something I didn't want to buy—I'll cancel and see what's going to happen." You have to address all three possibilities. We began by running teaser ads in *The New York Times, Advertising Age*, and *Ad Week* in June and July. We announced a new editorial service for September that would give overdosed readers "month-to-month resuscitation," a phrase George Lois at our agency came up with. But we did not tell them how we would do it, and that got a lot of curiosity going. We were careful not to scare anybody. We did not tell enough for advertisers to change their schedules. Then, on August 1, all advertisers in the September issue were told exactly what we were doing and that they had the option to cancel. None did.

Q: How did you describe the plan?
A: We had a four-page descriptive paper that recapped the reader's need, what we were doing to fill it, and how we would change the name to reflect the new service. The reception was excellent. September was the biggest issue we've had in two years. Not only did September advertisers stay, but advertisers scheduled for October and November moved up to September.

Q: The new section is now the first major feature. Have there been requests to run ads next to it?
A: There sure have. I tell them we want to wait until January to give the editors plenty of time to fine tune the section. If the demand's enough, we'll introduce a position charge.

Q: Good salespeople always sell their magazine as the best in the world. How do they explain why you're improving the unimprovable?
A: Americans are used to great products that suddenly become new and improved. Our advertisers do the same thing all the time in their own businesses.

Two kinds of changes

Q: Shouldn't we distinguish between basic change, which must be announced, and incidental, which should not?
A: I agree. There is a great deal of difference.

Q: Did you ever make changes without announcement?

A: When Clem and I came aboard seven years ago, we inherited a nice, gray, staid publication, tipped toward the financial with a lot of on-your-own-time articles. Clem said, "Our readers are trying to run businesses. When they read us, they want to think business. They have other magazines to read on playing tennis weekends. Let's stick with articles about running businesses." We also faced the fact that we were a monthly, choosing to concentrate on what we call "early-warning articles" to spot trends and alert readers to their significance. These changes were unannounced.

ANALYSIS

Evolution vs. Revolution

Since no two issues of a magazine can be identical, change is constant and pervasive in periodical publishing. Theoretically, what follows can be applied to every editorial decision. Practically, however, we have in mind extraordinary changes, i.e., changes readers and advertiser are not expecting and which are significant enough to require the publisher's approval.

We are not concerned here with how to judge the merits of a proposed change. That will differ with the purpose of each magazine and its positioning needs. The subject of this chapter is how to manage deliberate change after the decision to change has been reached.

Objectives

Successful changes will satisfy all four of the following objectives, though the relative importance of each will differ from case to case:

1. To improve profit. Changes can achieve this either by reducing expenses or by increasing income.

2. To attract different or merely additional readers. A change that expands a magazine's reader market is almost always advantageous. But it is also possible for a change to improve the reader market without expanding it.

3. To attract more or different advertising. Here, too, a publication's market can be improved in either quantity or quality. One reason for the huge success of *Architectural Digest* is that its change from a trade publication to a consumer magazine resulted in attracting not only a greater number of advertisers but a very different kind of advertiser.

4. To preserve current assets. So far as possible, a change should not alienate or confuse the readers and advertisers on whom the magazine now depends. Since a bird in the hand is worth two in the bush, any sacrifice on this level requires extraordinary assurances of compensating gains.

The secret to successful change lies in keeping all of these objectives clearly in mind both while planning and while implementing the changes. Each step, so far as possible, should advance all four objectives.

The key decision

No decision makes more difference to how a change is to be implemented than whether the change should be abrupt or gradual, as is evident in the changes Bob Potts has made at *Dun's*.

Frequently the very nature of the change will dictate whether it should be abrupt or gradual. *Time* magazine's overhaul of its graphics and type, in the late '70s, had to be made all at once. To change body type a little bit at a time would have been graphically disastrous. Enlarging the page size of a magazine is another example of a change that has to be abrupt.

When the best way to make changes is not so evident, studying the impact of abrupt vs. gradual change on the four objectives should lead to the right answer. Costs, for instance, were the principal reason for *The New Yorker*'s switch to electronic composition in 1980, and costs dictated that it be done all at once.

Expanding or changing one's reader market may at one time call for abrupt change, as Gruner + Jahr decided with *Young Miss*; at another, for gradual change —the route which president Thomas Wolf and editor Jim Reynolds chose in transforming *Hudson Home* from a trade magazine for builders to a consumer shelter book. In each case management had to decide which method would be more effective in advancing the primary objective.

When the advertising market is the principal objective of the change, and the purpose of it to open up an entirely new market or to attract many advertisers who have never used the magazine, an abrupt change is often preferable. Thus, when *Changing Times* decided to accept advertising, it was much more effective to take the step all at once than it would have been to try to edge into the market a few ads at a time.

Keeping current readers and advertisers happy is frequently the reason for making changes gradually, as was done with *Geo*'s editorial package, after Knapp Communications purchased it. But it can also result in a decision to change all at once, as in Bob Potts' opinion that it was important to convince current readers and advertisers that management was totally committed to the new concept.

The need to protect current assets is frequently the principal reason for choosing gradual change over abrupt change. Such assets need not be readers or advertisers. When Helen Gurley Brown became editor of *Cosmopolitan*, she gave relatively little consideration to current readers or advertisers. She did not have to because advertising and circulation were at such a low ebb, and because the magazine was 100% single-copy. The fact that her editorial changes were more gradual than abrupt, however, was still due to her need to protect current assets. In her case, it was the editorial staff which was especially important, due to her inexperience in magazine management.

Testing

Formal pretesting of a significant change should usually be done after making the decision whether to change abruptly or gradually. One reason is that abrupt changes have a different impact on the market than do gradual changes, and it is the impact that we are testing. The other is that gradual changes frequently can be tested in the very process of introducing them. Thus *Hudson Home*'s first subscription mailings to consumers simultaneously tested and advanced the change from business paper to consumer magazine.

No test should be undertaken without a clear decision on what you want to know. One can test for feasibility (Will it work?) or for fine tuning (Is this the best way to do it?). Tests that try to do both are almost always less effective than those that concentrate on one question. The biggest single danger in such tests is that conclusions may be based on the participants' opinions, which are easier to uncover than the subconscious attitudes and decision-making habits that really determine how a change will be received. Though this is especially true when focus groups are used, it is a problem common to every form of research which involves the subject as a conscious participant.

Again, the four fundamental objectives for all change should be considered. The cost of the test has to be weighed against the intended cost advantages of the change. If the change is meant to benefit current readers or attract more of the same, the test will be done with different subjects than if the change is aimed at attracting a different kind of reader. In some instances two tests may be required, one for the new readers, whom the change is supposed to attract, and another to judge the effect on current readers, whom you do not wish to alienate.

Like Bob Potts, smart publishers are not satisfied with pretesting major changes. They also conduct tests after the change is introduced for what Bob calls "fine tuning."

This brings us to a frequently overlooked consideration. Changes require strategy and strategy should always include contingency planning. The decision on how to implement the plan is incomplete—and fool-hardy—if it does not include decisions on what to do if things go wrong or results are not what was intended. One wonders if then publisher Chuck Colletti could have avoided complete defeat with *Cuisine*'s regional insert, "Cuisine New York" had he done more contingency planning.

Staff considerations

There are very few significant changes that do not affect and are affected by the magazine's staff. First there is the psychological impact. If the change does not originate with staff members, it must be sold to them. A change resisted internally is doomed. The staff, no matter how great its enthusiasm, has to be equipped to handle the change. This can mean more manpower, or different manpower. A new editorial feature may be a terrific idea, but it is no more than an idea until there is an editor or writer talented enough to make it happen.

Personnel problems usually include budget problems. Although advocates of change almost always emphasize long-term benefits, they frequently forget to project long-term expense. New people hired today will not be getting the same salaries a year from now.

Of course, changes in personnel (and cooperation from current personnel) are not restricted to the editorial department. A change to attract new advertisers may involve additional salespeople or more production personnel. A large gain in circulation may mean a bigger fulfillment department.

Among the effects that should be carefully calculated are those consequent on success. Success always affects personnel and may be very disruptive. Can the magazine handle more advertising, or a major increase in circulation? How will such increases affect the editorial staff, sales force, production department? More circulation or advertising, could force conversion from a manual to a computerized operation. Will present personnel adapt? Can the company afford to train or replace them? How much money will be needed for severance or early retirement pensions?

Announcing the change

The most common mistake made in planning a change is not in fully integrating and controlling publicity regarding the change. Promotion specialists, whether agents or employees, tend to value publicity in terms of the attention it gets rather than its overall effect on the objectives of the company. When *Ladies' Home Journal* reduced its circulation rate based by 500,000 in 1981, any announcement, beyond what was needed to avoid deceiving or angering advertisers, was a mistake. Publisher Tom Kenney's objective in making a wise and necessary change was not advanced by *The New York Times*'s pointing out that the magazine's rate base has dropped from 7 million to to 5 million since 1970.

As a general rule advance publicity is helpful in abrupt changes and harmful in gradual changes. There are exceptions, of course. A change in body type, for instance, should almost always be abrupt, but should almost never be announced. The final determinant should be how advance announcement will contribute to the change's objectives. Will it help or hurt?

To facilitate judging the advisability of advance announcement it helps to consider its positive and negative effects. An announcement avoids unpleasant surprise among current readers and advertisers, prevents harmful confusion or misunderstanding, forestalls misleading rumors, and most importantly obtains attention from prospects who might not otherwise notice. But it also can give rise to unfulfillable expectations, encourage prospects to hold back until they see what happens, confirm suspicions that the magazine is in trouble, and give the competition time to prepare its counterattack.

A major advantage of not announcing a change is that people respond favorably to pleasant surprises and take a proprietary interest in improvements they discover for themselves—the principal force behind word-of-mouth publicity.

Integrating strategic elements

In actual planning and implementation, the different aspects of a change should not be considered as independent elements. Almost always one of the four objectives of a change predominates, and should be the principal consideration in each step of the plan.

The way its new management changed the name of *New West* to *California* provides a good example of how the nature of a change, the way it is introduced, and the manner in which it is announced should work together. The change from fortnightly to monthly had previously been made abruptly. Editorial changes were already underway. The announcement campaign was reserved for the name change, and Keye/Donna/Pearlstein was engaged to promote it. The purpose, editor William Broyles said at the time, was to "reflect exactly what we are—not a magazine of the West, new or old, but of a very important and special state of the West, California."

Note that, with both *California* and *Dun's Business Month*, the purpose of the change was to reposition the publication, particularly with readers. In each case, the name change, the editorial changes, and the way these changes were announced were integral parts of a single strategy.

MANAGEMENT REVIEW

Check List for Implementing Changes

I. Decide which of the four essential objectives is the primary or direct purpose of the change.

_____ Improved profits (reduce expenses or increase income).

_____ Improved circulation (improved reader involvement or attract different advertising).

_____ Protection of current assets (preserve operational or marketing strengths).

II. Decide whether change should be abrupt or gradual.

		Abrupt	Gradual
A.	For more effective improvement of profits it should be	_____	_____
B.	For more effective improvement of circulation it should be	_____	_____
C.	For more effective improvement of advertising sales it should be	_____	_____
D.	For more effective protection of current assets it should be	_____	_____

E. To facilitate the primary or direct purpose of the change more effectively it should be _____ _____

Totals usually point the way to go: _____ _____

III. Decide on the wisdom of pretesting

A. Will pretesting   Yes   No
1. Improve profits? _____ _____
2. Improve circulation? _____ _____
3. Improve advertising? _____ _____
4. Protect current assets? _____ _____

B. Will the test under consideration   Yes   No
1. Reinforce the decision on whether to implement the change abruptly or gradually? _____ _____
2. Reveal what will really happen, not just what the participants say will happen? _____ _____

Even one no *is reason for reassessment.*

IV. Decide whether you are prepared for the change.

A. Is the staff prepared   Yes   No
1. Psychologically (understanding, acceptance, enthusiasm)? _____ _____
2. In manpower (number of people required by the change)? _____ _____
3. In talent (staff abilities required by the change)? _____ _____

B. Is the company prepared   Yes   No
1. To bear the consequences of success? _____ _____
2. With a fallback plan in case of failure? _____ _____

C. Will these adjustments advance   Yes   No
1. Improvement of profits? _____ _____
2. Improvement of circulation? _____ _____
3. Improvement of advertising sales? _____ _____
4. Protection of current assets? _____ _____

Even one no *requires reassessment of entire plan.*

V. Decide on the nature and extent of publicity.

		Yes	No
A.	Will the publicity advance		
1.	Improvement of profits?	___	___
2.	Improvement of circulation?	___	___
3.	Improvement of advertising sales?	___	___
4.	Protection of current assets?	___	___
B.	Does the publicity program facilitate	Yes	No
1.	The decision to change abruptly or gradually?	___	___
2.	The decision on how to pretest the change?	___	___

Even one no *requires reassessment of publicity plans.*

VI. Do all the elements of the implementation strategy effectively reinforce each other?

Yes   No

If no, try again.   ___   ___

CHAPTER TWENTY-TWO

How an Editor Should Think About Database Publishing

Featuring an Interview with Paul F. McPherson

President of McGraw-Hill Publications

There has been a lot of speculation, in the last ten years, on how data processing will affect publishing, particularly magazine publishing. There is no doubt that the computer has brought, and will continue to bring, some remarkable changes in how magazines are edited and manufactured. But learning to operate and adapt to electronic tools is not what worries editors.

What worries editors is what happens when electronic data processing becomes a competitor to magazine publishing. There has been a lot of talk about database publishing and how it will transform our business—and most of it either belittles the importance of editors or makes them sound obsolete.

Just what is database publishing? How close is it? How will it affect magazine publishing? And what should editors do about it? To get the answers, we approached Paul McPherson, then president of McGraw-Hill Publications, a magazine publisher more deeply into database publishing than any other company in the industry.

Paul McPherson got his Master of Business Administration degree from Babson College in 1952. His first jobs were all in sales: door-to-door for Fuller Brush, retail for Filene's department store, wholesale for Kraft Foods.

In 1955, McGraw-Hill hired him to sell classified advertising, and soon moved him to advertising space sales for *Chemical Week*. In 1967, he became publisher of the company's medical and educational publication. In 1969, he was appointed publisher of *Chemical Week*. In 1973, he was promoted to vice president and group publisher of the Process Industries Group.

Three years later, he was chosen executive vice president for McGraw-Hill Publications. In March of 1979, he became president of the McGraw-Hill's Information Systems Company. Seven months later he went back to the McGraw-Hill Publications Company as its president, a job he held until 1983, when the company underwent a major restructuring and he resumed the title of executive vice president.

INTERVIEW

Q: How do you define database publishing?
A: There are as many definitions as there are people. We opt for the broadest possible: a mass of data organized and made available by a publisher, with the choice of the medium depending on the market.

Q: In that sense it's nothing new.
A: No. What's new is the use of computers: the information is fed into a computer's data bank.

Q: What they call a database?
A: Any extensive statistical or reference material is a database, a source of information. All computerization means is greater sophistication in storage and use.

Q: Database publishing consultants distinguish three media categories: print, electronic and face-to-face. Do you find that helpful in a company with many databases?
A: Information is a basic resource. In the future, it will be the most-valued resource. That's why McGraw-Hill has become, and will increasingly become, an information company. Information can be communicated by publication in a magazine, or electronically or face-to-face in a conference or seminar. We do it in all those ways.

Impact of the electronic revolution

Q: I understand where the computer can help produce a lot of different products for communicating, but what does it do for marketing those products?
A: You can use the computer to transmit promotion about a service or a database. We have an electronic information service covering the petrochemical market. We've developed subscribers to that service through teletype messages, employing the very medium used to deliver the service as a way of selling the service.

Q: But teletype is not a computer.
A: The computerized database makes electronic access to the information feasible. McGraw-Hill's Data Resources Inc. provides, among other things, electronic economic models on the macro-economy. You can use them to develop your own business scenarios from your office on your own terminal.

Q: Isn't electronic access just another distribution technique?
A: Yes, but an increasingly prevelant one.

Q: Will it eventually replace magazines?
A: No. Magazines will survive. What you are dealing with in magazines cannot be duplicated by electronic access to a database, just as a magazine cannot duplicate the ability to manipulate large amounts of data, bring out information for a specific purpose, or interact information on-hand with information in the database.

Impact on the editor's function

Q: In most cases, what you are talking about involves direct access to the database by the subscriber.
A: You can have access in one way or another. They can send you preselected information from the database, or you can access it directly through a terminal.

Q: I'm trying to distinguish between the reader acting as his own editor by selecting from the database what he or she wants, and the editor putting together what the editor thinks the reader wants. Does this new medium eliminate the editor?
A: You can't have a database without an editor to develop, massage, interpret, format the data. Once that is done, you can access the information and select what you want, just as when you pick up a copy of *Business Week* and select what you wish to read.

Q: Then data can't be stored without being edited?
A: Compiling the data, deciding how to enter it, programming the computer for retrieval are all forms of editing. How that is done will be determined by the markets served.

Medium vs. source

Q: But the idea in database publishing is that the databank becomes the source for all kinds of media, whether magazines, books or wire services.
A: You're talking about an integrated information base. We haven't developed that yet. We have to determine whether it's the best route. Maybe there's a simpler, cheaper, more efficient way to go.

Q: I'd like to clarify our terms. If we define database as any collection of data, then even a magazine is a database. Are we talking about a source of information or the transmission of information?
A: We have to talk about both. You can't just store information. You have to transfer it from inside the computer to the user.

Q: That is true even of information stored in people's heads. Perhaps the distinction between the medium and the database is difficult to make because every medium is itself a database.
A: Whether we call it a medium or not, the importance of the electronic database is that is allows you to organize a vast amount of information which can be updated and retrieved instantaneously, and used in a variety of very selective ways, because you can interact with it.

Marketing comes first

Q: What you're describing is a new communications medium.
A: It's McGraw-Hill's objective to be a complete information company, which means to serve the business and professional community with information in every possible form. One form is the computerized database, and we're moving down that track as rapidly as we can.

Q: About five years ago, National Technical Information Service placed a terminal in the McGraw-Hill bookstore to provide electronic access to a huge bank of information from federal agencies and other sources. Business people were sup-

posed to walk in and pay to obtain information needed. It didn't succeed, because nobody had arranged to teach the businessman how to use such information. Most didn't even know what to ask.

A: The users have to know what they want.

Q: Which is a form of editing, and in most instances the users need someone to help them do this editing.

A: That depends on the user. When my staff economist wants information, he has no trouble using the Data Resources Inc. database.

Q: But he has to understand how the database works. It is no longer just a database for him, it's a medium he knows how to read.

A: That's part of the marketing process. Once you establish a database, you must continually teach people how to use it. When you enhance the database with additional information, you've got to show them how to use that.

Q: Is that so different from putting out a new directory? The directory is not going to succeed unless the people who buy it know how to use it. Part of marketing every medium is teaching people to use it.

A: Most people today are not yet at that point where they are comfortable with a video display terminal. They must be made comfortable before they can take full value from the system. A new generation will learn it in school.

Database publishing—theory vs. practice

Q: This interview will achieve something even if we only distinguish the electronic database as a new medium from database publishing as a system of storing information to generate new products. The electronic medium exists and its potential is being explored. The publishing technique is largely theory, having proved practical only in very limited applications.

A: My approach is to define the area of information. It should not be from horizon to horizon, but limited to a particular subject area, i.e., the database should be constructed to fill a particular marketing need.

Q: How do you determine when a market is ready for a database medium, particularly with direct access?

A: The market tells you. When I was president of McGraw-Hill's Information Systems Company, we integrated two companies in the real-estate information field, which provide brokers with listings of homes, property, etc. The information was fed into a computer, converted to electronic scan from which a weekly book was printed for brokers. It became apparent that brokers wanted immediate access to the information. So an on-line information service was established and has done very well.

Q: Is there an example of another medium using information compiled by a publication?
A: Our petroleum price service, for the informational needs of the oil business. We have both a publication and a newswire. That information is now being added to the database at Data Resources Inc., giving it additional exposure—for additional revenue.

Q: Multiple use of data is nothing new. Publishers have always turned magazine articles into books, used monthly figures to compile annual directories.
A: Electronic direct access is not all that different, but now we're working in a medium with which you can do many things that couldn't be done in print.

Q: Can this new medium carry advertising?
A: Several electronic information serices offer something like classified advertising. McGraw-Hill's Standard & Poor's distributes the "Blue List Ticker," a listing of bonds currently on the market, over the Telerate System. And the Publications Company has just initiated "electronic advertising" to newswire clients.

Q: A practical management question: what is the best way to set up the company? Should each medium be a separate profit center, or is it possible to organize the profit center around a body of information, a database?
A: At present, McGraw-Hill is organized primarily by medium, but we do have some organization by field of information. However, our book, publications and information companies are separate. What we've done is develop an inter-company task-force approach. Specialists from each company meet for synergistic planning.

Q: Although many of your newsletters are related to some magazine, you manage them in a separate division.
A: We found that by putting newsletter people together, you develop in-house talent capable of producing more newsletters, which are quite different from magazines.

Q: So the subject-matter of the database is not as important as the nature of the medium.

A: The market is the determining factor. For instance, we are currently conducting a broad evaluation to determine what informational needs of the chemical industry are not being met. What information does the manager and the engineer need that is not available from existing sources? Can we serve some of those needs as an extension of our chemical magazines?

Q: You have a Chemical Week *newswire. Is that run by the same people who run the magazine?*
A: It's a separate group within *Chemical Week*. The newswire is a good example of what we're talking about. It provides news vital to chemical-products marketers.

Q: In the petroleum field you have a newsletter and a newswire. Will the latter eventually replace the former?
A: No, because the readers need more information than can be put on a newswire.

Q: How would you recommend that small publishers think in terms of database publishing?
A: Most small publishers lack the resources to build an electronic database. To be successful with a database requires completeness. *The New York Times* discovered that with their information bank. They were forced to include a tremendous amount of information beyond what was in the paper. Small publishers have to work within their limitations.

ANALYSIS

Database—Chicken or Egg?

For no previous subject of these chapters has it been more important to distinguish between theory and practice than for the subject at hand: database publishing. In theory, it makes enormous sense to build a multimedia enterprise on what Paul McPherson calls "a mass of data organized and made available by a publisher for use in media, with the choice of the medium depending on the market."

In practice, however, we know of no company where the mass of data, or database, came first. Databases are always organized by publishers initially to develop a single medium, e.g., a specific magazine. The idea of using the database to develop other media is almost always an afterthought.

The nature of any collection of reference material is determined by the purpose of the collector. In fact, the more specific that purpose, the more immediately useful the collection. Hence most existing databases require extensive revision before they can be used for other purposes—for media other than the one for which they were initially created. The extent of this revision will, of course, depend on the new medium, but the fact that no database can be equally useful as a source for all media is the fundamental problem in database publishing.

The significance of EDP

As was agreed in the interview, database publishing is not a new idea. For years there have been publishers who have successfully sold different media developed from a single pool of information. But electronic data processing has given database publishing the appearance of a new idea. Today the term is used almost exclusively for situations where the publisher generates new products from a mass of information stored in a computer.

In theory, EDP has made database publishing appear irresistable—the foundation upon which all future publishing enterprises will have to be built. Computers make it possible to store, retrieve and manipulate huge amounts of information quickly, inexpensively and in a relatively small space. Moreover, the miracles of electronic technology make it possible to connect the database itself directly to production machinery, whether typesetting equipment, typewriters, teletype networks, television screens, or even electronically produced voices. So intriguing is the concept, and so strong its hold on publishers, that consultants like Bob Birnbaum and Paul Doebler can specialize in database publishing.

In practice, of course, there is much more to database publishing than selecting a field, putting all the information available about that field into a computer, and then taking it out in forms (media) that can be marketed at a profit. Information has to be obtained and evaluated before it can be stored. It has to be organized for storage and retrieval. Computer programs have to be designed to do this, and the programmer cannot do a proper job without knowing the purpose of the retriever. The medium that is to be developed from the database must exist before the database, at least in someone's mind.

Even such a large and apparently complex database (actually a network of databases) as that of the Source Telecomputering Corp., *Reader's Digest's* newly 51%-owned subsidiary, is designed for a relatively narrow market—in this case users of home computers (currently about 7,000 subscribe).

The very convenience and potential of an EDP database is a source of serious management problems. Publishers dive in and are swept along by a current so fast and so deep that it often is not only impossible to reach the goal, but even difficult to keep their eyes on it.

The database as medium

In theory, the best way to use a database is to provide customers with direct access to it. Let them do their own thing, both determining their own needs and satisfying them. In theory, a database with provision for direct access by customers is a universal medium which does its own marketing. The more information in the database and the more people with access to it, the more needs it should be able to fill—and the more money it should make.

The practical barriers to realizing such a scenario go far beyond the fact that many people are still afraid of computers and have to be taught how to use them. More fundamental: people often do not know their own needs. Recognizing needs is only the first half of creative marketing. The second is getting people to recognize those needs. The National Technical Information Service did not work because no provision was made for educating businessmen to recognize the need.

Furthermore, even a direct-access database has to be programmed for specific uses. As McPherson points out, the user of a direct-access database is not much different than a magazine reader. Both must select from material an editor has decided to present. And the ease and utility of selection and use depend on how an editor has organized the material.

Many experiments in direct-access database services fail precisely because the target market is too broad. The New York Times Information Bank learned this the hard way. Its function was so broad, the fields of information it chose to cover so unrestricted that it had to go far beyond the columns of *Times* to gather material just to make the database somewhat complete. Not only did this raise costs astronomically, but—as it turned out—the broader the scope the more difficult it became to market the service.

Target marketing is as vital for a direct-access database as for any other medium. The biggest mistake an editor can make is to give in to the temptation to create a medium that will communicate all things to all men—a temptation especially strong when dealing with the apparently infinite capacity of computers.

The database as competition

How will the computer as a communications medium affect the future of existing media, particularly print? The answer becomes less frightening if we remember that a direct-access database is just another medium.

The nature of each medium determines the kinds of information that can be presented, the form in which it can be offered, and how it can be organized. No one medium, including the direct-access database, can do everything equally well. Wire services will never completely replace newsletters. Direct-access databases will never make all magazines obsolete.

Each new medium, however, does replace certain functions of older media—those functions which the new medium can perform better than the old. The wire service does replace the newsletter as a means for rapid transmission of news. Leo Bogart, executive vice president of the Newspaper Advertising Bureau, sees a long future for newspapers, but predicts that certain newspaper features, such as stock-market quotations, baseball batting averages and movie timetables, will disappear because they will be better handled by the new electronic media.

One reason magazine editors should consider database publishing and direct-access database services is that planning for such a future prevents being trapped by the past. Studying the new, even the visionary, media helps an editor realize what a magazine can do best and how the publication may endanger its future by putting too much stress on what other media can do or will be doing better.

Five practical pointers

1. Don't invest in tools because they intrigue you. For the editor, both a database and a computer are tools. Whether separately or in combination, they are expensive to obtain and maintain. Successful publishing companies invest in them only if probability of payout justifies cost.

It is frequently advisable for a publication to take the first steps into multimedia publishing without investing in EDP. The database can be computerized later, when the operation grows complex enough to demand it—and sufficient revenue is generated to support it. Experience in using the database for the new products will also make programming easier and more effective.

2. Evaluate the database you now have. Every editor already has—and is using—some sort of database, even if it is only the back issues of the magazine. What is that material worth and to whom? How can it be reused?

The data you have already collected may be useful for reuse if it is supplemented by and combined with other information. How feasible is such an addition? Will the new product that can be generated from the altered database justify the cost of the alterations?

It is important to look beyond the editorial database. At the present moment the subscriber-information database developed by the circulation department or the market-research database created for the advertising sales force may be equally or more valuable than the editorial database—and more likely to be computerized. Consider the editorial mileage FOLIO: is getting out of The Folio:400, a database set up for promotion and sales to publishing-industry suppliers.

3. Be very specific in each new use for a database. When you market information, the medium is the message. From a marketing point of view, information is very much like food: customers want it processed. Food marketers don't sell wheat; they sell wheat flakes, bread, cake or cookies. Information marketers don't sell information; they sell books, magazines, tapes, records, wire services, electronic access, etc.

The database will have to be adjusted and manipulated for each new medium. Hence it is essential to envision the new medium with great precision, not only in physical terms (magazine, cassette, newspaper, book, television program, record, etc.), but in the way it will be marketed and used. Unless this is done, you cannot determine the work and expense involved in adjusting the database to the new product. In most cases, editors will find, when other factors are equal, it is advisable to run with the new media ideas that require the least changes in the database.

4. Let present customers lead you to future products. Marketers of information have a tremendous advantage. The communications business, of its very nature, generates feedback full of new-product ideas. Listen to your readers. Watch them.

What happens after the readers receive your magazine? Are the issues stored for reference, torn up, passed on, reproduced, junked? How frequent are requests for additional information? In what areas? Are readers meshing your material with other information, restructuring it for special uses? Can you publish it in a form that would make such uses easier for them?

Does your publication have a secondary market—other than your primary readers who are using the material? Would tailoring the same information to produce a medium primarily for them make sense?

Are there elements in your publication that meet the needs of your readers inadequately, e.g., news you provide weekly that they could use daily, leads that would be more useful if qualified, print that needs illustrations, illustrations that need moving pictures?

Every well-run publication encourages this constant analysis of how well it fills readers' needs. Good editors are asking these questions all the time. But it takes a farsighted editor to envision answers beyond the potential of the magazine itself. It requires the ability to think entirely in terms of market needs, untrammeled by preconceptions about specific media forms.

5. Learn as much about computers as you can. Editors cannot afford to ignore EDP—even when it is impractical to use it. Computers and computer technology have become as important to publishing as printing processes, distribution methods and promotion techniques. Good business judgment may require turning down or postponing EDP, but even that should not be done without knowledge.

In some instances, publishers will be better off, at least for the present, letting someone else put all or part of their database on computer. *Newsweek* and *U.S.News & World Report* allow Media Data to store their editorial contents for its clients. *Better Homes & Gardens* sells unpublished information gathered in preparing food articles by feeding it into the computers of Compu-Serve Information Service.

In other instances, computerizing a database may be worthwhile purely for internal purposes, e.g., to produce more accurate or thorough editorial data, or to organize it more effectively for readers. The New York Times Information Bank originated in an attempt to computerize the paper's morgue.

MANAGEMENT REVIEW

Two Check Lists for Database Publishing

I. **Evaluate management's approach to the entire area of database publishing in terms of:**
   A. Reasons for making such an investment.
      ____ Subjective interest, glamour are not affecting the decision.
      ____ Profit in developing the database is likely and significant.
   B. The value of the present database (or databases).
      ____ All possible databases in the company have been considered.

_____ The data is important to a significant market.

_____ The data can be reused in a new form.

_____ The new form has marketing potential.

_____ Required database additions and revisions will not destroy profit potential.

C. The search for new-product idea. Have the following sources been adequately used?

_____ Inquiries, complaints and other reader communications (including bingo-card and advertising response).

_____ Studies on how the publication is read.

_____ Data on pass-along and secondary readers.

_____ Studies on the publication's after-market (back issues, reprints, binders, etc.).

_____ Inadequate filling of reader needs (often revealed in editors' frustrations).

D. The new medium to be produced. Is the concept of the new product clear and specific with regard to the following?

_____ Form and characteristics of the medium itself.

_____ The manner in which it will be marketed.

_____ Costs, price and potential revenue?

_____ The way the database will have to be programmed and changed.

E. Management's knowledge of electronic data processing. Does management know the basics?

_____ What can and cannot be done.

_____ The cost.

_____ Which time-sharing services can be used as alternatives, and what they cost.

II. **Evaluate the following to determine whether or not it is advisable to establish a direct-access database:**

_____ The same norms of evaluation are being used as would be used for any new medium.

_____ There exists a real need for the information in this form.

_____ The market is large enough and can pay for the service.

_____ A plan (with costs) for educating the market to the need for the service is included.

_____ A plan (with costs) for teaching the market how to use the service is included.

_____ The database is large enough (or can be made large enough) to really serve the need.

_____ The database can be programmed to serve the need practically and cost-effectively.

ABOUT THE AUTHOR

Jim Mann is president of Jim Mann & Associates, a consulting firm specializing in the marketing problems of communications media, which he founded in 1974. He is also editor and publisher of MEDIA MANAGEMENT MONOGRAPHS, a monthly advisory service for periodical publishers, which he started in 1978.

Jim was formerly president and editor of THE GALLAGHER REPORT, having been with that publication from 1959 through 1974. It was during these 15 years that he perfected his expertise in developing and working in marketing and with media. In all the years he worked with the Gallagher letters, he was also responsible for promotion activities, including direct mail.

Jim has been an Adjunct Professor of Marketing, Advertising and Promotion at the University of New Haven's School of Business Administration. He was Director of the School's New Products & Concepts Laboratory until it was suspended in 1977. He has a Master of Fine Arts degree in creative writing from Fordham University and also studied writing at Columbia.

Jim has been writing professionally for more than 40 years. His articles have appeared in many different magazines, and he has written educational comics and several children's book.

He is also a member of the faculty of FOLIO MAGAZINE's two annual conferences, Publishing Week and Face to Face.